"An Interracial Movement of the Poor"

"An Interracial Movement of the Poor"

Community Organizing and the New Left in the 1960s

Jennifer Frost

NEW YORK UNIVERSITY PRESS
New York and London

NEW YORK UNIVERSITY PRESS
New York and London

Library of Congress Cataloging-in-Publication Data
Frost, Jennifer, 1961–
"An interracial movement of the poor" : community organizing and
the New Left in the 1960s / Jennifer Frost.
p.   cm.
Includes bibliographical references and index.
ISBN 0-8147-2697-6 (cloth : alk. paper)
1. Community development, Urban—United States—Case studies.
2. Economic Research and Action Project.   I. Title.
HN90.C6 F77 2001
307.1'412'0973—dc21   2001002977

New York University Press books are printed on acid-free paper,
and their binding materials are chosen for strength and durability.

Manufactured in the United States of America

10 9 8 7 6 5 4 3 2 1

For Paul and Cealagh

Acknowledgments

This is the best part of writing a book. I am most appreciative of the many activists of the 1960s New Left who took time out of their busy lives to talk with me about events some forty years past. Of particular help were Helen Garvy and Vivian Rothstein, who helped me locate people, and John Bancroft, Helen Garvy, D. Gorton, Nancy Hollander, and Stan Nadel, who provided photographs for the book. I also am grateful that Marge Grevatt aided Lillian Craig in recording and publishing her memoirs, and that Studs Terkel gave me permission to quote extensively from his books. The voices of Lillian Craig, Peggy Terry, and Dovie Thurman have enriched this book immensely.

Funding from the University of Wisconsin-Madison, in the form of a Graduate School Domestic Travel Fellowship, a Department of History Travel Grant, and a Marie Christine Kohler Fellowship, helped to support my dissertation research and writing. A Faculty Research and Publications Board Grant from the University of Northern Colorado allowed me to complete the book. The richness of the Social Action Collection at the State Historical Society of Wisconsin is what got me started on this project in the first place, and I have been aided over the years by archivists and staff, especially Harry Miller. It has been a pleasure to work with the editors at New York University Press, beginning with Niko Pfund, who encouraged me at the early stages, and ending with Jennifer Hammer, who saw the book through to completion.

I continue to appreciate the contributions of faculty, friends, and colleagues at the University of Wisconsin-Madison. Linda Gordon's work on women, social movements, and the welfare state and commitment to politically engaged scholarship spurred me on both before and after the completion of the dissertation. The comments and suggestions of Paul Boyer, Roger Horowitz, Marie Laberge, Gerda Lerner, Tom McCormick, and Tim Tyson guided my revisions for the book. Providing critical feedback at different stages were David Gerwin, Felicia Kornbluh, Steve Max,

David Myers, Peg Strobel, the readers for New York University Press, Alexander Bloom, and Rickie Solinger, my co-panelists at various conferences, including commentators Eileen Boris, Robert Fisher, Nancy Isenberg, and Tom Jackson, and my fellow participants in the 1996 NEH Summer Seminar for College Teachers on "The History of American Women through Social Movements," with Kathryn Kish Sklar and Thomas Dublin, in Binghamton, New York, and at the University of Houston's Black History Workshop on "The Civil Rights Movement: Local Perspectives," in 1997.

Family and friends, especially Marybeth Carlson, Eftihia Danellis, and Kathy Tatar, my siblings, Millicent and Jamie Frost, and my mother, Ann Frost, offered consistent and enthusiastic support over the years. Paul Taillon's immeasurable contribution to this project ranged from discussing the "big picture" to reformatting endnotes. I am most thankful to them all for sharing the vision and values that were behind this project and for keeping me focused on what is truly important.

Abbreviations

A(F)DC	Aid to (Families with) Dependent Children
AFL-CIO	American Federation of Labor-Congress of Industrial Organizations
CCAP	Citizens' Crusade Against Poverty
CCP	Cleveland Community Project
CORE	Congress of Racial Equality
CUFAW	Citizens United for Adequate Welfare [Cleveland]
CWLU	Chicago Women's Liberation Union
ERAP	Economic Research and Action Project
FBI	Federal Bureau of Investigation
IAF	Industrial Areas Foundation
JOIN	Jobs or Income Now
LID	League for Industrial Democracy
MAW	Mothers for Adequate Welfare [Boston]
MWRO	Massachusetts Welfare Rights Organization
NAACP	National Association for the Advancement of Colored People
NCU	National Community Union [Chicago]
NCUP	Newark Community Union Project
NSM	Northern Student Movement
NWRO	National Welfare Rights Organization
OEO	Office of Economic Opportunity
PREP	Peace Research and Education Project
SCLC	Southern Christian Leadership Conference
SDS	Students for a Democratic Society
SNCC	Student Nonviolent Coordinating Committee
UAW	United Automobile Workers
UPPC	Uptown People's Planning Coalition
VISTA	Volunteers in Service to America

Office of the Hill Neighborhood Union in New Haven, Connecticut, summer 1965. (Courtesy of John Bancroft.)

Introduction

During the summer of 1964, University of Michigan graduate Dave Strauss joined a community organizing project sponsored by the Students for a Democratic Society (SDS) on Cleveland's Near West Side. SDS—the organization that came to be regarded as virtually synonymous with the white New Left—began community organizing under the auspices of its Economic Research and Action Project (ERAP) in 1963. Inspired by the Civil Rights Movement, SDS activists entered low-income neighborhoods to pursue what they first called "community organization": bringing individuals living in the same residential area together into organizations to fight for their common interests. The ultimate and indeed lofty aim was to build "an interracial movement of the poor" to abolish poverty, end racial inequality, and extend democracy in America. Over the next few years, New Left organizers established thirteen official ERAP projects in predominantly black, white, and racially diverse neighborhoods; the largest, most successful, and longest-lasting projects were located in Chicago, Newark, Boston, and Cleveland. The son of Jewish Communists, Strauss had grown up in Cleveland and "it made a lot of sense to go to Cleveland, which I knew, and try to make a difference." He joined other organizers, including fellow Michigan graduate Sharon Jeffrey, as well as Swarthmore College graduates Oliver Fein and Charlotte Phillips, and stayed for two and a half years, through the fall of 1966.

One of the first residents encountered by organizers in Cleveland was Beulah "Boots" Neal, a welfare recipient. "What we did the first year for her was move her," Strauss recalls. "Every few weeks she was moving again, and we got to go and move her, her refrigerator and stove." For Neal, raising her children and dealing with the insecurities and injuries that stemmed from the marginal economic existence afforded by welfare left her with little time and energy for community activism. When Strauss first met her, he remembers thinking, "'This is absurd. Why are we working with this person?' . . . And then one day it

1

seemed like she just decided to commit to the stuff that Sharon kept talking to her about, and she did it with a lot of integrity." Neal was at a place in her life where she was willing to "say 'yes' to something positive." For Strauss, "the key thing" that spurred community people like Boots Neal to participate in ERAP was the time organizers spent with them. "Sharon Jeffrey and Charlotte Phillips had endless amounts of energy for other people, just one on one. . . . That really means a lot to somebody, [and] that respect got a lot back."[1]

In fact, Boots Neal ended up joining the Cleveland project's welfare rights group, Citizens United for Adequate Welfare (CUFAW). In November 1964 she took part in a vigil held by CUFAW to gain political attention for welfare issues when Governor James Rhodes was in the city. She and others carried signs with slogans such as "Is the Economy Great When Children Suffer?" and drew the attention of the local media. The following February, she reported in the Cleveland project's newsletter that CUFAW was in the midst "of fighting the County Commissioners for a free school lunch for our high school children." Taking charge of organizing a rummage sale to raise funds to pay for mailing supplies, transportation, and babysitters for the campaign, Neal contributed to what became ERAP's first tangible victory. Neal continued her involvement with CUFAW's successor, the Welfare Grievance Committee, and during the summer of 1966 helped recruit new members by passing out leaflets to recipients standing in line at the welfare department. "We are trying hard to better ourselves," she explained, "by working together as a group."[2] For Boots Neal, the Cleveland project provided impetus, focus, and resources for her community activism. The help and time New Left organizers gave to Boots Neal resulted in an active member of the Cleveland project.

Such successes, however, did not translate into the interracial movement of the poor SDS had intended to build. "At the time," Strauss remembers, the effort organizers put into people like Boots Neal "looked like a waste of time" for it did not produce what they had hoped. "I think most of us had the mass movement idea of change. The Civil Rights Movement . . . the Russian Revolution, sitdown strikes of the '30s. That's how you change things. It's hard to measure [what we were doing] against those things." By January 1967, when he left the Cleveland project, it was clear that ERAP had failed to achieve its goal of sparking a sustained movement for social change. And Strauss took this sense of failure with him, as did many other New Left organizers at ERAP's end. "I incorrectly felt that I hadn't any skills, that I hadn't learned anything. That wasn't true, but I didn't know that." Only later, reflecting back, did he realize that the "model we were using was actually a pretty good one, which is that you are probably going to change people one person at a time." "Moving Boots Neal," he now says, "was a good thing."[3]

The community organizing Dave Strauss and Boots Neal participated in was an important part of the activist repertoire of the New Left in the 1960s. Attention to one key example of New Left community organizing—SDS's ERAP—challenges the emphasis on the student and antiwar movements in histories of SDS, the New Left, and the 1960s. As the decade's largest New Left organization, with an estimated membership ranging from 30,000 to 100,000 at its height in the late 1960s, SDS played a prominent role in both movements. In scholarship, as in life, as the historian Charles M. Payne found for the Civil Rights Movement, these larger movements with their mass demonstrations, student sit-ins, and university takeovers eclipsed quiet, undramatic community organizing efforts.[4] Sharon Jeffrey chatting with Boots Neal and Dave Strauss moving refrigerators in Cleveland are not part of our collective memory of "the sixties," but they should be. These efforts not only belie the image of SDS members as "spoiled brats" with "disdain for the lives of ordinary people,"[5] they also demonstrate that the white New Left was not monolithic and that not all participants experienced it in the same way. For a small but significant group (perhaps three hundred people), that experience did not occur only on a university campus, in a homogeneous environment in terms of race, class, or age, or in isolation from communities.[6] Focusing on what organizers actually did in the community projects, the services they provided, and the relationships they established broadens, and complicates, our understanding of New Left activism.

As in the case of Boots Neal, these projects facilitated the community activism of local residents, especially women. In turn, residents challenged the assumptions of New Left organizers and determined to a significant degree the shape and outcome of ERAP. Most notably, the voices and actions of neighborhood participants illuminated how black, white, and Latino poor and working-class Americans defined the problems of and solutions to inner-city poverty in the 1960s. A number of the residents who became involved and took leadership in the projects had previous political experience, but their participation in SDS's community organizing unquestionably expanded their organizing skills, political knowledge, and self-confidence. Some, like Cleveland's Lillian Craig, Chicago's Dovie Coleman, and Newark's Thurman

Smith, used these attributes when they participated in community activism, the welfare rights movement, and government service later in the decade and after. Although the ERAP projects never mobilized great numbers of neighborhood residents, the stories of those they did mobilize reveal the power and possibilities of organizing from the "bottom up," of working with people, as Sharon Jeffrey did with Boots Neal, to see themselves and their capabilities in new ways.

The prominent place Sharon Jeffrey, Boots Neal, and Charlotte Phillips occupy in Dave Strauss's memories of ERAP indicates the importance of women in the neighborhood projects. As first documented by the historian Sara Evans, New Left women were the most accomplished organizers in the projects. Similarly, community women emerged as the largest and most active constituency. Together, they built and sustained the community projects, and, by designing campaigns around welfare rights, they achieved most of the projects' concrete gains, like the free school lunch program in Cleveland. As it turned out, SDS's community organizing became an important site for the emergence, and presaged the feminist and political content, of both the women's liberation and welfare rights movements.[7]

The fact and success of women's organizing were not part of the original vision for ERAP, however. In 1963, when ERAP planners formulated the strategy and goals for building an interracial movement of the poor through community organizing, they were most concerned about targeting the intertwined problems of class and race inequality, of synthesizing the aims of the labor and civil rights movements. Given the historical moment, before the "second wave of feminism," women's issues were not part of their political agenda or consciousness. Instead, ERAP planners took the position of men as the standard measure, and the initial strategy they settled upon focused on organizing jobless men around the issue of unemployment to demand full employment or a guaranteed income from the state. But once under way, the neighborhood projects shifted from this initial masculinist approach to one more inclusive of women. This development, how it happened, and what it meant for how participants came to define "politics" and "social movements" form the pivot on which the story of ERAP turned.

Realizing how important women and gender are to political organizing and social movement building was only one of many lessons learned by New Left organizers from the ERAP experience. Perhaps most important was the lesson captured in Dave Strauss's later understanding that "moving Boots Neal was a good thing." With a historical frame of reference that included successful examples of social transformation but little on past neighborhood-based activism, New Left organizers struggled with the contradiction between the small victories and contributions the projects achieved through community organizing and the social change that could have been effected by the mass movement they sought. Because ERAP never built the interracial movement of the poor, many left the projects feeling they had failed. Yet the tangible and intangible benefits New Left and neighborhood activists gained from their involvement in ERAP qualified this failure. In fact, consideration of these efforts in the context, and as a continuation of, the twentieth-century tradition of community organizing does so as well, given the mix of frequent defeats and limited achievements—including the personal and political development of participants—that characterize this tradition.[8]

Understanding ERAP as "mainly a flop in its avowed purpose, but not a total flop" acknowledges the various scholarly interpretations of SDS's community organizing.[9] Scholars concur on the neighborhood projects' ultimate, evident failure, and a number consider the ERAP experiment from the start to have been naive, misguided, even mistaken. At the same time, others credit these efforts with being an important chapter in the New Left's dedication to social change, embodying better than any other project SDS's democratic idealism, and contributing to later community organizing and social movements.[10] Of course, as this study reveals, these assessments do not necessarily preclude one another. This is particularly so because, although general patterns exist, ERAP was different in every location and a different experience for every participant. What these interpretations do indicate is that ERAP is at least mentioned by all scholars of "the sixties." Even so, the specific strategy, goals, experience, and lessons of New Left community organizing are largely forgotten. As an act of remembering, this study provides historical perspective and context for current efforts aimed at linking community and labor organizing and simultaneously targeting inequalities of race, gender, and class. By trying and failing to build an interracial movement of the poor, New Left organizers and neighborhood participants learned worthwhile lessons about politics, community organizing, and social movements. Although it may be romantic to see value in these failed efforts, perhaps this experience from the past will have some relevance for the future, leaving open the larger meaning and legacy of New Left community organizing, like that of the decade in which it occurred.

Office of the JOIN project in Chicago, summer 1964. (Courtesy of Stan Nadel.)

1

From Campus to Community

In December 1963 members of the National Council of the Students for a Democratic Society gathered in New York City for their regular quarterly meeting. For New Left activists, the year just ending had been a time of "vital politics" when a mood of possibility and urgency pervaded the nation.[1] That year, the Civil Rights Movement stood at its point of most effective pressure and protest. The Southern Christian Leadership Conference's victorious Birmingham campaign that spring, a long-awaited civil rights bill pending in Congress, and the historic March on Washington in August made this period, according to SDS leader Richard Flacks, "a very, very optimistic moment, probably the peak moment for my generation."[2] Other political developments, from rent strikes in Harlem to President John F. Kennedy's call for a reexamination of the tenets of the Cold War, fostered a sense among SDS members that significant social change was achievable in the near future in the United States. Yet a rising tide of white violence and backlash against the Civil Rights Movement tempered their idealism. They sought to play a role in both shaping the direction of social change and stemming reactionary forces.

At the National Council meeting, SDS members were to do just that. National secretary Lee Webb called for a discussion of "what kind of organization" SDS wanted to be. He had definite opinions. In his report to the National Council, circulated in advance as part of a set of working papers under a cover filled with slogans such as "Into the Ghetto Nearest You" and "What We Really Need Is a Good White Ghetto Two Miles from Campus," Webb admitted "a certain lack of objectivity." Black activism in the North and South, he argued, revealed the "strategic necessity" of organizing white Americans on the community level around economic issues. SDS could be a "catalytic force in this area," Webb believed.[3] After three days of reports, panel discussions, and workshops, the council finally took up the question of the organization's priorities.

In the first major disagreement over SDS's political direction, two proposals came before the National Council. Robert Alan (Al) Haber's urged SDS to maintain its focus on college campuses and the radical education of students, while Tom Hayden's prioritized community organization around poverty and civil rights. Former SDS presidents, Haber and Hayden were respected and influential leaders in the organization. The two men had worked closely together from 1960 to 1963, but their political approaches now diverged. Hayden wanted students to leave college for full-time work in northern communities. In this way, SDS would contribute to a "new insurgency" emerging on the local level across the country.[4] Haber strongly objected, arguing that the desire for community organization came out of "disgust with school, . . . alienation, sexual frustration or expectation, parental rejection." Hayden's proposed plan of action required far more research and refinement. After all, Haber contended, SDS "can't just take one generation of students and run off to the ghetto."[5]

Although it lasted only a few hours, what later was called the "Hayden-Haber debate" revealed a dilemma in SDS between campus and community organizing, a dilemma with which members struggled repeatedly throughout the 1960s. Should they stay on campus where their strength lay and build a base through student organization? Or should they move off campus and directly confront social inequalities by building cross-class movements in communities? Central to this conflict was the question of which location provided the best foundation for creating a movement for social change. In December 1963, culminating developments both within and outside the organization and reflecting a mix of personal and political motivations, SDS decided in favor of community organizing. As it turned out, however, this decision was only a temporary and uneasy resolution to SDS's locational dilemma.

The Freedom Movement

"The movement has changed from a Civil Rights Movement to a Freedom Movement," Bill Strickland of the Northern Student Movement informed those attending the December 1963 National Council meeting. As the Civil Rights Movement reached its peak that year, the early focus on segregation in the South broadened to include political and economic inequalities in the North and South. Setting the context for the deliberations and decisions on "radical political action" to follow, Strickland's presentation was the meeting's first, demonstrating the critical importance of the Civil Rights Movement in the early 1960s.[6] It is now well known that the struggle for racial equality gave the New Left its initial spark and direction; it certainly influenced SDS's move into community organizing in 1963.

This period was not the first time that the Civil Rights Movement had provided impetus and inspiration for SDS. In 1959 and 1960 Al Haber, then a student at the University of Michigan, spearheaded the emergence of SDS from its forerunner, the Student League for Industrial Democracy. Under Haber's innovative leadership, civil rights was one of the first issues taken up by the new national organization. When the black student sit-ins protesting lunch counter segregation in Greensboro, North Carolina, began in February 1960, Haber felt the need to "act *now*" and organized sympathy pickets in Ann Arbor.[7] He also recruited Tom Hayden. As part of this initial emphasis, Hayden was named SDS's southern field secretary and relocated to Atlanta in the fall of 1961 to be with his new wife, the civil rights organizer Sandra Cason (Casey) Hayden. His reports from the South, later published as the pamphlet *Revolution in Mississippi,* kept SDS members informed and conveyed a sense of gravity and immediacy about the movement.[8] Of all the causes SDS could have taken on at this early point, such as peace or academic freedom, civil rights had the greatest moral and emotional power and, eventually, the greatest impact on national politics.[9]

The Civil Rights Movement—especially the direct action and student arms of the movement, the Congress of Racial Equality (CORE) and the Student Nonviolent Coordinating Committee (SNCC)—provided a training ground for SDS activists. For some, like Johns Hopkins University student Kim Moody, civil rights organizing preceded their membership in SDS.

> The thing that caught my imagination really was the Civil Rights Movement, particularly the sit-ins in Greensboro. [It was] right around my birthday, and it sort of struck me, here are these black students my age doing this revolutionary, radical thing. I thought that's what we all needed to do.

When he arrived in Baltimore from Chicago as a freshman in 1960, Moody, the son of Republican parents, "made a point of finding the Civil Rights Movement." Baltimore was a segregated city, "very much a southern kind of city," with a mass movement in the early 1960s. He ended up contacting and working with Baltimore CORE and the SNCC chapter at nearby Morgan State, a historically black college, and participated in weekend sit-ins to integrate lunch counters. Later, in 1962, Moody helped found the SDS chapter at Johns Hopkins.[10] Shared political activism fostered close personal and organizational ties between SDS and other student organizations focused on civil rights.

Particularly important to SDS was SNCC, which had been formed in 1960 out of the Greensboro sit-ins. SNCC members dedicated themselves to a politics of nonviolent direct action that brought more young people into and invigorated the Civil Rights Movement. Joining SNCC meant a willingness to risk physical harm and arrest, because "truth comes from being involved and not from observation and speculation."[11] Full-time organizers went into areas of the Deep South most feared by civil rights activists, such as Mississippi and southwestern Georgia. Through these difficult, often frustrating, and always dangerous efforts, SNCC organizers met and came to identify with poor, uneducated, rural black southerners.[12] They shared the philosophy of the longtime civil rights activist Ella Baker, that meaningful social change came only from the participation and leadership of these people at the grassroots.[13] SDS's *Port Huron Statement* later defined and codified this belief as "participatory democracy," a true democracy in which people share in the decisions shaping their lives. This principle guided the internal structures and political goals of both organizations.[14] By embodying a commitment to "putting your body on the line" for the values in which one believed, SNCC's activism created a mystique that inspired and intrigued members of SDS. As Tom Hayden asked in the spring of 1963, "Can the methods of SNCC be applied to the North?"[15]

As with SNCC, SDS enjoyed a close relationship with the Northern Student Movement (NSM), sharing information, members, and projects. NSM began in 1961 with the explicit intention of raising money for SNCC and initially focused its campus protests, education programs, and fund-raising drives on the southern Civil Rights Movement. Of increasing concern, however, were the race- and class-based problems plaguing blacks in the North, including high unemployment, inferior schooling and housing, and police brutality.[16] During the summer of 1963, the organization established community projects in eight black neighborhoods in cities such as New York, Boston, and Detroit. These projects were first dedicated to one-on-one tutorial programs as a way to call attention to racial and class inequalities in education. But

NSM organizers soon concluded, "it is useless to provide educational resources to people who feel powerless to significantly improve their environment" and began to participate in broader community action, including rent strikes in Harlem.[17] Together with NSM and SNCC, SDS members felt compassion for and solidarity with others and sought to realize the values of equality and democracy in all areas of life—social, political, and economic—for all of America's dispossessed.

In 1963 a dramatic upsurge in local civil rights movements in the North and South increasingly drew SDS members into action. During the spring and summer of 1963 students at Swarthmore College in Pennsylvania joined the SNCC affiliate in Cambridge on Maryland's Eastern Shore to protest segregation and inequalities in employment and housing.[18] Nick Egleson, who came from a liberal East Coast background, visited Cambridge as a reporter for the Swarthmore student newspaper. "It was a completely segregated town, in which the poor people were all black and lived on one side of town." In June mass arrests and violent clashes between police and demonstrators culminated in a riot, and the National Guard was called in to restore order. Egleson was "quite amazed at what I saw, which was not what was supposed to be going on in the country. The city was under military guard, there were jeeps with armed soldiers in them, patrolling the streets." Such experiences had a profound personal and political impact, changing the lives of students such as Egleson.[19] Personally witnessing racial and economic injustices that so contradicted American ideals of democracy and equality renewed and strengthened the moral commitment and political dedication of young New Leftists.

By the fall of 1963 SDS sought new ways to participate more fully in and further the aims of the Civil Rights Movement, just as it confronted black economic inequality and escalating white violence. Although black leaders historically had advocated a dual agenda aimed at social welfare and racial discrimination, during the 1950s and early 1960s they prioritized legal, civil rights over economic, class-based goals.[20] In 1963 campaigns throughout the country revealed the "contradictions" between the movement's goals "to desegregate public space and the daily struggles of the black poor."[21] That fall, a broad consensus emerged on the need for a new civil rights agenda focused on the simultaneous pursuit of racial and economic justice.[22] At the same time, southern extremism, violent confrontations, and so-called massive resistance to racial change escalated in 1963. Assassination, bombings, arson, and police brutality prompted

President Kennedy to call civil rights America's "moral crisis" and to send his civil rights bill to Congress in June.[23] In this changing and tense situation, and as a response to the forces of racial progress and reaction, SDS members formed in September what would become their vehicle for community organizing: the Economic Research and Action Project.

The new ERAP would investigate and organize around the problem of economic inequality and the potential for economic democracy in the United States. Envisioning the project as a strategic complement to the work of civil rights activists, Tom Hayden and Lee Webb met to discuss ERAP with SNCC's Stokely Carmichael soon after the March on Washington in August 1963.[24] Although a powerful event both politically and morally, the "March on Washington for Jobs and Freedom" concentrated more on freedom than on jobs. For SDS, critical of the legalism of civil rights liberalism, this further demonstrated the need for a project such as ERAP to make economic demands that went beyond the "symbolic" demands of the Civil Rights Movement. "'Civil rights' mean little if for the mass of Negro people there are no roads up out of the ghetto."[25] Carmichael strongly supported ERAP and urged Hayden and Webb to organize poor whites primarily, reflecting both an emergent black nationalism and a belief that poor whites were the core of white backlash. If white resistance was mostly spurred by economic resentment, as many SDS members held, then ERAP's focus on economic issues could be a way to cross racial barriers and bring together black and white Americans.[26]

ERAP integrated SDS's passionate concern for racial equality with the social democratic heritage and trade union funding of its now estranged parent organization, the League for Industrial Democracy (LID).[27] Part of the project aimed to "create a viewpoint sympathetic to labor and its history, yet at the same time to be critical." SDS knew that the labor movement was not monolithic but had both "good guys and bad guys."[28] While critical of conservative and often racially discriminatory unions, such as the building trades and many of the old American Federation of Labor unions, they considered more progressive unions, such as the United Automobile Workers (UAW) and the United Packinghouse Workers of America, to be important political allies. For their part, these unions saw SDS as the student organization "closest philosophically to the labor movement." Aiding SDS's relationship with both unions were personal and familial ties, and in the summer of 1963 the UAW provided five thousand dollars to initiate ERAP.[29] The historian Nelson Lichtenstein notes that this period "may well be taken as the moment when the discourse of American liberalism shifted decisively out of the New Deal–Fair Deal–laborite orbit and into a world in which the racial divide colored all politics," but ERAP still sought to bring the two together.[30]

Although charting a new direction for SDS, ERAP continued the organization's male-dominated leadership. While women constituted between 32 and 39 percent of SDS's general membership throughout the decade, they consistently were underrepresented in leadership. The year 1963 marked the highest percentage of women on SDS's National Council— 26—a number that would plummet the next year to 6 percent.[31] Similarly, men controlled ERAP's leadership and early orientation. Al Haber became the first director of the project and took primary responsibility for the research component on campus in Ann Arbor. Joe Chabot headed up ERAP's action component, left the University of Michigan, and moved to Chicago to begin to organize unemployed young white men in the community around economic concerns. Of the six members on the new ERAP Supervisory Committee, Sharon Jeffrey was the only woman.[32] Nevertheless, her role in ERAP proved to be crucial.

One of Haber's first recruits to SDS, at a time when the national convention drew only a handful of students, Jeffrey helped to build and set the agenda for the young organization. She grew up in a household oriented toward trade unionism, socialism, feminism, and Democratic Party politics and always considered herself a "rebel." She and her mother, Mildred, who worked for the UAW in Detroit, linked the union and SDS. As a student at Michigan, Jeffrey sought "intellectual discussion around significant philosophical, political, and social issues." Yet she also was an activist; "I was marching in union picket lines at the age of five." SDS was perfect for her. She could commit herself to an idea with "vision and meaning," like participatory democracy, and seek to implement it through organizing.[33] As a consequence, when in the fall of 1963 Hayden and Webb urged the National Council to consider "a vital project" for ERAP, one with more "room for participation" from SDS members, Jeffrey supported them.[34]

The direct impetus for this "vital project" came from the activism of Swarthmore students in nearby Chester, Pennsylvania. During the fall of 1963, fresh from their experiences in Cambridge, members of the SDS-affiliated Swarthmore Political Action Club joined with the local National Association for the Advancement of Colored People (NAACP) Youth

Chapter, Chester parents, and high school students in forming the Committee for Freedom Now. Using a range of protest tactics, including a boycott, marches, pickets, and sit-ins, the Committee for Freedom Now protested de facto segregation in the public schools and experienced hundreds of arrests. Realizing that the northern movement was "really a movement of poor people," Swarthmore activists decided that if they wanted to achieve lasting social change they needed to mobilize Chester residents at the grassroots around economic issues.[35] They formed several neighborhood organizations in November by "going door-to-door, making leaflets, going to meetings, trying to find community leaders" and began to work on improving housing conditions. These efforts convinced them that to succeed in Chester the movement needed both white allies and a national orientation.[36] A visit to Swarthmore and Chester in the fall greatly impressed Lee Webb, who was in the middle of his first and only term as SDS national secretary. Frustrated with the office work and routine, Webb felt he "ought to be out *doing* something with his life instead."[37] Chester provided an answer: community organizing.

The National Council Meeting

"I want SDS to be an organization that is an initiator," Lee Webb argued in his report in advance of the National Council meeting in December 1963. "For too long we have been a parasite on the more active organizations, i.e. SNCC and NSM." By expanding ERAP's action component, Webb believed they could define a new arena of political activity for SDS. Modeled on the experiences of activists in SNCC, NSM, Cambridge, and Chester, ERAP organizing was to be full-time, based in the North, concerned with economic issues, and focused on whites.[38] But first Webb, Hayden, and their allies needed to convince the National Council—over very sound objections—to take the four-month-old ERAP project in a new direction. Discussions at the meeting over whether to prioritize community over campus organizing or action over research and education culminated in the Hayden-Haber debate.

For advocates of transforming ERAP, the community constituted the best site for radical organizing. If SDS members wanted to connect with civil rights activists, they needed to go where they operated, at the grassroots. Danny Schechter, an NSM and SDS member, pointed out how NSM's community location contributed to an impressive series of rent strikes in Harlem that fall, and Jesse Gray, a local rent strike leader, urged SDS to supply more organizers for the movement.[39] The presence of representatives from NSM as well as SNCC, two student organizations that paradoxically operated mostly off campus, buttressed the case for what they then called "community organization." So, too, did a relative lull in student activism during the 1962–63 academic year. Even enthusiasm for university reform, one of SDS's major campus-based issues, had waned, because students preferred to "devote their efforts to more pressing and substantive issues."[40] This orientation away from campus organizing fit with SDS's increasingly critical and less hopeful stance toward the function of the university in American society. How could the New Left create social change from a base on campus when the university was imbedded in "the system"? Instead, activists were coming to believe that students needed "to stand outside . . . [and] develop alternatives to the system."[41] By remaining on campus, many felt, ERAP would blunt its radical edge.

Others disagreed. Before 1963 SDS had considered students a necessary part of any coalition for social change and the university an important "base for assault upon the loci of power."[42] Many continued to hold these views, and the consensus at the National Council meeting was that students were the organization's constituency and that developing students to be lifelong radicals should be SDS's main purpose. Yet Nancy Hollander from the Michigan chapter warned that SDS was losing its student base through a lack of campus-based programs. "[U]nless we recapture the campus base we will never reach these potential radicals," she argued. SDS still had to build the solid, continuing chapters and membership needed for a successful student organization.[43] ERAP could contribute to this task by remaining on campus. Chapter reports, like that from Baltimore, demonstrated how campus and community economic activities could be integrated, as ERAP originally intended.[44] Moreover, Joe Chabot's bleak report on mobilizing unemployed whites in Chicago recounted only problems, impossibilities, and the need for "something positive." His progress—or rather lack thereof—contrasted sharply with successes in Chester. But the model for community organization in ERAP was Chicago, not Chester; white organizing, not black; economic issues, not civil rights. Chabot's experience raised serious questions about the efficacy of expanding ERAP's community efforts.[45]

As participants at the meeting discussed the best location for ERAP, they also asked whether the project's focus should be research and action equally, or action primarily. For those interested in community organization, the upsurge in civil rights activism during 1963 demanded SDS's move into full-time, direct action. They feared that SDS was being left behind by the pace of events and increasingly took part in community activism on their own, apart from SDS.[46] Sharon Jeffrey chose to work on direct action with CORE, voter registration with the National Student Association, and community research with NSM. "If SDS was going to survive and have any lasting future for itself, let alone have an impact on things," she felt at the time, "it was going to have to change, from an intellectual to an action orientation."[47] This desire for action reflected an existential spirit as well as SNCC's influence. Participation in direct political action constituted a means of self-assertion, of moral struggle and commitment, and could be personally transforming. Taking action also radicalized students. Speaking perhaps of his own experience in Cambridge, Nick Egleson argued, "action was a way of attaining commitment."[48] Community advocates thought ERAP should be dedicated not to theory and analysis—what SDS was known for already—but to getting students into localities where exciting work was being done.

For proponents of maintaining ERAP's original focus, the upsurge in activism that year called for sober thought and reflection. They believed that ERAP should be dedicated to studying and formulating programs around economic and political problems. "Action should only be undertaken," Al Haber contended, "after research had determined what a radical program should be." As ERAP director, Haber wanted the project to be an "independent center for radical thinking," aiding the education of student radicals. Over the long run, radical research and education would have greater political impact than recruiting students for brief stints as community organizers.[49] Kim Moody stressed the interrelated nature of research, education, and action. A multi-issue and pluralistic program always had been one of SDS's strengths and, in fact, had positioned it well to capitalize on the interests of students like Moody in the early 1960s. The initial design for ERAP—concerned with both "research" and "action"—reflected an experimental, project-oriented approach to politics.[50] After only four months, the results were not in on the ERAP experiment, and shifting ERAP's emphasis to full-scale community action seemed premature to some SDS members.

Finally, late on the third day of the National Council meeting, Hayden and Haber brought forward and argued for their respective resolutions: community organization around poverty and civil rights versus the radical education of students, combined with research and action, on campus. Opposing views of SDS's place in progressive politics fundamentally shaped their advocacy of community or campus activism. As the "new insurgency" began to challenge mainstream institutions at the grassroots, Hayden asserted, "the presence of radicals" could contribute to a "revolutionary trajectory" where "day to day reforms can lead to revolution." This rhetoric revealed Hayden's "infatuation with SNCC's revolutionary élan," as the historian Clayborne Carson has put it.[51] It also conveyed his sense of the historical moment and SDS's political importance. With support from SNCC's Stokely Carmichael and the UAW's financial coffers, ERAP could bridge the two most important social movements of the day, civil rights and labor. A crucial opportunity for creating social change would be lost if SDS did not act, he believed, making community action both necessary and urgent. Less tied to the Old Left and old social movements, with parents unconnected to either socialism or labor, Hayden was not a traditional leftist. "[H]e didn't have any politics," Sharon Jeffrey later observed. "He didn't understand economics."[52] That Hayden and others, such as Lee Webb, felt alone on the U.S. Left reflected both the political uncertainty caused by the general collapse of the Old Left during the McCarthy era and generational rebellion and hubris on the part of many young New Leftists.[53]

Haber believed that Hayden's assumption of a "revolutionary trajectory" was incorrect and therefore could not provide the political perspective needed for community action. He stressed SDS's limited financial resources. The organization could not "do all things," and members simply could not afford to support ERAP as a full-scale action project.[54] Haber also criticized Hayden for exaggerating SDS's political role and potential for creating social change. "[T]he brute fact," he wrote in his report on ERAP to the National Council, "is that *as radicals* we do not have influence." This "desire for influence" led SDS members to participate in actions, like demonstrations and marches, that squandered their political energy; prioritizing community organization would do only more of the same.[55] In contrast to Hayden, Haber maintained relations and an affinity with the old social movements of organized labor and the Old Left; his father had been a liberal economist, labor arbitrator, and LID supporter. He regarded SDS in a more modest fashion, as only a small and specific part of the Left with a responsibility for organizing college students. That responsibility, for Haber and members like Don McKelvey, was what SDS needed to prioritize.[56]

The debate between Hayden and Haber occurred in such an intense and rancorous atmosphere that its ramifications were felt for months. The tone and language of these two key participants revealed the high level of discord. Hayden, for example, belittled the position of the campus contingent when he argued that SDS should make the move into communities and "leave all that academic crap behind it."[57] For his part, Haber criticized the entire debate over ERAP as "recklessly irresponsible," blaming "poor National Council planning" on the part of Lee Webb for the fact that it even took place.[58] The debate also signaled the end of Hayden and Haber's early collaborations. The enthusiasm for community organizing in SDS owed much to Hayden's insistence and confidence, while, at the same time, it isolated and worried Haber. To Hayden, Haber "represented an inconclusive intellectualism that was frustrating the birth of SDS as an active force." At the same time, Hayden's new direction "wasn't easy for Al," according to Jeffrey. "So all of a sudden, he was going to be left out. He was no longer going to be a leader."[59] The personal dimension of their political differences exacerbated the tense mood at the National Council meeting.

In the discussion that followed, the debate between Haber and Hayden came to be summed up as a contest of priorities between theory and practice, between "an ethereal, intellectual focus" and a "hands-on organizing" one.[60] Hayden, as did SNCC, emphasized direct political action and "putting your body on the line" and concluded that "strategically relevant theory is in part an outcome of experiencing political action." Haber remained focused on developing concrete goals and political strategy, arguing that the call to action reflected "momentum rather than theory."[61] SDS members admitted that Hayden's proposal for community organization did not measure up to the standards of practical politics; it was "too vague about the radical function" and lacked a clear political strategy. Yet they felt that Haber's position on research and education underestimated the strength and success of SDS's campus base and was ultimately "negative and limiting, as well as cold."[62] If Hayden's proposal needed more theoretical grounding, then Haber's required an expressive outlet for organizing energy. In the end, the requirement for the latter trumped the need for the former, and the National Council voted twenty to six to devote SDS's energies and funds toward full-time community organization.

Why did a majority of those in attendance at the meeting support Hayden? Not all agreed with everything he argued, but for many, communities were clearly the place they needed to be. "Once you'd seen what was going on in Cambridge," Nick Egleson notes, "my recollection was it didn't seem like much of a debate."[63] To Dave Strauss, then a student at Michigan, "Hayden easily won that as far as I was concerned." Strauss grew up in an environment where racial equality was a main concern, due to his parents' involvement in the Communist Party. While still in high school in Cleveland, Ohio, he participated in civil rights activities and joined SDS only when civil rights organizing became prominent. "I wanted to do something that felt right and relevant." As a consequence, he "never understood" Haber's opposition to transforming ERAP. "[T]he Civil Rights Movement is exploding all over the place and we're sitting there saying, you know, 'Wait a minute, if we just stay on campus we're not gonna be there when we're needed.' It seemed to make sense."[64] Like Egleson and Strauss, the rest of the Swarthmore and Michigan contingents lent particularly strong support to community organization both at the meeting and later.

SDS members' readiness to relocate from campus to community stemmed from personal concerns as well as political commitments. Underlying the development of ERAP into a full-scale community action project, Hayden believed, "was the more personal question of where to locate ourselves, what to do with ourselves."[65] A significant minority of SDS leadership and membership already had completed, or were about to complete, their undergraduate educations. Hayden, Haber, Webb, Moody, and Strauss all fit this profile. They now were deciding how to relate to SDS as adults rather than as students. Jeffrey, too, had graduated from college and suggested that SDS think "about forming an adult group to effectuate change."[66] Members needed something to "graduate into," and ERAP provided a compelling option and sense of purpose at this point in their young lives. After ERAP's first summer in 1964, an estimated one-third of organizers did not return to campus in the fall.[67] As a student organization, SDS encountered this issue throughout the 1960s, and members periodically proposed the formation of an adult New Left organization. At this point, however, ERAP's new direction gave older members a place to go and obscured the need for such an organization.[68]

One more point about the Hayden-Haber debate deserves attention. Despite its importance for the future of SDS and the personal and political lives of individual members, there was no written record of women taking a stand for or against community organization in discussions before or during the debate. That women's views on this issue went unrecorded in the official minutes was not because women were insignificant members of SDS. Nor was it due to women's absence from the meeting or lack of definite opinions about ERAP's direction. All four women who were national officers on the National Council were proponents of community organization. As SNCC workers, both Betty Garman and Mary Varela had supported grassroots efforts over the years. Sarah Murphy, a freshman at the University of Chicago who had been active in SDS as a high school student in New York, believed "the experimentation was necessary." And the fourth woman member was Jeffrey.[69] Also in attendance at the meeting, probably as SDS chapter delegates, were Carol McEldowney, Nancy Hollander, Nada Chandler (the official minute taker), and Joan Wallach. Both McEldowney and Hollander joined ERAP projects the following summer, and it is likely that they too supported the community side of the debate.[70]

What primarily accounted for women's lack of prominence at the meeting was SDS's now well-known male-dominated leadership.[71] Of some fifty speakers named in discussions leading up to the Hayden-Haber debate, only six were women, although they constituted about one-third of registrants. Many women held themselves responsible for not having the self-confidence to articulate their ideas in such public settings.[72] But others blamed an aggressive style of debate. This style of argument and exchange proved alienating for many SDS members, male and female, but it inhibited the participation of women especially. Women with the vocabulary to do so explicitly attributed this style to traditional ideas about masculinity and to the sexism of men in SDS; such attributions were particularly true of women who were red-diaper babies and familiar with Old Left concerns about "the woman question" and "male supremacy." As one woman furiously wrote in an anonymous evaluation of the December 1963 National Council meeting, "The NC can be partly explained by . . . SDS diseases—male supremacy, agenda debates, jargon—diseases which are carryovers from bourgeois society."[73]

SDS's competitive culture clashed with its stated dedication to implementing the principle of participatory democracy at the most basic level of discussion and decision making. Although this male culture subsequently created the contradictory conditions that contributed to the emergence of feminism among women, not all women in SDS experienced it the same way and not all felt silenced.[74] Still, in 1963 it meant that women's opinions on the direction of ERAP were not registered fully until the vote for community organization and after.

Consequences and Meanings

Even after the December 1963 decision in favor of transforming ERAP into a full-time action project, SDS members continued to disagree strongly about whether the campus or the community should be their organizational focus. Conveying the intensity, as well as the personalized nature, of this division during the spring of 1964, Richard Flacks observed, "strategic questions are being turned into matters of basic moral principle; . . . personality clashes are becoming ideological conflicts and vice versa; fairly vituperative labels and stereotypes are coming to replace honest confrontation of opposing views."[75] No doubt, the Hayden-Haber debate and the decision about ERAP generated a deep factional cleavage; so "disgusted" was Haber that for the first time in seven years he did not attend SDS's national convention in June 1964. Even so, the issues at stake and resulting conflicts were greater and more dramatic for leaders like Hayden and Haber than for the general membership of SDS.[76] The consequences and meanings of ERAP's new direction extended well beyond the campus-community split.

The push to make community organization a top priority divided SDS, but the division did not have to be so sharp. Proponents of community action were accused of believing the "notion that the campus is really unimportant compared to the ghetto."[77] Certainly Hayden did when he insisted that all SDS members leave the university for full-time work in communities and that future developments might necessitate the transformation of SDS into ERAP.[78] Hayden's political style, his "tendency to factionalism and personal power politics," fueled these conflicts.[79] Even decades later, SDS activists remember the "factionalism" and "hostility" that accompanied the move into community organization as unfortunate and unnecessary.[80] Due to limited personnel and financial resources, SDS leadership viewed the dilemma between campus and community activism as a zero-sum game, whereby the endorsement of one option precluded the other. But for most SDS members at the time—on campus and off— these were complementary rather than mutually exclusive options. ERAP was primarily for those who had completed their undergraduate work, while SDS's primary task remained that of creating and educating student radicals. In some locations, notably Boston, this complementary perspective dominated.[81]

Still, SDS's shift in priorities had real political consequences for the organization. With much of the leadership opting to participate in ERAP, it contributed to a generational overturn in the organization. At the time, it was perceived to "not be a good thing for the organization to have the best speakers, the best writers leaving."[82] After the Hayden-Haber debate, when the National Council prioritized community organization, followed by peace and disarmament, university reform, and electoral politics, funding and staff were allocated accordingly.[83] This situation led "southern hillbilly SDSer" Jim Williams to warn that the ERAP "tail" was now wagging the SDS "dog."[84] Williams came from Louisville, Kentucky, and a strong trade union and Southern Baptist family; his father called himself a "socialist" and "would explain from the Bible that Jesus Christ was a socialist." Williams was in a unique position in that he both criticized and gave support to ERAP's new direction. He believed SDS needed to give more attention to political education and elections, but he also directed an ERAP project in Louisville during the summer of 1964. From his vantage point, ERAP was "a tremendous drain on the organization. There was no way the organization could maintain higher and higher levels of support for ERAP without doing away with everything else."[85]

Perhaps most important, this ordering of priorities left SDS unprepared for subsequent political developments, particularly the explosion of the Free Speech Movement at the University of California-Berkeley in the fall of 1964 and the escalation of the war in Vietnam in early 1965. Yet it cannot be said that SDS "proceeded to abandon" the campus just as the student and Vietnam teach-in movements began to take off; in December 1963 those developments were nearly a year away.[86] Even in Berkeley, the year preceding the Free Speech Movement was dominated by students organizing off campus, protesting racial discrimination in Oakland and San Francisco, and helping welfare mothers and public housing tenants.[87] SDS's attention returned to the nation's campuses after 1964. Although this change in locational focus would not be SDS's last, it convinced many members at the time, as well as scholars of the New Left since then, that Haber and other critics of community organization were correct: SDS should have maintained campus-based organizing as its top priority all along.

Beyond the conflicts over location and focus, the decision to transform ERAP had implications for gender relations in SDS. At the most basic level, the community projects brought together a core group of women. In fact, ERAP drew many of SDS's "leadership-type women."[88] Although SDS's male-dominated culture often reproduced itself in these projects, a few, such as the Cleveland project, offered women an environment quite apart from that culture. Jeffrey, for one, sought the opportunity to work in such an environment. "I did not want to be in a project that would be dominated by strong male personalities."[89] Whether or not the community proved more conducive to female leadership than did the campus remains to be seen.[90] There is no question, however, that women emerged as the most accomplished organizers in the community projects and, in turn, participated more readily at the national level. "What happened," Marya Levenson of the Boston project later noted, "was that a group of us who were women became much stronger. . . . And so when it came to appearing in SDS national things, I had no question I could talk."[91] Moreover, organizers such as Jeffrey and Carol McEldowney, also in Cleveland, wrote and published often about their experiences and, as Sara Evans argues, commanded respect within SDS as a whole. ERAP provided a set of political experiences and an organizational base from which women could challenge male domination and sexism in SDS and in the larger society.[92]

The move from campus to community also connected SDS to a wider spirit of community organizing in the United States, both past and present. "Virtually every serious left-wing student movement since the early nineteenth century has gone through a similar stage, sending students out from the university 'to the people' as revolutionary agitators."[93] Jim Williams even likened proponents of community organization within SDS to "a bunch of Narodniks," Russian students who had done the same a century before.[94] Beginning with the Progressive Era settlement movement, social reformers and activists throughout the twentieth century, spurred by a desire to contribute to broader social movements, chose to locate their organizing efforts in communities.[95] During the 1960s a wide range of political, social welfare, church, labor, and government entities shifted their focus to the local and communal level. For example, Mobilization for Youth in New York, of which SDS was well aware, spearheaded a social welfare project to prevent juvenile delinquency by encouraging community participation among youth. That students and young people were not alone became even more clear as New Left organizers established themselves in neighborhoods. The massive shift of organizing sites to the community contributed to what came to be called the "backyard revolution" of the mid-1960s and 1970s.[96]

This array of community organizing efforts challenged the idea of the workplace as a uniquely privileged arena for social struggle, an idea that reflected the theoretical position, held by many Marxists, that working-class exploitation was an outcome of domination and coercion at the "point of production."[97] For the most part, the U.S. labor movement located in the workplace rather than the community, overlapping the locus of organizing with the locus of power that created workers' grievances. Because the workers on those shop floors tended to be white and male, they were the constituency privileged in workplace organizing.[98] Taking the community approach of civil rights activists, including SNCC and NSM, SDS proceeded from the fact that this location no longer seemed most appropriate to the conditions and constituencies of the 1960s. The demands of the Civil Rights Movement in particular did not arise solely from, nor was its constituency located solely in, the workplace. Although very aware that the "roots" of local problems "lay elsewhere," civil rights activists in the South such as Ella Baker and Septima Clark operated at the community level.[99] This understanding of the community as an important site for organizing more fully incorporated women's activism, challenged male-defined notions of "workplace," and revealed the community as a place of work for women.

In the end, ERAP represented SDS's most direct attempt to respond and contribute to the Civil Rights Movement, but the project also expressed a desire to go beyond SDS's essentially supportive role. From campus, they could act on their solidarity in only limited ways—fundraising, bringing speakers on campus, holding conferences—which over time for some, like Judith Bernstein, began to feel "a little one-dimensional." A student at the State University of New York-Binghamton, Bernstein "was very impatient at the university. I felt that I was too isolated from what I perceived to be an emerging struggle, emerging changes."[100] Other SDS members expressed an impatience with their position as "faceless friends of SNCC supporters" and sought to take on activities and challenges that would allow them to make their own mark.[101]

This desire dovetailed with a growing understanding of themselves as whites needing to find new ways to relate to the civil rights struggle.

For those who viewed white students as "intruding or at least tagging along" on the Civil Rights Movement, ERAP's emphasis on economic issues and organizing whites created "possibilities for the white student."[102] With the advent of Black Power later on, these possibilities appealed even more to white activists, especially those working in the black movement, like Casey Hayden and Vivian Rothstein. In the midst of reconsidering her place in SNCC as the organization discussed limiting the number and role of whites, Hayden, a longtime SDS member, saw focusing on white Americans "as a way to keep working in alliance with SNCC folks." Vivian Rothstein, a student at Berkeley, worked in Mississippi with CORE during the summer of 1965. By that point, the "racial tension was really extreme," and she "got the message that white people should organize whites."[103] Working with this group also was imperative. Along with many liberals and leftists, SDS feared that poor whites had "great potential for the right," but if "organized around an intelligent program" they could be "a new force for better things." This argument made sense to Dave Strauss. "A lot of civil rights organizations were starting to say, 'People need to work with whites.' 'That's us. We're white, why don't we do that?'"[104]

After the December 1963 National Council meeting, SDS began to do just that, transforming itself from primarily an organization of intellectuals into a sponsor of grassroots, community activists. ERAP dominated SDS's attention throughout the spring. Rennie Davis, who had left his graduate program in labor and industrial relations at the University of Illinois and was living in Ann Arbor, took over from Al Haber as ERAP director and assembled a staff of twenty-five students in Ann Arbor to plan and prepare for the summer of 1964.[105] Meanwhile, events beyond SDS's organizational boundaries sustained the mood of possibility and urgency among proponents of community activism. SNCC was preparing for Mississippi Freedom Summer, and President Lyndon B. Johnson was soon to declare his "war on poverty." "'The times they are a-changing' and we are part of it," exclaimed Richard Flacks, perhaps inspired by the folk celebrity Bob Dylan's brief appearance at the National Council meeting.[106] Now all they needed was a strategy and goals for ERAP, specifically for building a social movement through community organizing.

ERAP brochure, 1964. (Courtesy of Helen Garvy.)

2

Building a Social Movement

They go beyond civil rights. They are interested in economics and
Marx, but by no means limited to Marx. We have emerged from
the beat period and are under way!
—Holgate Young, International Association of Machinists, 1964

The strategy and goals for ERAP first appeared in the position paper entitled *An Interracial Movement of the Poor?* The pamphlet was written by Swarthmore SDS leader Carl Wittman, who based
it on his experiences as an organizer in Cambridge and Chester, and
edited by Tom Hayden.[1] Although 1963 is the standard date given to
An Interracial Movement of the Poor? by scholars, Wittman and Hayden wrote and circulated the paper only after SDS made the decision to
prioritize community organization. This correction gives credence to
the contention of Al Haber and others that the decision for community
organization reflected "momentum rather than theory" and "preceded
the elaborate ideological justification for it."[2]
Even though SDS's initial decision to move from campus to community could be seen as more impulsive than strategic, *An Interracial Movement of the Poor?* remains an important document. It outlined a strategy
for building a social movement through community organization and argued for goals that would challenge the intertwined problems of poverty
and racism. Synthesizing insights and lessons from the labor movement,
the Old Left, and the Civil Rights Movement, the ERAP strategy and
goals were designed to "galvanize the quiescent populists in the ranks of
labor and liberalism" and indeed did inspire enthusiasm and secure funds
from the likes of the labor leader Holgate Young.[3] This synthesis owed
much to Carl Wittman, the son of Communist parents and an avid student of history. Wittman's strategic thinking was shaped by a tacit dialogue with Marxism and the "achievements and failures" of earlier social

movements.[4] With ERAP, SDS members for the first time formulated and put into practice a political strategy with definite goals.

Wittman and Hayden's paper revealed further dilemmas for SDS. Most centrally, did ERAP need a concrete, overarching "metastrategy" that claimed to account for and predict historical social change, or should organizers maintain strategic flexibility, view organizing strategies as alternative hypotheses, and decide between them by trying them out? At the time, Wittman and Hayden were working this through, and *An Interracial Movement of the Poor?* could be read, and was, as both too definitive and too open-ended. Yet the overall tone was tentative. The question mark in the title indicated as much. "What follows," Wittman and Hayden stressed, "is a set of working notes, not a 'blueprint' about which we are confident."[5] This stance invited and provoked discussion, criticism, and elaboration within SDS and ERAP over the spring of 1964. Even so, heading into the first summer of organizing, many questions remained unanswered about ERAP's strategy and goals.

Defining Goals for ERAP

In the broadest sense, Wittman and Hayden wanted to conduct a true "war on poverty," arguing that President Johnson's War on Poverty would not be won because it was "not intended to redistribute power and wealth." More modestly, building on an analysis of poverty developed within SDS—not only by advocates of ERAP—over 1963 and the spring of 1964, they laid out two concrete reform aims for ERAP: national economic planning with democratic participation and full and fair employment or a guaranteed annual income from the state.[6] An attempt to pursue social justice through policy making, these goals integrated an expanded welfare state with citizen participation and empowerment. Although only the first step on the way to the creation of the new society SDS sought, one "which guarantees political freedom, economic and physical security, abundant education, and incentives for wide cultural variety," these aims reflected the New Left's moral and visionary commitments to race and class equality and to participatory democracy. They also fit with items on the more conventional agenda of the liberal-left coalition in the early 1960s.[7]

Along with most Americans, SDS did not directly address the problem of poverty until its "rediscovery" in the early 1960s. Although

John Kenneth Galbraith discussed the "national disgrace" of poverty in his 1958 book *The Affluent Society,* Americans generally ignored the issue of poverty during that decade in favor of examining "the challenges of abundance," explained Paul Booth. An SDS leader at Swarthmore whose parents had been in the Socialist Party, Booth developed research expertise on issues related to the political economy, and his writings, especially as the director of the organization's Peace Research and Education Project (PREP), shaped SDS's perspective on poverty. "The problems of the affluent society, of suburbia, of the organization man and the status seeker," he noted of the 1950s, "were popularly understood as the outstanding social ills of the nation."[8] Relative affluence and confidence in the economy, paradoxically, contributed to the emergence of poverty as a "problem" in the media and in public consciousness in the early 1960s.[9] The combination of the Civil Rights Movement and publications by two influential figures on the American Left, Michael Harrington's *The Other America* in 1962 and Dwight Macdonald's subsequent review of the book in the *New Yorker* in 1963, put the issue of persistent, hard core poverty on the national and SDS's political agenda.

SDS's understanding of the problem of poverty drew on these studies of "the other America." The poor constituted one-fifth of the national population, about 36 million people, according to Harrington and other researchers. Because poor Americans constituted a minority of the population and were isolated geographically, however, they were "invisible." The majority of poor Americans were white, but African Americans earned only 40 percent of what whites earned and constituted 22 percent of the poor—double their proportion of the population.[10] Although most contemporaries assumed the continuation of economic growth, leftists and liberals began to question the assumption that growth would solve persistent poverty—that, in fact, "a rising tide lifts all boats." This questioning, while it reflected a structural insight, moved reformers in two competing directions. One, which led to the War on Poverty, focused on "blocked opportunities" as the cause of poverty among individuals or specific groups, like racial minorities. The second, followed by SDS, emphasized the structural causes of poverty.[11] For SDS, the existence of poverty and unemployment revealed the contradictions of capitalism, specifically the inadequacy of the "free enterprise economy" to ensure full employment and the equitable distribution of resources.[12]

SDS further contended that economic developments and automation during the decade would lead to even greater, permanent unemployment—creating a situation similar to that of the Great Depression of the 1930s. This analysis of automation and unemployment borrowed directly from Harrington, academic scholars, and labor spokesmen. At a National Committee for Full Employment conference in June 1963, SDS members heard Ray Brown, an economist with the Federal Reserve System, predict that the high number of "baby-boom" workers entering the labor force during the 1960s, combined with an increase in automated manufacturing, would leave eleven million Americans unemployed by 1970.[13] Expressing the prominence and gravity of automation fears, A. J. Hayes, president of the International Association of Machinists, warned that "automation presents the United States . . . with a threat and a challenge second only to the possibility of the hydrogen bomb." These concerns contributed to an upsurge in legislative and intellectual activity around national labor market issues.[14]

This upsurge appeared to dovetail with the activist approach of the Democratic administrations of Presidents Kennedy and Johnson. No longer dedicated to their original faith in the invisible hand and a limited state, postwar liberals saw Keynesian economics as fully within the proper realm of public policy liberalism. By the end of the 1950s, prominent economists, like Leon Keyserling, were calling for national commitments to an increased rate of economic growth and to the repair of the country's public sector. Kennedy's proposed tax cut and Johnson's 1964 declaration of an "unconditional war on poverty in America"—to lesser and greater degrees—responded to this call.[15] Moreover, in June 1963, eight months after the sobering Cuban Missile Crisis, Kennedy proposed a relaxation in U.S.-USSR tensions and began negotiations for an unprecedented ban on nuclear testing, resulting in the Test Ban Treaty of 1963. If this brief thaw in the Cold War reoriented national priorities toward domestic needs, cuts in defense spending would follow and make federal funds available for social reform. The defense budget, as Booth put it, was "*the* major stumbling-block to the beginning of a politically meaningful debate on full employment and urban development."[16] These developments formed the backdrop for SDS's proposals for "radical alternatives at the national level for combating poverty," including "rearranging existing economic and political structures."[17]

ERAP planners first urged national economic planning: direct government intervention in labor markets and manpower policy. "It is time for a reexamination of the way in which resources are presently allocated in our society." To this end, the United States needed to develop institutions of local, state, and national planning.[18] Hardly novel, planning had been long part of the postwar social democratic agenda and advocated by prominent labor leaders, such as Jack Conway, executive director of the AFL-CIO Industrial Union Department, and Walter Reuther of the UAW, who pushed for "democratic national planning"—unsuccessfully, as it turned out—as part of the War on Poverty.[19] In fact, ERAP's goal of national planning met with criticism from those who saw it as simply a reiteration of the New Deal vision. "I get only a limited feeling that you have a new vocabulary or new ideas for today," one critic wrote, after receiving ERAP's first publication. "Too much of your brochure reads as though it were the 1930s."[20] Economic planning also implied bureaucratic, centralized, top-down policies, and thus stood at odds with SDS's commitment to participatory democracy.

To counter this possibility, SDS advocated national planning that was organized democratically, or "publicly-controlled," as Wittman and Hayden put it.[21] At this point, SDS was grappling with the "macro-political meanings of participatory democracy" and attempting to envision a state and economy open and responsive to people's voices and needs.[22] Political participation and national planning could be integrated through a variety of "public groupings," including citizen lobbies and worker participation in business management. Although this proposal was reminiscent of industrial democracy from the World War I period—when SDS's parent organization adopted the name League for Industrial Democracy—ERAP planners focused on the era of the New Deal and believed participation made their proposal new.[23] And, indeed, the liberal vision of national economic planning during the 1930s was that of expert management of the economy through centralized state bureaucracies, not of restoring power to individuals and communities. Thus, ERAP director Rennie Davis concluded, "we're working toward something quite apart from the corporate state of the New Deal."[24]

SDS members, along with Harrington and others, also believed that participation would ameliorate the "culture of poverty." A much misunderstood concept advanced by the anthropologist Oscar Lewis, the culture of poverty resulted from "a creative coping" on the part of the poor, included both positive and destructive traits, and was reproduced generationally, as parents passed on their worldview to children.[25] SDS emphasized the emotional and political effects of the culture of poverty: passivity, self-blame, and isolation. Although SDS and Lewis located the causes of poverty in the structure of capitalist economic relations, many contemporaries employed the concept to buttress arguments about poverty as the product of group culture or racial inferiority, of individual faults or moral failings.[26] Al Haber, who was in the midst of conducting research on poverty and developing a demonstration project for the War on Poverty outside Ann Arbor, vigorously countered such views. "Poverty exists not because some people are lazy, indolent, free loaders, or inferior. It exists because of the way the productive and distributive systems are organized and controlled."[27] Through participation, poor Americans could reverse the political powerlessness and social marginalization they felt and lived. This reversal would allow them not just to see and take advantage of "economic opportunity," as the War on Poverty would have it, but to challenge the very "systems" that kept them in poverty.

Beyond democratic national planning, ERAP proposed two specific solutions to the problem of poverty. The first was production-based and, therefore, oriented toward full and fair or nondiscriminatory employment; the second was aimed at the system of distribution and thus concerned with a guaranteed income apart from employment. Public jobs were the only certain source of employment for whites, African Americans, and other racial minorities; nothing compensated for "joblessness except . . . a job," Wittman and Hayden observed.[28] But if the U.S. government would not honor such a commitment, it should insure a decent level of income for all Americans. "The social value that income is a reward for productive work can no longer be maintained in an economic system that cannot provide work for all its members." SDS's assumption of continued economic growth and automation reinforced this perspective.[29] The emphasis on public job creation and guaranteed income differentiated ERAP's agenda from that of the War on Poverty, which considered but rejected such proposals after pressure from business interests and focused instead on education and training. SDS's emphasis was captured in the ERAP slogan "Jobs or Income Now!"[30]

The advocacy of solutions aimed at both production and distribution reflected one of SDS's central and persistent questions about the changing economy: did automation and the loss of manufacturing jobs mean different kinds of work or more leisure time? The organization preferred the former; "We are for jobs rather than income."[31] In contrast to President Kennedy's 1963 proposal to increase unemployment compensation benefits—a more distributionist policy—Paul Booth thought "it urgent to give fulfilling work to the unemployed."[32] SDS's productionist orientation reflected the fact that "work is more suitable to American political culture," as Bob Ross puts it. An early member of SDS at the University of Michigan, with parents who had been part of left-leaning trade union politics in New York until McCarthyism set in, Ross agreed with making "the federal government the employer of last resort."[33] ERAP wanted these public jobs to require skill and imagination and confer dignity upon workers, for SDS members believed that work had the potential to be a rewarding experience. As they had argued the year before in their *Port Huron Statement,* work should involve "incentives worthier than money or survival" and be "educative, not stultifying; creative, not mechanical; self-directed, not manipulated."[34]

In defining their goals, however, ERAP planners—overwhelmingly male—failed to include the role of gender in poverty. During this period, women disproportionately numbered among the poor; in 1960 about 58 percent of all poor adults were women.[35] Due to women's unequal position in the labor market and responsibility for children, they were particularly vulnerable to poverty. Yet in one proposal, women were absent from SDS's list of eight "social groups" who experienced poverty; in another, the category of sex was excluded from the catalog of six "factors" that correlated with low income. Listing the "fatherless family" among those "who are the poor" was the closest ERAP came to considering the poverty of women.[36] New Left intellectuals were not alone, however, for the scholarly discourses about poverty they drew on were, as the historian Michael B. Katz has noted, "surprisingly male-centered." In the mid-1960s the nuclear family, with a breadwinning husband and dependent wife and mother, remained the American ideal for family and gender relationships. According to this ideal, the cause of men's poverty was the lack of work; the cause of women's poverty, the lack of men's support. In these years before the second wave of feminism, mainstream assumptions about masculinity, femininity, and the role of the welfare state led to the assumption, reflected in ERAP literature, that women's poverty equaled disrupted male wage earning.[37]

As a result, ERAP's goals were masculinist, for the worker ERAP planners had in mind was definitely a man. "Our goal should be the creation of new jobs, enough for every working man," or a guaranteed income that exploded "the myth that a man's worth is determined by his economic contribution."[38] Based on assumptions about the respective responsibilities of women and men, SDS assumed that full employment or guaranteed income would shore up men's breadwinning status and thus solve the poverty of women and children. Missed in this formulation was the fact that many men did not conform to the role of breadwinner, while many married women and mothers found it necessary to work outside the home, and their numbers were rising.[39] Similarly, the War on Poverty set out to end male joblessness. New poverty programs aimed to counter "the postponement of full responsibility and manhood" among the poor; initially the work training program Job Corps was designed for young men only.[40] Although ERAP planners and liberal policy makers differed on how to resolve the problem of poverty, they shared a common gender ideology, which left them unprepared to deal with the specific position of low-income women once ERAP and the War on Poverty were under way.

As defined, ERAP's goals found an important audience among civil rights activists and other liberal-left contemporaries. The historian Clayborne Carson credits SDS with encouraging "the shift in the focus of SNCC's activities from civil rights to economic issues." In late 1963 SNCC requested a speaker from SDS to discuss the "integrated nature of problems of unemployment, the vote, and cultural poverty" for blacks, and in early 1964 held a "Demonstration for Jobs and Food," which called for creating jobs around community needs to guarantee work for all African Americans.[41] Later that spring, SDS was invited to participate in the "Ad Hoc Committee on the Triple Revolution." This committee of prominent social scientists, labor leaders, and political activists issued a public memorandum that argued that developments in the areas of nuclear weapons, civil rights, and industrial automation and cybernation constituted a "triple revolution." These developments would restructure the U.S. political economy and necessitate a national full employment policy and, for those not covered by such a policy, a guaranteed minimum income. Reflecting SDS's input, the statement concluded that "unshackling of men from the bonds of unfulfilling labor frees them to become citizens, to make themselves and to make their own history."[42] This memo may have "made only the back pages of the press," but it revealed a now forgotten attempt to define a social-democratic alternative to the welfare state. The Ad Hoc Committee, as well as SNCC, confirmed and validated ERAP's aims.[43]

ERAP's goals also resonated with organized labor, liberal foundations, and individual leftists, securing crucial financial support. During the spring of 1964 the project raised the "incredible" sum of nearly $20,000—a sum equivalent to $100,000 in 1997 dollars.[44] Loyalty to SDS's parent organization, LID, certainly encouraged donors, but supporters also saw ERAP's approach to poverty as a vital complement to the Civil Rights Movement. There was substantial agreement among the liberal-left about the importance of "economic demands going beyond breaking down juridical Jim Crow," according to Michael Harrington.[45] Moreover, ERAP inspired and impressed donors. At one fund-raising meeting with educational directors for the International Association of Machinists, "tears almost came to their eyes as they thought about their experiences in the 1930s. They were quite surprised that someone was trying to organize and help the poor and unemployed." To the labor leader Jack Conway, ERAP was "visionary, . . . sober, intelligent and realistic." "If this exciting effort fails," W. H. Ferry, the pacifist A. J. Muste, and the journalist I. F. Stone pointed out, "it will not be for lack of talent, energy, or savvy, but for lack of funds."[46] Such generous endorsements and the financial support they brought spurred on ERAP advocates.

Spelled out in only the most general terms, ERAP's call for jobs and income, planning and participation may have been "a formula for a mixed economy with a social democratic direction," but the "glimmer of a decentralist alternative" was significant.[47] Instead of settling for a more equal distribution of resources and incomes in the absence of popular power, or assuming that an expanded welfare state could not also be a more democratic welfare state, ERAP planners, together with other SDS members, held that the expansion of public authority to resolve the problem of poverty needed to be accompanied by the extension of political participation, especially to the poor themselves.[48] For SDS, economic questions could not be separated from political ones, nor economic justice from democratic participation. Material resources alone could not solve the problem of poverty; citizen participation and empowerment were crucial, beginning with the social protest and organization of poor Americans.

Formulating the ERAP Strategy

"We believe," Wittman and Hayden argued, "that nothing less than a wholly new organized political presence in the society is needed to break the problems of poverty and racism."[49] They were talking about a social movement of poor, racially diverse Americans, and *An Interracial Movement of the Poor?* laid out a strategy for building this movement through community organizing. Their strategy had three components that reflected the priorities of both practical and personal politics: an understanding of poor Americans as the agents of social change; a role for SDS members as catalysts of social change; and a commitment to establishing community organizations around the issue of unemployment.

In formulating a strategy, SDS needed to settle the question of "agency," that is, which groups were able to effect social change in the United States. According to Marxist theory, the organized working class was to be the agent of social change, but ERAP challenged this Old Left emphasis. Many SDS members considered even liberal trade unionists to be "fat and happy," well integrated into America's postwar affluence and consensus. Labor's social integration meant that the movement had abandoned its role as the foremost agent of social change; it was no longer positioned to challenge fundamental economic structures and relations. This belief was in keeping with the influential sociologist C. Wright Mills's "Letter to the New Left," published in the United States in 1961. Mills argued that the New Left must reject "the labor metaphysic," or the idea that labor is "The Necessary Lever" to bring about social change.[50] Kicking the labor metaphysic may have been part of what made the New Left "new," but not all SDS members agreed. Bob Ross "didn't share that estrangement from labor," while from Baltimore Kim Moody and Peter Davidowicz continued to see organized labor "as the most vital agency of social change in our society." The ERAP strategy, however, assumed that organized labor would not "be a mass political force" campaigning for "progressive economic change."[51]

After dismissing the organized working class as social agents, ERAP advocates might have considered themselves and their fellow activists. Yet they rejected this role for students. Throughout the twentieth century, leftist student groups in the United States had agreed with the Marxist notion that neither students nor intellectuals, as small, generally well-off groups, were positioned to bring about social change.[52] For the New Left, this rejection signaled personal discomfort with seeing themselves—students or young people—as agents. Behind this discomfort, former SDS members recalled, lay feelings of guilt and shame about SDS's race and class privilege. Although there are no exact numbers, members were overwhelmingly white and tended to be middle-class; about one-third were Jewish.[53] However, not all SDS members came from privileged backgrounds. Despite being college-educated and thus "culturally middle-class," many were the first in their family to attend college. Jim Williams noted that members of the University of Louisville chapter were "primarily working class [and] interested in getting into the middle class—not donning sackcloth and ashes, as the ERAP . . . crowd suggests."[54] However, believing that their own grievances were not legitimate, that the middle class could "not produce the revolution," the ERAP crowd—"in the best Bourgeois Adventurist tradition"—looked to the society's most oppressed.[55]

As a consequence, ERAP planners settled upon poor Americans as the agents of social change. "The elimination of poverty . . . requires the mobilization of all the power of the 75 or 100 million Americans who suffer it or suffer over it." Civil rights and community activism in the North and South during 1963 indicated that poor and unemployed blacks could be organized in their own interests. Wittman and Hayden saw a latent capacity for acting and exerting power also existing among poor whites, Mexicans, and Puerto Ricans.[56] A sense of cultural alienation that encouraged some members of SDS to romanticize and identify with poor Americans contributed to this understanding of the "radical potential of the poor." Seeing impoverished citizens as removed from the dominant U.S. culture of consumption and progress, as even "antimodern" in orientation, and estranged from the political system, Hayden contended that "students and poor people make each other feel real."[57] Although to a certain degree naive and unrealistic, identification with the poor constituted a rejection of the materialist values of "the affluent society" and a move toward the humane and moral values of "the counterculture." It also was part of what the historian Doug Rossinow has called the New Left's "search for authenticity," for "inner wholeness."[58] The substitution of "the poor" or "the unemployed" for the proletariat as the radical agent came to be called the "Erapian hypothesis."[59]

In the Erapian hypothesis, either through intention or by default, only men appeared to demonstrate radical agency. To prove that "the unemployed present a potential force," Wittman and Hayden called for organizing in areas where "men are being laid off." Others argued against the idea that "jobless men are incapable of sustained social action."[60] ERAP's romanticized image of poor Americans was gendered as well. For many young men, the poor—meaning men—represented an untamed masculinity, unencumbered by restraints and responsibilities, that countered the dominant domesticated masculinity of the postwar period.[61] Young women, too, were drawn to this image of oppositional manhood, an attraction to "dramatic, unpredictable, possibly dangerous" men from "the other side of the tracks" that allowed them to explore new versions of femininity and sexuality.[62] Yet the Civil Rights Movement disproved this implicit understanding of agency as an attribute of men. SNCC's organizing in Mississippi, for example, resulted in more participation from women than men in rural communities.[63] The prominence, leadership, and evident agency of low-income black women belied the assumption that poor, unemployed men alone were radical agents and, thus, should be ERAP's sole constituency.

In the end, advocates of the agency of the poor within SDS contended that the organized working class no longer was the privileged social movement constituency. They remained committed to a class-based strategy but were beginning to see that, like the Civil Rights Movement, the social movements and politics of the 1960s did not fit the old categories. Jim Williams believed that class struggles had "been diverted into new, unexplored channels, with completely new forms and effects." The participants were now "dispossessed economic groups," such as racial minorities and the "technological unemployed."[64] But the search for "a surrogate universal" in SDS did not end with ERAP. Like debates over whether the campus or community provided the best location for contributing to social change, debates over the agency of social change continued, with various groups—blacks, revolutionary youth, the "new working class"—considered over the decade of the 1960s.[65]

After deciding upon the agency of poor Americans, ERAP planners began to define a role for students as organizers and catalysts of social change. Such a role was necessary because, while poor blacks, whites, and other racial minorities were "*objectively* ripe for radical action" as a class, the effects of the culture of poverty and the existence of white racism prevented them from doing so.[66] "The poor are not a class. In an ultimate sense, they have common roots and interests, but in day to day life they are separate, discontinuous."[67] This understanding stemmed from the Marxist distinction between "class-in-itself" and "class-for-itself," which recognizes that occupying an objective class position cannot be equated with a subjective consciousness of class membership. By demonstrating that poverty was structural and crossed racial lines, ERAP would catalyze class consciousness and solidarity among poor, racially diverse Americans, aiding the transition from a "class-in-itself" to a "class-for-itself." "Their common consciousness of poverty and economic superfluousness," wrote Wittman and Hayden, "will ultimately have to bring them together." This aim may have been "exuberantly optimistic" about overcoming racial differences and entrenched white racism to unite low-income people. Yet, as Paul Booth remembers, it "seemed to be analogous to what we knew had occurred under certain circumstances in union organizing."[68]

SNCC's organizing among poor black southerners provided SDS with a compelling model for the role of catalyst. Activists in SNCC and SDS defined the role of social movement catalyst as that of an initiator, not that of a leader or a vanguard in the Leninist sense, a definition that stemmed from their critical stance toward any form of domination or authoritarian control. "The people on the bottom don't need leaders at all. What they need is to have confidence in their own lives," SNCC organizer Bob Moses argued.[69] With this perspective, ERAP organizers would enable, rather than guide or direct, low-income community residents toward building a social movement. They had an "image of an organizer who never organized, who by his simple presence was the mystical medium for the spontaneous expression of the 'people.'" Behind this image was a romantic populism, a belief in the poor, in the words of the historian Michael Kazin, that "once empowered, they would pursue tolerant, egalitarian ends," a belief soon to be called into question.[70]

The role of catalyst greatly interested New Left activists, as became clear during recruitment for ERAP Summer 1964. "We are asking each person . . . to consider [whether] one should devote a summer, if not a lifetime, in a personal engagement with the problems of America's dispossessed."[71] The call to service resonated with many young people, as it did for volunteers for the Peace Corps and Volunteers in Service to America (VISTA). Dave Strauss heard John F. Kennedy propose the idea of the Peace Corps during a campaign swing through Michigan in the fall of 1960. "It meant something to hear . . . everybody should be serving the people in the world." David Palmer also heard Kennedy's speech, and he ended up serving both in the Peace Corps in Africa and later in Cleveland with ERAP. The local press in Trenton, New Jersey, an ERAP location in 1964, made the same connection, calling New Left organizers "the Domestic Peace Corps."[72] Also appealing was something that drew radical students of the 1930s into activism as well: the promise of a new community of friendship and shared purpose.[73]

As a consequence, ERAP was "swamped" with applications. Although a small number compared to SNCC's 1,000 volunteers for Mississippi Freedom Summer, the project placed some 120 organizers in the field that first summer, a number equal to 20 percent of SDS's total membership.[74] Lack of evidence makes it impossible to calculate how many women and men initially applied to ERAP, but they were recruited in proportions roughly equivalent to their numbers in SDS. Thus, men outnumbered women two to one in ERAP as a whole, a male to female balance ERAP planners deemed "favorable."[75]

Both men and women saw the role of catalyst as a way to meet personal needs and define a political identity. Like many reformers in the past, they developed a social movement strategy that included a prominent position for themselves; they would be not merely "secondary or supportive, but the catalyst of the movement." Part of a search for meaning and authenticity, the role offered an opportunity to create "radical life vocations" where work could be personally engaging and politically significant.[76] SNCC already had forged the way, and, unlike radical student activists of the 1930s, at this point SDS members found a career in the labor movement not as compelling an alternative. "Working in poor communities is a concrete task in which the split between job and values can be healed," Hayden contended.[77] For these reasons, a number of prominent ERAP advocates came to consider community organizing as a permanent career path. "For those who want to take sides," one such organizer urged, "I believe the time is at hand when real vocations exist through which we can realize our values and realize ourselves. Organizing . . . can be a way of life if only we make it so."[78]

Yet creating radical life vocations in community organizing had different meanings for men and women during the 1960s, a time of ambivalent, perhaps transitional, gender attitudes.[79] For men, community organizing involved a rejection of the professional career track that was clearly in their futures. Critical of a "future demarcated by occupational boundaries, in a society increasingly dominated by white-collar jobs [and] air-conditioned offices," they, as had the Beats before them, implicitly challenged the masculine ideal of domesticated breadwinner.[80] Hayden felt divided between "trying to mimic the life of James

Dean or something like that" and being "in the Establishment—ambitious young reporter who wanted to be a famous correspondent."[81] Although they shared a critique of middle-class professionalism, the men who went into ERAP differed as to whether they saw the traits and skills demanded by corporations and white-collar occupations as emasculating, as did contemporary academic sociologists and social critics, or viewed the "male" worlds of business and politics as harsh and competitive.[82] Either way, they sought alternatives to the professional career track.

For many women, community organizing held greater appeal than the distinctly unsatisfactory future of marriage and motherhood, poor jobs and low pay.[83] "There was no place to go," Sharon Jeffrey recalled feeling after college. For Vivian Rothstein, the role of organizing among the poor "meant that your world expanded."[84] After graduating from Smith College in 1964, Carol Glassman, the daughter of lower-middle-class Jewish parents, was living at home, working as a waitress—"the only job you could get if you couldn't type"—and debating whether or not to go to Europe. At Smith she had taken a course on problems in the American economy, written a seminar paper on poverty, read Harrington's *The Other America*, heard the SNCC freedom singers, and become aware of NSM's organizing projects. Then she and her friends Merble Harrington and Harriet Stulman, who all had attended Smith, met Lee Webb at the SDS national office in New York and heard about ERAP.

> It really is like I was an adding machine and all the stuff had been put in and nobody had pushed the equals button, and that conversation with Lee, there it all was. That was the first time I really felt like all the things I thought and felt just came together in some way that made sense to me.

She became "very excited" about working with ERAP. "It had the same feel to me [as Europe] in terms of adventure and going out differently into the world."[85] The role of organizing among the poor opened up life possibilities and options for Glassman, Jeffrey, and other women.

ERAP provided a timely alternative to the traditional career or family track laid out for male and female college graduates in the early 1960s, and both women and men pursued community organizing as a vocation. But men in SDS understood that they were giving up power to do so, while women felt that they were gaining power.[86] Moreover, such organizing—unchaperoned, political, and sometimes dangerous—could be seen as part of the process of "becoming a man," "seeing the world," or "testing one's mettle," as the sociologist Doug McAdam argues. Young women, however, were not expected to have such adventures; thus, just by volunteering for ERAP, women transcended traditional gender expectations.[87]

The final component of the ERAP strategy involved building community organizations. Because the eradication of poverty necessitated the meaningful democratic participation of poor Americans, ERAP's introductory brochure asked, in an oft-used metaphor, "can the newly articulated poor achieve a permanent voice in the political arena?" Having or finding one's "voice" allowed for the definition and expression of needs and interests and was equated with political participation. Yet poverty robbed the poor of their voice; it limited their "full exercise of democratic rights."[88] Organization building would overcome the experience of oppression, the culture of poverty, that left the poor feeling powerless, isolated, and alienated, allowing poor community residents to realize and act on their radical agency as individuals and as a community. Community organization, then, would give "voice to the voiceless." Echoing a political tradition that harkened back to Thomas Jefferson, through John Dewey, and to C. Wright Mills, Wittman and Hayden believed that neighborhood-based forums and discussions would establish a basis for participatory democracy, social change around class and race inequalities, and "possibly the seed for a different society."[89]

Assuming "particular classes have innate interests," ERAP planners believed that once poor Americans found their voice they would raise economic issues and thus would be recruited and radicalized most with the issue of unemployment.[90] "Key" to the issues of civil rights and peace, unemployment, according to Wittman and Hayden, meant that "the movement is immediately political." It also led logically to ERAP's goals: jobs or income.[91] Leaders of the U.S. Communist Party during the early years of the Great Depression also considered unemployment to be the "tactical key to the present state of class struggle" and would tap into "the spontaneous discontent that was sweeping through the urban unemployed." Once organized, the 1930s Unemployed Councils raised demands equivalent for the time period to those of ERAP, including demands for "work or wages," public jobs or unemployment compensation.[92] Aware of these obvious similarities, ERAP advocates researched and reported on the Unemployed Councils but disagreed about the usefulness of historical comparisons. For some, the councils were hardly "relevant," while for others they were ERAP's "model."[93]

Like the Unemployed Councils, organizing around unemployment in ERAP privileged a constituency of men. The Chicago project proclaimed itself "an organization of employed and unemployed men who are demanding government policies which guarantee everyone a decent job or income."[94] This masculinist strategy implied that women's organizing and even women organizers were unnecessary. In 1964 the Chicago project's list of summer staff needs included a project director, a research director, educational staff, a service coordinator, and two to five organizers. Revealing both the low priority given to mobilizing community women and the gender stereotyping of women's work in the projects, they added to the end of the list "a girl to handle office work and perhaps handle organizing focused on women."[95] In this way, ERAP initially departed from more traditional approaches to community organization. Throughout the twentieth century, local organizing efforts disproportionately involved women as the caretakers of families and communities. Moreover, these efforts focused on issues stemming from the spheres of distribution and consumption, such as slum housing, rather than from the sphere of production, as did unemployment. ERAP's gendered strategy meant that organizations comprised of neighborhood women devoted to community issues would not at first be recognized as legitimate or political.[96]

In the end, ERAP's various community organizations aimed to forge ties to the civil rights and labor movements and establish an interracial movement of the poor on the national level. These ties among movements would place ERAP and its agenda on the national political scene, the locus of decision-making power in American society.[97] How ERAP was going to move from the local to the national level was not laid out with any specificity, however. "I think there was just a huge amount of squishiness there," notes Fran Ansley, who later organized in Cleveland and Chicago. "Somehow all of this would magically build and build and build." Jim Williams agrees. "For the life of me, I didn't see how an organization of five hundred students was going to be able to build and sustain a national organization of poor people."[98] Even so, what needs to be emphasized is that, for SDS, community organizing was not an end in itself, but a means to exert political pressure in order to eradicate poverty, achieve racial justice, and extend participatory democracy into low-income communities.

Criticizing the ERAP Strategy

An Interracial Movement of the Poor? was circulated and read while the planning and preparations for ERAP Summer 1964 took place. As logistical arrangements for the summer proceeded, including recruitment and the selection of ten project sites, sharp criticism from SDS members and other commentators emerged in response to Wittman and Hayden's newly formulated strategy. Although they agreed with the larger goal of building an interracial movement of the poor, few were happy with the strategy for how to achieve it. Critics singled out different aspects of the strategy for criticism, revealing two competing approaches to what precisely constituted a political strategy for building a social movement within ERAP.

For those concerned with formulating a concrete, overarching "meta-strategy," ERAP lacked clarity and specificity and failed to answer questions of method, tactics, and outcome. Exactly what approach, these critics asked, would ERAP organizers utilize to mobilize poor neighborhood residents? And how precisely would local community organizing efforts transform the U.S. welfare state?[99] Steve Max considered the ERAP strategy and goals "too vague." A red-diaper baby, Max had worked as a community organizer in East Harlem in 1960 and 1961 as part of a grassroots political organization with a specific goal: to oust the Democratic machine and elect to public office the first blacks and Puerto Ricans in the area.[100] "Clearly we need to start formulating specific immediate demands," another critic contended. "No one throughout history was organized on the basis that if they only united, then a program would be generated. Quite the reverse." Without an organizing blueprint, Jim Williams believed, ERAP was impulsive "ghetto-jumping."[101]

These critics cited the notion of poor Americans as the agents of social change and the lack of results from the ERAP pilot project in Chicago as further evidence of the strategy's unfeasibility. The poor were unlikely agents simply on a mathematical basis: all the poor, even if organized, were still a minority (20 percent) of the country. "These men . . . are in limited supply. They don't form a constituency."[102] Imprecision in the use of "the poor" and "the unemployed" also provoked censure from those who remained committed to "the labor metaphysic" and believed that ERAP should organize not the poor but rather temporarily unemployed workers. Kim Moody reminded his colleagues that it "was not the miserably poor that rebelled in the '30s, but primarily those who were employed."[103] Meanwhile, in Chicago the project's original organizer, Joe Chabot, had been joined by Danny Max and Lee Webb. They located their project office on Chicago's North Side near an unemployment compensation center, which they leafleted to reach and organize unemployed men. But they had little to show for their efforts. Of a symbolic apple-selling demonstration designed to recall the Great Depression held in late May, Rennie Davis reported, "Hell, we've been working at this now since September and finally spring 25 guys into the streets."[104] Clearly, Wittman and Hayden's strategy needed to be revised.

Other detractors regarded the ERAP strategy as problematic for precisely the opposite reasons. For them, the problem was the strategy's definitive, determining character; they mistrusted metastrategies that claimed to account for and predict historical social change. "In short," Paul Potter later argued, "ERAP substituted a kind of closed, vulgar Marxism for the more hopeful tentativeness of earlier SDS proclamations." They rejected any hint of economic determinism and, instead, advocated a varied, situational strategy, consistent with the New Left's experimental approach to politics.[105] How else, they asked, could ERAP maintain its commitment to participatory democracy? Should not the ERAP strategy emerge in the process of inspiring community residents to organize around the issues and goals they themselves defined as important? Ken McEldowney, a graduate of the University of Michigan who was around "even before SDS was SDS," argued against following a rigid political strategy. "What you need to do is to organize people around the issues that mean something in their lives, that are important to them." A member of the ERAP staff preparing for the summer, McEldowney took this view with him when he volunteered for the Cleveland project.[106] Only with a flexible approach would ERAP measure up to the New Left's standard of participation.

These detractors believed that the priority of organizing around the issue of unemployment made the ERAP strategy too deterministic and looked to events in Chester to bolster their position. They contended that the projects should take up any issues of concern to neighborhood residents. A reworking of the ERAP strategy to include a multiplicity of organizing issues, unlike unemployment alone, would encompass the full range of needs that existed in poor communities.[107] The ideas behind ERAP's expanded political strategy were developed first in

Chester, where Swarthmore students continued to engage in community organizing with local civil rights activists. Residents there created a list of demands that included not only full and fair employment but also equal and improved education, adequate housing, and universal medical care, indicating that multiple issues were necessary for effective grassroots organizing.[108] Wittman concluded that residents, "although most concerned about employment, will be most active in those areas where local changes can bring about improvement, i.e. public services, housing, and schools." At this point, ERAP began to consider "a working conception of what a radical, multi-issue, community-based organization means."[109]

Developments beyond SDS's orbit broadly supported both critical perspectives. Those arguing for a flexible strategy and multiple issues drew on a theory of "community unions" that transplanted the traditional trade union model of organization from the workplace to the community. During the spring of 1964 the political scientist James O'-Connor argued that community unions focused on housing, education, and welfare rather than a lack of jobs "will be the appropriate mode of working class organization and struggle."[110] The language later used in ERAP demonstrated the influence of this concept, with projects named the Newark Community Union Project, the Cleveland Community Union, and the JOIN (Jobs or Income Now) Community Union in Chicago. At the same time, black activists in CORE and Mexican American farmworkers in California sought to create a "new kind of union" or a "civil rights union" to organize "the unorganized," the poverty-wage workers in the ghettos and fields, whom most labor unions ignored.[111] These efforts did not come to fruition until 1965, but they fit logically with the thinking of those who wanted a more concrete strategy and to organize workers. In fact, SDS members in Baltimore, such as Kim Moody and Peter Davidowicz, already were cooperating with similar CORE and AFL-CIO initiatives in that city.[112]

ERAP volunteers came from those who agreed with Wittman and Hayden's strategy, as well as from both groups of critics. Of the original paper, Paul Booth says, "I was sold on that," and for Bob Ross it "seemed like exciting stuff . . . strategically clever to me." Ross headed to Chicago that summer, and Booth set up the Oakland, California, project the following year.[113] Paul Millman, a red-diaper baby who grew up in a housing project in a working-class, integrated neighborhood in Brooklyn, "loved the idea. If I understood the strategy at the time, it seemed to me . . . they were talking about an interracial movement of working people. It was in keeping with my background, with how I was raised, and it was great." He too went to Chicago.[114] ERAP also attracted those like Carol Glassman, who stressed "the need to listen to the community to learn what the issues should be" and participated in projects first in Philadelphia and later in Newark, and recruited strong advocates of organizing around unemployment, including Kim Moody to Baltimore.[115]

As the summer of 1964 began, major questions remained about ERAP's strategy and goals. Of the ten projects established that summer, only three—Baltimore, Philadelphia, and Chicago—intended to implement the original strategy and goals. Proposals for the projects in Chester, Louisville, Newark, Trenton, and Cleveland opted for strategic flexibility and presented a range of possible organizing issues, not just unemployment. Summer organizing projects in Boston and Hazard, Kentucky, were more consistent with ERAP's orientation toward "joblessness through automation," but they were not official ERAP projects. The initial organizing project in Boston was sponsored by PREP, not ERAP, and would focus on the unemployment not of the poor but of defense industry workers. The Hazard project, cosponsored by SDS, the Committee for Miners, and the Appalachian Committee for Full Employment, would provide support for unemployed miners as well as mount a legal defense for leaders facing trumped up charges after engaging in a wildcat strike.[116]

An Interracial Movement of the Poor? then had failed to achieve what it set out to do: establish consensus within SDS about ERAP's purpose and aims. But this fact did not deter ERAP advocates. "Our major problem," Carl Wittman maintained, paraphrasing Karl Marx on philosophers, "is not to analyze the situation, but to change it." "Nobody knew if the analysis was true or not," Jeffrey recalled. "But it sounded good, and it fit. And therefore we could justify doing these projects."[117] What really began to provide ERAP organizers with answers to their strategic questions were encounters with actual neighborhood residents in the specific community projects.

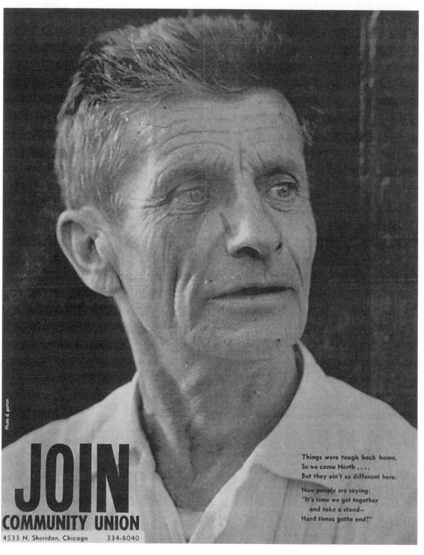

Chicago JOIN poster featuring John Howard, 1966. (© D. Gorton.)

3

Communities and Constituents

"Cleveland is coming along," wrote Sharon Jeffrey in May 1964 of her experiences over the past month. "I have learned lots about the white community in my short time and about unemployment, but it is dam[n] as hell to develop a program. The white poor represent but a minor, minor part of the total city population, that a movement of the interracial poor is highly unlikely. Well, we shall see."[1] This conclusion did not augur well for an ERAP project in Cleveland, and it could have dissuaded Jeffrey, along with Case Western Reserve University medical students Charlotte Phillips and Oliver Fein, from founding one. Only a few days later, however, they wrote confidently of the range of program possibilities they saw for the project, including "a community newspaper; working with a group of mothers who have formed a protest group on welfare; organizing jobless youth; voter registration and education; and organizing parents around problems in education."[2]

This experience was repeated throughout ERAP during the summer of 1964. As New Left organizers entered low-income, inner-city neighborhoods, they encountered communities and constituents that challenged assumptions central to their social movement strategy. SDS's strategy for building an interracial movement of the poor through community organizing privileged unemployment as an issue and unemployed men as a constituency. Yet organizers soon learned that unemployment was not always the most immediately felt, or considered by residents to be the most important, problem in the neighborhoods. Nor were jobless men the only significant community constituency. In addition, ERAP's assumption that the primary barrier to poor Americans realizing and acting upon their social agency was a lack of political consciousness and organization underestimated both the myriad barriers to, and the already existing sources for, political activism in the communities. These lessons would spur ERAP organizers to rethink and revise their social movement strategy.

Setting Up

Although eventually there were thirteen official ERAP projects, the four largest, longest-lasting, and most successful projects were located in Chicago's Uptown, Newark's Clinton Hill, Cleveland's Near West Side, and—by 1965—Boston's Roxbury-North Dorchester.[3] The persistence of these particular projects had much to do with why New Left organizers selected these sites in the first place. As major U.S. cities at a time of "urban crisis," Chicago, Newark, Cleveland, and Boston were on the national political agenda and recipients of national media attention and federal grant dollars. During the postwar period, southern migration, competition from the growing suburbs, deindustrialization, urban blight—and the responses they engendered—reshaped metropolitan America, nowhere more than in these four aging cities.[4] ERAP project locations "were 'almost out of a textbook' in the sense that conditions seemed to demand organizing."[5]

More important, perhaps, these four cities were also places where organizers wanted to be. The selection of Boston and Cleveland as project locations permitted New Left activists to remain in school, while the Chicago and Newark projects allowed them to live in or near attractive and interesting cities. Many organizers, from urban backgrounds themselves, enjoyed residing in large metropolitan areas. At the end of ERAP Summer 1964, Newark organizers asserted, "We are happy here. We do not want to leave."[6] Personal connections brought Dave Strauss back to Cleveland and kept southerner Jim Williams in his hometown of Louisville. "Being north of the Mason-Dixon always gave me a little hard time." Organizers also considered with whom they wanted to work. For Ken McEldowney, Cleveland was the clear choice. "I felt closer to the people there. Not because of any scientific reasons."[7] Without the combination of a prominent urban location and personal satisfaction, ERAP projects elsewhere uniformly and quickly failed.

Wherever New Left organizers ended up, they shared a commitment to creating community in their projects and aimed to integrate themselves into the neighborhoods by living and working in the area. Like the Progressive Era settlement workers before them, they believed "you gotta live with the folk if you're ever gonna understand them and they trust you."[8] Yet they went further, seeking to moderate class differences between themselves and the communities by adopting the style and standard of living of those around them. They chose to live at a subsistence level, often at the level of a welfare budget. Kathy Boudin, who grew up in a family committed to making "a better society," had just finished her junior year at Bryn Mawr. She joined the Cleveland project for half of the summer of 1964 and later returned in November 1965. "My experience in Cleveland—for better or worse—led me to feel that I had to live a life immersed in the community, almost like a vow of poverty taken by nuns. So that in my personal choices for myself, I was living out the ideals of equality."[9] ERAP's "voluntary poverty ethic" provoked both admiration and sarcasm from commentators. "It looked as though the students had ironed the wrinkles into their shirtsleeves," one noted of organizers in Chicago.[10]

To make this vision of community work, ERAP set up many but not all of the projects as experiments in communal living. In the tradition of SNCC, organizers pooled resources and shared finances. Corinna Fales spent the summer of 1964 in Chester. "It was amazing. We had no money. I had five bucks to me, and I remember showing up and Vernon [Grizzard] saying, 'Okay everybody, we've got to live communally now, hand over what you got.'" This requirement was not easy for Fales. Although her father had been a university professor, upon his death the family became impoverished, and she attended Goucher College on scholarship. In Chester she thought, "Oh my god, I have to hand over this five bucks which is my only feeling of security in the world."[11] To save money, project members often resided in the same house or apartments, although some women roomed with local families, as SNCC did in the South. They also ate meals together and circulated "recipes for a semi-starvation diet" that included creamed chicken over biscuits and hot dogs with baked beans. "I don't eat tunafish casserole," says Paul Millman, looking back, "because on the [Chicago] JOIN project we once ate tunafish casserole for, I think, forty-one days straight." And Fales remembers "buying ten to fifteen pound bags of chicken hearts. You got tired of eating chicken hearts which I couldn't stand to begin with . . . but there was a lot of spirit, there was a lot of energy."[12]

ERAP's "ethic of community" anticipated what would become a tenet of the hippie counterculture of the 1960s. A number of the ERAP projects were not only "organizing communes" with a common ideology and a strategy for social change but also "utopian communes" with the aim of exploring new ways of living.[13] Reflecting ERAP's integration of the two communal types, Carol Glassman wanted the long-range vision for organizing to be to "transcend the limitations of what some refer to as the greed of man, where one can begin to love."[14] Despite ERAP's radical egalitarian and transformative implications, projects often failed to challenge the sexual division of labor, in which women continued to perform many of women's traditional tasks, such as cooking and serving meals.[15] There were significant exceptions, however. In Cleveland, organizers, male and female, rotated household chores, with cooks labeled "potato keepers" and "broom keepers" in charge of cleaning. The term "keepers" instead of "directors" was meant to convey that authority and responsibility were "evenly dispersed throughout the group." And in Newark men too were to "do their share."[16] Even so, ERAP's "new" way of living generally coexisted with older patterns of gender relations.

Organizers in all the ERAP projects shared a significant obstacle to setting up a community project: financial support. ERAP planners spent the spring of 1964 raising funds on a national basis and regularly appealed to the SDS membership for support, but as the summer began every local project faced inadequate funding. They estimated that an average of two hundred dollars per month per organizer was needed and encouraged volunteers to bring that amount with them. Still, they did not want distinctions to be made between "those people on the project who can and cannot support themselves."[17] In the end, ERAP organizers solicited funds from sympathetic individuals and organizations in the various metropolitan areas. Dave Strauss connected the Cleveland ERAP project with the local Left. "My parents' friends sort of provided a network of fund-raising for us in Cleveland. We had to raise a lot of money locally and lot of those Old Left folks provided us either money or food and stuff like that."[18] ERAP also sponsored fundraisers in the communities, and, depending on their personal financial situations, individual organizers took part- and full-time jobs.

Organizers also lacked concrete knowledge about the communities they were entering. Due to a lack of time, funding, and, perhaps, patience, most of the project proposals were written without even a visit to the chosen location. Lee Webb explained this phase of the planning and preparations for the summer. "We bought the census tracts, got a book about cities from the library, and we sat down and wrote the proposals for all the different cities."[19] SDS's analysis of poverty and the culture of poverty also produced and reinforced generalizations about the lives and conditions of poor Americans. "None of my reading or class work prepared me to know the ghetto, or know concrete economic realities," Tom Hayden recalled of his experience in Newark. At the time, he described poor Americans as "the scorned, the illegitimate, and the hurt," revealing how sincere empathy can border on conde-scension and victimization.[20] The consistent use of terms such as "the poor" and "the unemployed" in ERAP revealed an abstract—and es-sentialized—knowledge about low-income community residents.

Images used in publicity for the projects helped "to construct mean-ings" of "the poor." In the tradition of documentary expression, ERAP used these images to make visible the "invisible" poor of "the other America," persuade and convince viewers to identify emotionally with the subject, and see poverty as a problem that could be solved with po-litical commitment.[21] The style of ERAP's photographic images re-flected a historical frame of reference of the 1930s, as did the expecta-tion of increasing unemployment and discussions of the New Deal and the Unemployed Councils. Along with the folk music revival, the publi-cation of the second edition of James Agee and Walker Evans's *Let Us Now Praise Famous Men* in 1960 played a part in "the New Left's ap-propriation of depression iconography."[22] This book influenced Todd Gitlin and Nancy Hollander's *Uptown* and D. Gorton's photographs for the Chicago JOIN project.[23] Photographs of an unemployed black worker selling apples and demanding "jobs now" and John Howard, a white resident of Uptown who had endured and wanted to end "hard times," sought to evoke the mood, economy, and politics of the 1930s. They also conveyed meanings that dovetailed with ERAP's interracial and masculinist strategy and goals.

Overall, plans for ERAP Summer 1964 were based on partial knowl-edge and faulty assumptions. During the spring, some organizers noted the need for local research before the projects began. A few called for a comprehensive research program based in ERAP's national office, but this proposal was resisted by most. Jeffrey believed that research was a low priority at this early point, and that organizers should wait until "*after* the summer to know what kind [of research] we need." Later that summer, when Cleveland organizers adopted an ambitious pro-gram of research, they still emphasized that "[r]esearch is viewed as augmenting community work, not substituting for it."[24] ERAP organiz-ers in the individual projects later would survey the communities to gain crucial information, but at the start they were generally unin-formed about the complex realities—the urban context, population makeup, physical environment, concerns of residents, as well as the barriers to, and sources for, political activism—of ERAP's communities and constituents in Chicago, Newark, Cleveland, and Boston.

Chicago's Uptown

Established in the fall of 1963, the Chicago project was ERAP's first "action" project. For the first year, through the summer of 1964, the project focused on implementing the original ERAP strategy: organizing the unemployed on a citywide basis. Organizers there included Joe Chabot, who later left the project, and Lee Webb, who had been in Chicago since the spring. They were joined that summer by Stan Nadel, Bob Ross, Rich Rothstein, and, continuing ERAP's close, even familial, connection to the labor movement, Toni Helstein and Leslie Woodcock, the daughters of Ralph Helstein and Leonard Woodcock, officials in the United Packinghouse Workers of America and the UAW, respectively.[25] After a difficult summer with little to show for their efforts, organizers decided to try the approach taken by other ERAP projects. They would select a neighborhood in which to locate the project and begin to organize on a community level. Their decision-making process involved sorting by neighborhood the index cards they had filled out when contacting unemployed Chicagoans. The winner, Uptown, had the highest stack of cards, and they chose to set up a project there.[26] By the winter of 1964–65, New Left organizers had installed themselves in the neighborhood as part of the Chicago JOIN project, working out of a storefront office in central Uptown, and living in apartments scattered throughout the area.

Uptown, Chicago's "white ghetto," had the highest concentration of poor white residents in the city and was considered to be "a poverty pocket" in the larger metropolitan area. Encompassing 120 square blocks about five miles north of downtown Chicago and south of Evanston, Uptown was the primary destination of Appalachian migrants to the city in the decades following World War II, when over three million Appalachians migrated north and contributed to the postwar "southernization" of the northern white working class.[27] Like Newark, Cleveland, and Boston during the postwar period, Chicago's manufacturing sector declined due to the twin forces of deindustrialization and suburbanization. Major industries, such as meatpacking and International Harvester, left the city, making employment more difficult to secure for Chicago residents.[28] Such developments contributed to sharp differences in wealth between the city and the suburbs, as was true nationally. In 1960, for example, 60 percent of metropolitan families with incomes under $3,000 lived in the central city, while 55 percent of those with incomes over $10,000 resided in the suburbs.[29] For recent migrants—black or white—job discrimination and a lack of networks worsened these economic disparities, as New Left organizers in Uptown soon learned.

Uptown residents came from a range of ethnic and economic backgrounds. Although whites, mostly southern and Appalachian migrants, comprised the majority of residents throughout the decade, Native Americans, Latinos, and African Americans began to account for more of the population. In 1960 Uptown's Latino and African American residents together constituted less than 2 percent of the total neighborhood population; by 1970 they had risen to 13 percent and 4 percent respectively. "Every block," as Rich Rothstein wrote, also held "a mixture of working class and underclass."[30] When Chicago's unemployment rate was reported as less than 3 percent in December 1964, with rates for white workers even lower, New Left organizers conducted their own survey. They found that nearly 48 percent of residents in one five-block area of Uptown were unemployed and that more than one-third of Uptown residents received some form of public aid. Another study, part of the city's War on Poverty, determined that 51 percent of heads of households in the community were either unemployed or had incomes below the poverty standard of $3,000.[31] One difficulty was the lack of full-time work close by. "There are a lot of jobs in the suburban areas," one community woman pointed out, "but often the unemployed in Uptown do not have transportation to these jobs."[32] Of their economic situations, Uptown's southern migrants stated, "Chicago is like home in one way: both have 'hard luck and misery.'"[33]

Uptown's physical environment was as heterogeneous as its population. With the so-called Gold Coast bordering Uptown's east side along the lakefront, dilapidated houses and high-rise apartment buildings, flophouses and first-rate hotels were all within walking distance of each other. There was one predominantly African American block in the neighborhood as well, "the remnants of the servant quarters of rich homes along the Outer Drive."[34] A citywide housing shortage following World War II prompted Uptown's landlords to subdivide many of the spacious homes and huge old apartments into smaller units. These conversions contributed to overcrowding, with some 12.4 percent of units having more than one person per room; Uptown contained one of the most densely populated square miles in Chicago.[35] Poor maintenance combined with overuse and overcrowding produced a neighborhood in a state of decline. Run-down tenements, broken windows, and uncollected garbage were common, as were the "whiskey bottles wrapped in paper bags [that] seemed to grow in every front yard." Junior Ball, an Uptown resident, complained about the lack of safe, clean places for children's recreation. "If the kids don't have a place to play besides the streets, the biggest part of them will wind up getting hit by cars or go to the lake and get lost or get into some sort of mischief."[36] "Ten years ago," Uptown resident Isabel Green recalled, "when I had made this my residence, this place—the North side—was a lot cleaner and a better place to live in than it is today. It has fallen down immensely."[37]

Concerns about employment prospects, housing conditions, and police relations predominated among the Uptown residents contacted by ERAP. Many had serious problems with notorious day labor agencies, "Manpower" and "Ready-Men." "If you're lucky, you may wind up with 8 dollars before you take out car fare, lunch, and taxes," one Uptown resident related. "The tops I ever got was $1.25 an hour. A family man can't make it on that."[38] Residents complained, too, about the high cost and poor state of housing and neglectful, indifferent landlords. "We are tired of the filth from rats and roaches, bad wiring, bad plumbing," Dorothy Perez angrily stated, "and promises, promises, promises."[39] The relationship between the community and Chicago police also was becoming a prominent issue. Uptown residents—especially racial minorities and young men attracted to street life—protested rude, rough, and violent treatment by police. "Because our clothing is not very good, a week does not go by without the police stopping us on the street and making us put our hands up like a thief," one Puerto Rican resident revealed. "We know we need police protection, but who is going to protect us against them?"[40]

ERAP organizers saw a number of barriers to building a strong community organization that could deal with these problems in Uptown. Finding common ground for the neighborhood's heterogeneous population would prove difficult for ERAP. "There are different communities within the community," Judith Bernstein commented.[41] Uptown also had the highest rate of transiency in the city, and many migrants remained attached to their homes in the South rather than making a commitment to the neighborhood. An Uptown resident of ten years was still likely to list their residence as "Pike County, Kentucky."[42] And, in general, New Left organizers found Uptown residents to be uninterested in politics or activism. "They don't talk to each other about their problems and have no history of struggle for a solution." Political apathy and transiency in the neighborhood resulted in low levels of voter registration. And this result, combined with the "Gold Coast" voting bloc, meant that Uptown's ward, the Forty-eighth, had a Republican alderman, one of only five in a city dominated by Mayor Daley's political machine.[43]

Even so, organizers recognized sources for community-based activism in Uptown. The neighborhood contained social welfare institutions that sought to foster community among residents, including a branch of Hull House opened in 1962. Casey Hayden, a SNCC staff member on loan to the Chicago project during the summer of 1965, learned of a network of women in the neighborhood:

[A]ll the women have some other women who are on welfare or very poor and they sort of follow each other around the city. . . . [T]hey are always in debt to each other, there is a circle of two, three, four people who are always lending each other money, because the check is late or they have to take a taxi and there is nothing left for that. . . . It just seems that there are a lot of natural ways that people relate and a real consciousness of shared problems.[44]

As Hayden discovered, strong ties of kinship and friendship existed among Uptown's southern migrants and, in fact, had contributed to collective action against mistreatment by local police well before ERAP arrived.[45]

As the Civil Rights Movement moved north, it began to have an influence on residents in Uptown as well. In 1963 Chicago CORE targeted de facto segregation arising from residential patterns, and subsequent overcrowding, in the Chicago school system. They demanded an end to the policy of using temporary, portable classrooms (called "Willis wagons" after the school superintendent) to accommodate a growing black student population, rather than allowing African American children to enroll in less crowded schools in white areas.[46] One Uptown resident who participated and was arrested in the school protests was Peggy Terry. Terry, who had migrated from Alabama to Chicago in 1956, came from a strong union family, but one also sympathetic to the Ku Klux Klan. "Funny thing," she recalled, "my father . . . always spoke out and stuck up for the workingman. Walked off many jobs, without a penny in his pocket. But he had this blind spot when it came to color." The Montgomery Bus Boycott of 1955–56 "absolutely changed my life," and she later joined Chicago CORE. Terry would become an influential leader of the Chicago JOIN project.[47]

Newark's Clinton Hill

The project in Newark's Clinton Hill neighborhood was one of the first to be planned and established for ERAP Summer 1964. It developed from foundations laid by Stanley Aronowitz, a socialist and trade unionist who had influenced SDS's move into community organizing by connecting SDS to current debates and agitation around labor and economic issues.[48] Through his contacts with the Clinton Hill Neighborhood Council and both the National and Newark Committees for Full Employment, Aronowitz arranged for these groups to sponsor and work closely with Newark ERAP.[49] Although this arrangement only lasted until August 1964— when New Left organizers "seceded" and formed their own organization, the Newark Community Union Project (NCUP)—it initially provided New Left organizers with an important base, source of funds, and personal connections in Newark. With some thirteen full-time organizers from schools such as Michigan, Swarthmore, Amherst, and Howard, and informally directed by Tom Hayden and Carl Wittman, NCUP would become one of the most prominent projects in ERAP.[50]

Newark organizers built their project in a community in flux. Clinton Hill was located immediately south and west of the city's central business district and the Central Ward, the heart of the black ghetto. Although blacks numbered only 10 percent of the city's population in 1940, that percentage rose as part of the extraordinary population shift that occurred when African Americans, 90 percent of whom lived in the South in 1910, migrated north during the postwar period; by 1960, half of all blacks lived outside the South. The combination of black in-migration and white suburbanization made Newark the first northern city with a "minority" majority by 1966.[51] Economically, the city was a mix of service employment for suburban commuters and unemployment for city residents. As the financial and economic center of the state of New Jersey, Newark employed some 200,000 workers from outside the city in 1960, while a long-term decline in manufacturing produced a citywide unemployment rate of 15 percent by 1964, with rates as high as 20 to 40 percent in some of Newark's black neighborhoods.[52] High incidence of tuberculosis, maternal and infant mortality, and crime made the city "a Mississippi of the North, in terms of poverty levels and inbred racial hostility."[53] "Newark is just like the South," resident Betty Moore noted, "right here they look down on you, give you a funny eye, make you feel you're not wanted."[54]

Mirroring citywide population developments, the racial composition of the Clinton Hill neighborhood underwent a "dramatic changeover from white to black" in just a single decade. Considered a white district in 1950, Clinton Hill had a majority (56 percent) of black residents by 1960. Black in-migration also contributed to a rise in the neighborhood's population, from 33,400 in 1950 to 41,289 in 1960.[55] Clinton Hill was touted by neighborhood and city leaders as an interracial, cross-class neighborhood, noted because it had the highest proportion of homeownership of any predominantly black community in the city. New Left organizers found, instead, that the neighborhood was really three. The "upper hill"—the area furthermost from downtown and the Central Ward—was occupied predominantly by white homeowners; the "middle hill" was more racially integrated, with residents who owned their own homes and who rented; and the "lower hill" was comprised overwhelmingly of blacks, with a tenancy rate of over 80 percent and the highest male unemployment and lowest family incomes in the neighborhood. Finding problems most acute in lower Clinton Hill, organizers soon decided to focus their efforts there.[56]

These inequalities were worsened by the city's urban renewal policies, which transformed the physical environment of the neighborhood in the mid-1960s. Assuming that urban decline was a physical and not a social problem, Newark was one of the first U.S. cities to launch an urban renewal program and was viewed at the time as the "nation's most respected 'urban renewal city.'"[57] As was the case nationally, Newark failed to replace the low-cost housing demolished during renewal, much less to keep up with the housing demands of new migrants to the city. Clinton Hill received most blacks dislocated by this process. This influx exacerbated overcrowded conditions, encouraged the subdivision of homes and apartments into smaller units, and resulted in rents that were next to the highest in the city.[58] At the same time, the Newark Housing Authority declared Clinton Hill, with the fourth highest number of dilapidated buildings in Newark, "blighted" and slated it for future urban renewal. Renewal would displace an estimated 13,500 families, including both new arrivals and many homeowners, both black and white, who would be unable to purchase comparable housing elsewhere. The blight declaration and renewal plans contributed to further housing deterioration. Landlords stopped making repairs, city garbage collection dropped off, and "rats, roaches, bad heat, rotten plumbing gets worse." Of the old neighborhood, one resident recalled, "It was a nice place to live—clean. Clinton Hill sure has changed."[59]

Of the myriad neighborhood problems, Clinton Hill residents were most concerned about urban renewal, but they also worried about their children's welfare and employment prospects. The dearth of recreation facilities in the area, combined with a constant stream of traffic on nearby Clinton Avenue, made playing outside dangerous for children. "One hears of accidents regularly," the Newark project reported. Residents wanted traffic lights at two intersections where numerous children had been injured or killed over the years.[60] They also complained that the dramatic increase in the number of students in the school system (up 14,000 between 1950 and 1960) had resulted in double sessions, overcrowded classrooms, run-down facilities, and textbook shortages.[61] Community residents were frustrated by the lack of accessible, well-paying jobs, as well as the prevalence of discrimination in employment. "We figure we're going to get a better deal up here," one woman migrant from the South attested. "But when you come here, it's the same way. You still can't get anything better than housework, factory work . . . dirty work, paying very little wages."[62]

Despite these problems, ERAP organizers perceived many sources for activism in Clinton Hill. The findings of a 1963 survey indicated that two-thirds of current residents hoped to remain in Newark and 90 percent preferred not to move from their present homes—convenient to church, work, social activities, and friends. This dedication to the neighborhood also existed among the newer, so-called urban renewal migrants to Clinton Hill, although such dislocation usually worked against "the development of community pride and the sense of civic investment."[63] An important source for neighborhood activism was one of ERAP's sponsors, the Clinton Hill Neighborhood Council. Founded in 1955 "to stabilize an integrated housing and school situation," the council was committed to improving area conditions, but it also was dominated by homeowners who often had little in common with Clinton Hill's large tenant population.[64] New Left organizers observed that homeowners "still tend to look down on tenants and condemn their indifference," but they hoped the shared threat of urban renewal would bring both groups together in the Newark ERAP project.[65]

As organizers contacted community residents, they found many with political and organizing experience. Through the Clinton Hill Neighborhood Council, a core group of residents had participated in a campaign against the city's "blight" declaration, which halted—temporarily—Newark's plans for urban renewal in Clinton Hill.[66] A former council president, Louise Patterson, later became an important community leader of the Newark project, while Jesse Allen, another community leader, was a former union shop steward. An increasing civil rights presence in the city furthered the mobilization of black residents as well. Only five years before, the black community had felt "dependent upon [the] Demo[cratic] machine . . . [but] recently a new strength and consciousness" had emerged.[67] A number of black political candidates sought office, at a time when only one of ten city officials was African American. Meanwhile, CORE launched a campaign to protest employment discrimination in Newark and regularly picketed City Hall and local business establishments. For Clinton Hill residents Bessie and Thurman Smith, for example, this civil rights spirit both excited them and encouraged them to participate in the Newark project.[68]

Cleveland's Near West Side

Organizers with the Cleveland ERAP, in contrast to those in Newark, began with a focus on organizing poor whites. Oliver Fein and Charlotte Phillips, who were attending medical school in Cleveland, were the first to suggest a project on the city's Near West Side. In January 1964 Fein proposed "to remain in Cleveland, and start (or try to initiate) some commotion at the 'poor white' base."[69] He and Phillips began to research the possibilities for such a project, and by the spring, Sharon Jeffrey had joined them as the full-time director of the project. They rented a rambling frame house in the heart of the predominantly Appalachian part of the neighborhood, recruited other organizers for the summer, including Kathy Boudin, Nancy Hollander, Ken and Carol McEldowney, and Dave Strauss, and established contacts with local political and labor activists, who offered support in the form of free meals, furniture, clothes, and mimeo machines.[70] By adopting the name Cleveland Community Project instead of the Cleveland Research and Action Project, they avoided an unfortunate acronym. "*CRAP* (yeechh! what a name)," exclaimed one ERAP staff member. By the beginning of ERAP Summer 1964, the project was set.[71]

The Near West Side was a community confronting the problems of growing poverty. The neighborhood was situated close to downtown, to the west of the Cuyahoga River, which geographically and racially divided the city of Cleveland. Although the city prided itself on having "no Negro problem," the 1960 census labeled Cleveland one of the most segregated metropolises in the country.[72] As blacks grew from 9.7 percent of the total city population in 1940 to 28.6 percent by 1960, they crowded into neighborhoods on the East Side. Ohio's location also made it a "principal target of genuine hillbilly migration," and over 80,000 Appalachian migrants moved into Cleveland, locating mostly in the West Side's "Hillbilly Heaven."[73] At the same time, 100,000 residents—largely white, ethnic, middle- and working-class—left Cleveland for the surrounding suburbs. With this loss of taxpayers and subsequent erosion of the tax base, as one commentator put it, "the city became increasingly brown, black, and broke."[74]

Like Chicago's Uptown, the Near West Side was inhabited by a heterogeneous population, ethnically and economically. Long dominated by Eastern Europeans, in the 1950s the neighborhood began to attract a growing number of Puerto Ricans and Appalachians.[75] Residents with stable working-class or lower-middle-class employment and incomes coexisted with those who lived in extreme poverty, were unemployed, and were on welfare. As New Left organizers discovered, the Near West Side had unemployment rates that ranged from 8 percent on some blocks to up to 19 percent on others, when the citywide rate was 5.5 percent. And since 1956, the number of welfare and general relief recipients had increased 96 and 35 percent, respectively.[76] The diverse population meant that community residents and conditions were not uniformly impoverished, however. "Some organizers were surprised to see that the 'Spanish-Harlem-type-treeless' poverty did not exist in the Near West Side."[77]

Situated on Cleveland's "white" West Side, the neighborhood was not experiencing the severe population and housing pressures faced by the "black" East Side, or Clinton Hill in Newark, in the early 1960s. Yet, with 91 percent of the housing built before 1919 and 40 percent classified as dilapidated or deteriorating, the Near West Side contained many a home, as community resident Marty Ruddenstein described her residence, "that looks like it might fall down if a strong wind blew." "It's got cracks between boards and glass is missing in the front door," she continued. "Wind and rain come in the windows."[78] Most (63.5 percent) of the housing on the Near West Side was rented, and negligent, absentee landlords contributed further to deteriorating housing conditions. One neighborhood resident spoke of a room in her apartment where "the ceiling was half torn away and when tenants upstairs flushed the toilet the debris came down all over the furniture. It took me four weeks to get that fixed."[79] Poor housing conditions also existed at Lakeview Terrace, a nearby housing project, where residents demanded immediate rat extermination and a general health check of the project.[80] The narrow alleys and densely packed housing of the Near West Side created a gloomy environment. Cleveland organizer Mimi Feingold, who had worked with CORE in Louisiana, believed that "[r]ural poverty had it all over urban poverty."[81]

Although housing was an issue on the Near West Side, welfare concerns predominated among residents. Women recipients of the Aid to (Families with) Dependent Children (A[F]DC) program, a joint federal-state public assistance program popularly known by the pejorative "welfare" by the early 1960s, struggled to get by on the low budgets allocated by the state of Ohio.[82] In the early 1960s, to deal with expanding costs due to rising numbers of recipients, Ohio reduced welfare benefits from 90 percent to 70 percent of the minimum standard of need set by the state in 1959. The state's actions occurred at a time of national alarm about rising municipal welfare rolls; real spending on the program would double between 1960 and 1967.[83] With these cuts, Ohio, the sixth richest state in the United States, ranked thirty-fifth in average payment per recipient in 1962.[84] Low welfare budgets failed to cover the cost of school clothing and lunches and, it was believed, contributed to a school dropout rate for teenagers in the neighborhood of 40 percent.[85] "[T]hey can't give our children the necessities," complained Dorothy Hammer, a Near West Side resident. Yet welfare officials "spend money for detention homes rather than . . . to feed our children so they won't have to go there." "The price of poor people's food has gone up, but our food budget has not been increased," Gwendolyn (Louise) Gaston declared. "So what do we do? Starve, steal or has it come to the place we have to stand on the corner and beg?"[86]

As did organizers in Chicago's Uptown, Cleveland organizers viewed the heterogeneity, high residential mobility, and political apathy of neighborhood residents as barriers to community organizing. "The Near West Side community is characterized predominantly by atomization and fragmentation," observed Phillips and Fein. Ethnic and economic heterogeneity proved divisive and often prevented neighbors from associating together. The fact that over half of the population had moved into the area in only the last ten years compounded the situation.[87] High residential mobility further undermined any sense of community on the Near West Side. Residents traveled back and forth between Appalachia and Cleveland looking for work, contributing to an annual turnover of

102 percent at Hicks elementary school, for example. For New Left organizers, this lack of neighborhood ties resulted in political apathy. "On the whole," Jeffrey commented, "people are isolationist, non-joiners, live independent of org[anizations] and institutions." In addition, most of the local institutions, such as churches and clubs, catered to former residents who now lived in the suburbs.[88]

Still, sources for community activism existed on the Near West Side. The Inner-City Protestant Parish, a group ministry supported by various denominations to work with the poor on an interracial basis, had a branch in the neighborhood. Reverends Paul Younger and Don Armstrong had developed "a program that recognizes not only spiritual needs, but material and political problems as well." After meeting with them, Cleveland organizers happily reported that these "energetic and young ministers with political perspectives . . . wish to work with us this summer."[89] As it turned out, Catholic and Protestant churches dedicated resources and energy to community action initiatives in a number of cities over the decade of the 1960s, and several ERAP projects encountered helpful inner-city ministers. Reverend Younger earlier had organized a welfare rights group, called Citizens United for Adequate Welfare, comprised mostly of women. Lillian Craig had been a member of the group. "The bonds went very deep" among the members, and she and others remained interested in welfare organizing and would participate if the group was restarted by ERAP. "When SDS came," Craig later recalled, "I was ready for something."[90]

The Civil Rights Movement also contributed to a mood of political possibility in Cleveland. "The Negro community is beginning to feel its oats here," Fein wrote in early 1964.[91] On the East Side, Cleveland CORE participated in a national CORE drive to "end bias in the building trades" and as part of the United Freedom Movement demanded a policy of integrated schools to compensate for de facto residential segregation, as was the case in Chicago. In April activists, including Phillips and Fein, picketed the Board of Education and protested at a school construction site, where, tragically, Reverend Bruce Klunder, a white CORE member, was killed by a bulldozer. CORE also targeted racial discrimination in housing. During the winter of 1963 the organization sponsored an assault on slum housing on the East Side, including a series of tenant actions and rent strikes.[92] This level of civil rights activism prompted some residents on the Near West Side to begin to consider ways to improve their own situation.

Boston's Roxbury–North Dorchester

The first SDS organizing project in Boston was sponsored by PREP and sought to organize middle-class, defense industry workers in suburban New Bedford. During ERAP Summer 1964, it focused on researching the possibilities. By that fall, however, SDS members at nearby universities such as Radcliffe, Harvard, and Brandeis wanted to contribute directly to the Civil Rights Movement by engaging in community organizing along the lines of the ERAP model in Boston's predominantly black neighborhoods.[93] Along with members of the Northern Student Movement, they began by supporting black social worker Noel Day's campaign for Congress and volunteering for two "action centers" in Roxbury and North Dorchester. Mike Ansara, a Boston native beginning his freshman year at Harvard, worked as an organizer for Day. "Our notion here was to use the congressional campaign as a springboard for organizing around tenant issues, housing issues—that was rents, slum landlords, and lead paint — also welfare issues, and a bunch of block associations."[94] New Left activists soon were organizing neighborhood block groups in the Dudley Street area, and, during the summer of 1965, the Dudley Street Action Center became a full-fledged ERAP project, with local foundation and campus chapter support, a storefront office, three apartments, and at least six full-time organizers: Sarah Eisenstein, Pat Hammond, Marya Levenson, Roger Manela, John Mendelhoff, and Jean Tepperman.[95]

There organizers encountered a depressed, transitional neighborhood buffeted by urban change. Located about two miles south of downtown, the Dudley Street area straddled the historic towns of Roxbury and Dorchester. As the Boston project reported, despite "brave talk about the 'New Boston,'" the city was losing population and jobs to the suburbs.[96] Between 1940 and 1970, 31 percent of Boston's middle-class, white residents moved to the suburbs, while defense and electronics firms boomed in outlying areas along Route 128. At the same time, the city's black population rose 342 percent, as African Americans from the South migrated north. They arrived in Boston just as traditional industries such as shoe and textile manufacturing were leaving.[97] These developments left city residents, like those of Roxbury–North Dorchester, in increasingly segregated neighborhoods, with fewer employment options, a shrinking tax base, and poorer public services.

As Boston's growing African American population expanded from the South End into the neighborhoods of Roxbury and then North Dorchester, earlier residents—predominantly working-class Italians and Irish—began to leave the Dudley Street area. Blacks' proportion of the neighborhood population rose from 5 percent in 1950 to 53 percent in 1970, while "white flight" reduced the white population from 95 to 45 percent. In 1960, although African Americans represented just 9 percent of total city residents, they were concentrated into just a few neighborhoods like Roxbury–North Dorchester, where they made up 20 percent of the community.[98] As the racial composition shifted, the neighborhood's median family income fell below the city's, and two census tracts in the area were among the poorest in Boston. With this information, New Left organizers disputed official 1964 unemployment figures that indicated a lower rate (4.6 percent) in the Dudley Street area than that of Boston as a whole (5.8 percent). "Casual observation of the street corners, bars and candy stores . . . [revealed] these figures are misleading." They surmised that most unemployed residents had simply given up looking for a job and, therefore, were excluded from such figures.[99]

Roxbury–North Dorchester's postwar development from a working-class, white community to a low-income, black community expanded the black ghetto in Boston, a development that was accelerated by Boston's urban renewal policies during the 1950s and 1960s. As elsewhere, these policies targeted the black communities in the South End (and later in Roxbury). So-called Negro removal resulted in a reduction in low-cost housing and dislocated entire neighborhoods in Boston.[100] Due to housing discrimination, these displaced black residents were forced to squeeze into the few neighborhoods open to African Americans. As a consequence, Roxbury–North Dorchester's "three-deckers"—houses with the "tiniest of yards" and flimsiest of construction—were split into even smaller apartments, resulting in overcrowding and deteriorating conditions. In their ERAP project proposal, Boston organizers noted, "much of the area looks as abandoned as a medieval city attacked by the black plague. There are deserted houses, cars, stores, furniture, vacant lots, and people."[101] Of these conditions, community resident Yvonne Ruelas wrote a poem. "Should I not be more better off in the North than in the South?/ You said if I could make it across the Mason-Dixie line, my life would be better, I would not be so far behind."[102]

In meetings with New Left organizers, residents articulated a range of concerns about these neighborhood conditions, but they were most distressed about welfare, children's welfare, and urban renewal. Given Boston's low welfare budgets and high grocery prices and rents, community women felt that their budgets should be raised, especially the rent allowance.[103] Recipients were allowed to pay only a certain amount for rent; this rent allowance then was calculated as part of their welfare benefits. Landlords familiar with the policy recruited welfare recipients into their apartments, charged the maximum amount, and, with no economic incentive to maintain buildings, let conditions deteriorate. In this way, the rent payments of welfare recipients actually subsidized slum housing in Boston and elsewhere. Welfare recipients also were reluctant to complain or report housing violations for fear of endangering their welfare benefits. Of tenants in one substandard building, Boston community resident Flossie Wilder commented, "Most of the girls are on ADC. They are afraid to speak up."[104] Additionally, the prevalence of abandoned houses, vacant lots, and abandoned cars in the neighborhood posed great dangers for children and underscored the need for area playgrounds. Children further suffered from the area's severely overcrowded, de facto segregated, and poorly staffed schools.[105] Dudley Street also was slated for future urban renewal, and community residents feared the consequences.[106]

As ERAP organizers began their work in the neighborhood, they discovered significant sources for political activism. As in Newark's Clinton Hill, residents of Roxbury–North Dorchester were committed to remaining in the community. This commitment was true of low-income women welfare recipients as well as middle-income community residents who desired to stay in a central location, near their place of work and the city's downtown. Middle-income blacks also feared encountering racial discrimination in Boston's predominantly white suburbs, even with open housing legislation. Instead, these residents sought to make their community "a more satisfactory place to live" and were eager to participate in community organizing.[107] The neighborhood's problems also had garnered attention from the Ford Foundation–sponsored Action for Boston Community Development, later to participate in the city's War on Poverty.[108] Further, a number of Roxbury–North Dorchester institutions, including St. Ann's Rectory and Episcopal Church, Denison House, and the Ward 8 Betterment Association, helped foster a sense of community in the area.[109]

Importantly, Boston's Roxbury–North Dorchester neighborhood was a site of political and civil rights activism well before ERAP arrived. Boston CORE and the NAACP, as well as the Boston Action Group— a coalition of local civil rights, community, and political organizations —already had mobilized apartment tenants around rent strikes, parents around education issues, and voters around progressive political candidates. CORE conducted a successful rent strike in 1962, and the NAACP launched a school campaign in 1963 and 1964 that accused the city of de facto segregation and proposed busing students from three area schools.[110] Moreover, the 1964 Noel Day congressional campaign's office and volunteers laid the foundation for ERAP in Roxbury–North Dorchester. As it turned out, the core group of women welfare recipients initially active in, and later leaders of, the Boston ERAP's welfare rights group, Mothers for Adequate Welfare, all had been involved in the CORE, Boston Action Group, and Day campaigns. They not only had political experience, but also were, according to one observer, "respected members of the community."[111]

As these profiles show, Chicago's Uptown, Newark's Clinton Hill, Cleveland's Near West Side, and Boston's Roxbury–North Dorchester were neighborhoods in the midst of urban crisis. Profound demographic and economic changes were reshaping these neighborhoods in the mid-1960s. All four were destinations for southern migrants, although, mirroring national trends, Uptown and the Near West Side in the Midwest received whites primarily and Clinton Hill and Roxbury–North Dorchester in the Northeast attracted more African Americans.[112] They also were located in cities that were losing jobs and population to the growing suburbs, experiencing deindustrialization, and shifting to a service economy—just as new migrants arrived, seeking work. Urban blight and crowded, deteriorating housing characterized the neighborhoods' physical environments, while city leaders' response to these changes—urban renewal—only exacerbated their decline.

Lessons Learned

Upon entering these communities and encountering constituents, ERAP organizers found that their knowledge of both was superficial and inadequate. In all the projects, they discovered that their experiments in communal living, with a large group of young, single women and men residing together, drew disapproving attention and set organizers apart from community residents. "When they know we are all living together, everybody has this idea of things going on in the apartment," Newark organizer Carol Glassman observed. "[W]e weren't living the way the rest of the community would live." In Cleveland, communal living supported "a variety of rumors about prostitution, communism, and bootlegging."[113]

Their initial ignorance of the social mores of these communities highlighted the cultural distance that existed and needed to be overcome between ERAP organizers and those they hoped to mobilize.

Organizers also learned lessons that challenged assumptions central to the original ERAP strategy. The constellation of concerns articulated by community residents indicated that unemployment was only one of many problems associated with poverty and the urban crisis. Residents named welfare, housing conditions, urban renewal, children's welfare, police brutality, along with unemployment, as significant concerns. As veteran community organizer Saul Alinsky believed, "The urban crisis was many-problemed."[114] The barriers to organizing in the communities also were far more complicated than the lack of political consciousness and organization New Left organizers had expected to find. Neighborhoods were not always communities, for residing in the same physical space did not necessarily translate into social ties. Each neighborhood had a heterogeneous mix of residents with different class, racial, and/or ethnic backgrounds, making it difficult to find common ground. High residential mobility further undermined a sense of, or commitment to, community, and meant organizers could not count on an existing "enclave consciousness" or attachment to a home territory.[115]

Despite these barriers, and to the surprise of organizers, sources for political activism existed in every neighborhood. Not all residents were as passive and isolated as the culture of poverty concept indicated. Residents with leadership and organizing experience, such as Peggy Terry in Chicago and Louise Patterson in Newark, and church and community organizations, like the Inner-City Protestant Parish in Cleveland and the civil rights "action centers" in Boston, contributed greatly to the establishment of local ERAP projects. An increasing civil rights presence, as the Civil Rights Movement moved north, provided inspiration and an important model for social change in all the cities. Moreover, in sharp contrast to the expectations of ERAP planners, neighborhood women constituted a crucial source of activism. In the course of fulfilling their caretaking duties, women struggled daily with community conditions and, indeed, identified problems as part of their domestic responsibilities. They also generally established the friendships and networks that tied the neighborhoods together.[116] Women's prominence and activism defied ERAP's intention of organizing only a constituency of men, and, as it turned out, community organizations in Uptown, Clinton Hill, the Near West Side, and Roxbury-North Dorchester could not be built without them.

Cleveland "Rat March," August 1965. (Courtesy of John Bancroft.)

4

Organizing from the Bottom Up

At the beginning of the summer of 1964, New Left organizers moved into neighborhoods and set up ERAP projects without an organizing blueprint. They may have disagreed about the precise strategy for ERAP, but they knew they wanted to build an interracial movement of the poor. What they were unsure of was how to use the method of community organizing to achieve this aim. They had engaged in political action on campus and in the Civil Rights Movement, worked with SNCC, CORE, and NSM, and organized in cities such as Chester and Chicago. Yet they had not established permanent, ongoing, grassroots organizations anywhere, nor did they have a clear idea of exactly how to go about doing so. Indeed, in discussions over SDS's move from campus to community, members assumed they would need to involve themselves in "developing techniques for sustained community organization."[1] The lack of an "organizing technology," a model "specifying step-by-step guidelines for creating neighborhood organizations," shaped the experience and outcome of every ERAP project.[2]

There was such a model available, however: Saul Alinsky's. The founder and philosopher of modern community organizing, Alinsky first developed his approach in Chicago's "Back of the Yards" neighborhood beginning in 1939 and further elaborated it through projects sponsored by his Industrial Areas Foundation (IAF) into the 1970s. He sought to restore democracy on the local level through citizen participation, by organizing residents outside the conventional party system to gain greater representation, exert political power, and thereby solve community problems.[3] Initially inspired by the neighborhood-based organizing efforts of the Congress of Industrial Organizations and the Communist Party's Unemployed Councils, by the late 1940s, in the context of Cold War anticommunism and his own aversion to dogmatic, authoritarian ideology, Alinsky touted his model as "nonideological organizing."[4]

Although Alinsky's commitment to citizen participation was hardly the nonideological organizing he claimed it to be, neither was it SDS's vision of participatory democracy or ERAP's national strategy to end inequalities of class and race. Moreover, a backyard barbecue hosted by the labor leader Ralph Helstein during the summer of 1964 to introduce Alinsky to Todd Gitlin, Tom Hayden, and Lee Webb did not go well, with Alinsky "dismissing their ideas and work" in ERAP "as naive and doomed to failure."[5] These differences, along with the evolution of the Back of the Yards Neighborhood Council into an organization opposed to residential integration—something Alinsky himself criticized—led most ERAP organizers to reject the Alinsky approach. "We didn't know what we were doing," Vivian Rothstein recalls, but "we knew we didn't like the Alinsky model." For many, it was "valueless," "too apolitical," even "liberal."[6] This rejection left them to work out the nuts and bolts of community organizing on their own, through trial and error, once they were in the field canvassing communities, recruiting residents, and building neighborhood organizations. As it turned out, they reproduced certain elements of the Alinsky model in the process.

What ERAP and Alinsky shared, in particular, was the definition of the role of the organizer. Both conceived of the organizer as "catalyst." Yet an inherent, even paralyzing contradiction lay at the heart of this concept for ERAP organizers. Seeing themselves as political initiators rather than leaders, as social movement catalysts rather than a vanguard, they, like SNCC, repudiated the manipulation and exploitation that so often accompanied political organizing. For many, "the right kind of organizing" was more about "teaching" than anything else.[7] They were committed to organizing from the "bottom up" and ensuring grassroots participation; in keeping with the dedication to participatory democracy, "Let the People Decide" became the favorite ERAP slogan. Yet organizers were outsiders who entered unfamiliar communities with a definite purpose and their own agenda. How could they both supply New Left direction and strategy and build community projects based on equality and democracy? Could one aim be achieved without hindering the other? This dilemma between providing "top-down" leadership and encouraging "bottom-up" participation was not an exceptional experience for organizers, past or present. In ERAP, managing this dilemma meant that the community organizing process was as much about learning as teaching.

Canvassing and Surveying Communities

ERAP organizers viewed informal canvassing and formal surveys as the first stage of organizing a community from the bottom up. Canvassing and surveys involved going through the neighborhood, attempting to talk with residents about their concerns, and soliciting their opinions about community problems. They used this undertaking to introduce themselves to neighborhood residents and gather detailed information about communities and constituents. Similarly, the Alinsky model called for spending the first few weeks "hanging out" in the neighborhood and getting a feel for the community.[8] In ERAP, women proved to be the most effective in this process. The friendship, hostility, discomfort, and learning that characterized these encounters formed a microcosm of the entire ERAP enterprise.

Every ERAP project began with canvassing. Because this first contact was so important, a few of the projects even wrote scripts. The Chicago project encouraged organizers and other volunteers to begin with "Hello, I'm from JOIN, an organization in this neighborhood which is concerned about housing, school, and employment problems. We were wondering if you could give us a few minutes to tell us what you think the chief needs of this area are."[9] In his memoirs, Tom Hayden recounted the "formal rules" for Newark's rap:

> [W]hen the door opens, smile, speak politely and quickly, saying something like, "Hello, I'm Tom Hayden, from the Newark Community Union Project. We're knocking on doors trying to get people together to do something about [high rents, rats and roaches, the lack of garbage collection, streetlights, etc.]. Do you mind if I ask you some questions about how you feel about these issues, and whether you would like to join us in doing something about them?"[10]

As these scripted introductions indicated, organizers realized that the first impression was crucial, especially in neighborhoods wary of outsiders—much less young, educated, and, in black neighborhoods, white outsiders. After the door was opened, "you had fifteen seconds to establish trust" with community people, Vivian Rothstein notes.[11] Personal appearance and self-presentation were important. The Trenton project urged organizers to dress appropriately. "We will wear conservative clothes (no shorts or loud plaids, guys, and no tight slacks or shorts for the girls)."[12]

As canvassing proceeded, they learned to adapt their approaches to fit varying circumstances. Organizers canvassing in Chicago's Uptown felt that residents mistrusted their motivations. To build trust across barriers of class and ethnicity, they began to explain to residents why they personally were involved in political and civil rights activism. But this only went so far. Because they feared imposing their views on or alienating residents on this initial contact, many organizers kept their political strategy and goals hidden. Similarly, some labeled their first project reports "confidential," restricting their circulation to New Left activists and allies. "There are things which we felt were true that we do not feel we can discuss in the community at this time," one project's members later wrote in the *ERAP Newsletter*.[13] This "desire for secrecy" was much debated and later repudiated. Still, it exposed how, in the attempt to make a good—and politically safe—first impression, organizers interjected a measure of dishonesty into these first relationships with their constituency.[14]

As a way to introduce ERAP to the neighborhood, canvassing brought mixed results. Not all residents were eager to talk. "A door slammed makes it very difficult to knock on another," Nancy Hollander wrote from Chicago. Some encounters were even less anticipated than a slammed door. After an evening of canvassing, one Chicago organizer listed the "names of individuals contacted the night of January 18, who were too drunk to converse but might be worth following up."[15] Canvassing certainly failed to yield an introduction or conversation with every knock on the door, but positive meetings balanced the negative ones. "That was a bad building," Carol Glassman reported after a day of canvassing in Newark's Clinton Hill. "I got more doors slammed in my face, more grouchy people, just opening [the door] a little bit and looking out at you." In another building, however, "one family was very receptive, agrees with you and talks and adds to the conversation."[16] "The first door I knocked on in Newark was 61 Hillside Avenue," Hayden recalled of meeting Bessie Smith. Smith—who upon introducing herself always added, "like the famous singer"—invited him in, and they spent several hours discussing a variety of community issues. As homeowners and proprietors of a camera shop, Smith and her husband, Thurman, were well-respected, stable members of the Clinton Hill neighborhood, and they agreed to create a block club on Hillside Avenue as part of the Newark project.[17] Such experiences made the overall experience of canvassing more bearable and at times even rewarding.

The racial makeup of the neighborhoods shaped canvassing interactions. Black nationalism was not yet a dominant sentiment in these communities, but it was on the rise, and the issue and role of white organizers in black neighborhoods were on the agenda of several civil rights groups, including SNCC. The Trenton project, which did not last past the summer of 1964, confronted this situation with a local CORE leader. "Mr. Lewis mentioned bitterly that there are very few Negroes in SDS and implied that we whites were trying to tell the Negroes who actually have the problems what to do."[18] Recognizing the validity of this argument, black organizers, like Marv Holloway, Junius Williams, and Phil Hutchings, joined the Newark project, yet whites still dominated the project staff over the years. The Baltimore project took a unique approach, setting up two offices, one in a black neighborhood, the other in a white area, half a mile apart on the city's east and southeast sides. They also decided on a segregated staff; Kim Moody focused on organizing whites. "We talked about it a lot, about whether it was the right way to go." Most of the black activists involved, like Bob Moore and Walter Lively, felt that white organizers would not be effective among African Americans. Once the two offices had mobilized their respective constituencies, they would hold integrated meetings together, which happened by the end of the summer of 1964.[19]

Despite such racial concerns and conflicts, ERAP organizers generally reported feeling more comfortable in poor black than white communities, accounting for the abandonment of ERAP's sole focus on organizing whites. This comfort stemmed from experiences in the southern Civil Rights Movement, the New Left's romanticization of poor African Americans, as well as actual circumstances and particular residents in these neighborhoods. Tom Hayden and Carl Wittman reported that Newark residents treated organizers with "remarkable alacrity and warmth." For Corinna Fales, who grew up on campus and near Lincoln University in Pennsylvania, the first black university in the country, "Newark was really my home when I was there. I did not want to leave it, even for a weekend."[20] At the very least, community residents recruited into NCUP viewed positively the presence of organizers in their neighborhoods. Terry Jefferson and Anita Warren, for example, felt that "they've given up so much to come here and help us."[21] In Cleveland, it was black women working on welfare rights who invited the project to expand to Glenville, on the city's East Side, and organizers were very willing to go. Experiences among Appalachian migrants on the Near West Side in Cleveland or in Chicago's Uptown compared much less favorably. Oliver Fein perceived the culture of Glenville's black population to be far more "vibrant, unifying, and supportive" than the "individualistic" orientation of Near West Side residents, while in Uptown, organizers reported, "despair hangs heavier here than in the Negro ghettos, and has a silent, sullen, hostile expression."[22]

Moreover, the social and cultural distance between New Left organizers and white community residents was vast. A shared racial identity as whites was rarely meaningful in the case of Jewish SDS activists, revealing not only class but also ethnic and racial differences within whiteness.[23] In Chicago Rich Rothstein, a New Yorker and Jewish, often encountered anti-Semitism and prejudice among Uptown's southern white population and received a beating at the hands of neighborhood "toughs." Leni Zeiger Wildflower, also Jewish, saw "the whole ghetto around" as her enemy. Only nineteen years old, she feared for her safety, especially when she experienced sexual harassment from two "huge men" who were "after my ass."[24] By the same token, organizers from similar regional and cultural backgrounds felt a measure of compatibility with ERAP's white constituency. Rennie Davis grew up in the Blue Ridge Mountains of Virginia and found it fairly easy to work in Uptown. "I could put on a southern accent. . . . I had a pretty good feel for the culture and I didn't feel intimidated. I liked it. It was an easy fit for me."[25] Still, there was nothing "real easy or automatic or sentimental" about white organizers from the South relating to Appalachian migrants in the ERAP neighborhoods—Appalachia was not the same as Atlanta.[26]

In every project, barriers of class and education existed. Although organizers were asking about the problems in the neighborhood, they already had ideas about what they thought the problems were and what should be done about them. "Why would an organizer be there," Rich Rothstein asked self-mockingly, "if he didn't assume that he was better than the ghetto residents, had some superior knowledge?"[27] Combined with the fact that, as outsiders, they did not always understand those they wished "to organize," this attitude could lead to patronizing and condescending behavior. Jean Tepperman, a student at Harvard who worked with the Boston project during the summer of

1965, "vividly" remembers one of the overly simplistic leaflets they often distributed while canvassing. "It said, 'The Emerson and Mason schools are bad. Why are they bad?' . . . The idiotic phrasing was our idea of how to write for people without very much education."[28] Eric Mann, a Cornell graduate and former CORE activist, also underestimated the intelligence and educational skills of community residents when he joined NCUP in 1965. "I'm knocking on a door and the door [opens], and this guy's reading this book *The Myth of the Negro Past* by [Melville] Herskovits. And . . . my jaw must have dropped, because he said, 'You never saw a black man who could read.'"[29] Contact with residents challenged organizers to confront their unacknowledged, even unconscious, stereotypical assumptions about low-income Americans, despite sincere empathy for those less privileged than themselves and strong personal and political commitments to equality.

Canvassing, then, was a challenging endeavor for New Left organizers. Carol Glassman found it "creative," because it "puts me into very human relations with people," while another woman described her experience in Cleveland as "getting up every morning and jumping in ice water."[30] Individual personalities had much to do with differing responses. Ken McEldowney learned he "lacked the patience" to be an organizer. Others were uncomfortable with bothering people, with the element of "harassment" involved in organizing.[31] The absence of training for organizers in ERAP also meant that many had no idea what they were supposed to be doing, felt "scared" and "inadequate," and ended up leaving the ERAP projects.[32] But community organizations needed people to fill a variety of roles, not just knocking on doors. Tepperman, who went on to organize in Chicago with JOIN after graduating from Harvard, sought such an alternative role. "The problem that I had was that I did not have the right kind of personality to be an organizer. I was shy and took rejection very personally. I was not good at it." She ended up devoting herself to research and writing for the project.[33]

But successful canvassing, it turned out, had something to do with gender. In general, women had an easier time than men. During the first summer of organizing, the Cleveland Community Project reported, "some of the boys . . . felt that it was easier to get responses when a girl was present." Vivian Rothstein believes that women did not "threaten people" and were comfortable with being "facilitators" for others, a characteristic that fit more with women's socialization than men's.[34] "Each sex will inherently have its own advantages and disadvantages," Cathy Wilkerson observed after her experience in Chester. The fact that canvassing door to door often resulted in meeting neighborhood women, who tended be home during the day when organizers came to call, also advantaged women organizers. As Jewish immigrant women knew when mobilizing housewives for consumer protests earlier in the century, the door-to-door canvass was a crucial way to reach other women; women also excelled at this vital task as block organizers with the Cincinnati Unit Experiment, which lasted from 1917 to 1920. In ERAP, Wilkerson noted, women "feel more at ease in the wash-tub situation or in small-talk over coffee which is useful just to get to know and establish a friendship with the women."[35]

In addition to introducing organizers to residents, canvassing generated much-needed information about the neighborhoods. When organizers sought specific data, they used formal surveys. With their social-science-oriented educations, a number of SDS members were familiar with the survey as a research tool, seeing it as a "Poor Man's Rand Corporation" and an indispensable way "to take stock of the human needs of a community."[36] In Newark and Chicago organizers conducted housing surveys and compiled long lists of violations; they later used this information to demonstrate the need for greater city inspection and code enforcement. The Cleveland project wanted to know which group on the Near West Side constituted the largest constituency? had the most children? were on welfare? were the most residentially mobile? In combination with research at the local tax assessors and planning boards, about pending legislation and the structure of local government, surveys yielded critical data about housing, employment, education, and social services in the neighborhoods.[37] Like settlement and other Progressive Era reformers before them, New Left organizers believed that surveys could spark consciousness about community needs, provide data for convincing others that action was necessary, and be used to challenge the technical expertise of government officials. By producing a "distinct kind and form of knowledge" indispensable to the goal of social reform, surveys were political instruments.[38]

Beyond "hard data," organizers wished to know the thoughts and perceptions of residents about their neighborhoods and personal situations. They wanted to understand, on a human scale, the structural forces of the urban crisis. Surveys would uncover "what the real problems are" and "what bothers people most." Responses would "add flesh to statistics and get at community attitudes."[39] Buttressing ERAP's use of the survey was the growing understanding that facts and statistics yielded only partial truths; that it was residents who could identify the real problems in a community. In their answers, residents presented their definitions of problems and conveyed their understandings of how power functioned in society and the causes of their powerlessness. And their "perceptions . . . about the neighborhood and their own 'condition'" differed greatly from organizers' assumptions and knowledge.[40] Cleveland resident Lillian Craig remembered how she had needed to teach the "SDS kids" the practical realities of being poor. "They were book-wise and common sense foolish," she recalled. In ERAP over time, the subjective, experiential knowledge of community residents became as legitimate as, if not more important than, the academic knowledge of New Left organizers. Rennie Davis made this clear when he called for a collection of writings on poverty from community people to complement SDS's more academic pamphlets on the subject.[41]

Canvassing and surveys prompted New Left organizers to recognize the political content and legitimacy of residents' views. This recognition allowed ERAP's organizing agenda to begin to emerge from communities and constituents rather than from the analysis and strategy of SDS members. Only by taking the "pulse of the community," Cleveland organizers concluded, would they be able "to determine priorities" for the project.[42] As it turned out, this viewpoint fit with the first step of the Alinsky model: surveying a neighborhood to discover specific grievances, which then would form a basis for community organization.[43] It also had been articulated in criticisms of the ERAP strategy over the spring of 1964 and was far more consistent with the commitment to organizing from the bottom up than was dictating strategic priorities from the top down.

Recruiting for ERAP

Canvassing became ERAP's principal means of recruitment, of ensuring grassroots participation in the neighborhood projects, and continued as long as the projects lasted. "Every day we would go knock on doors and talk to people," Sharon Jeffrey recalled. "That's what the work was. We would try to engage them in conversation."[44] Through canvassing and conversing, they sought to convince local residents of the benefits of organization. As it turned out, community women responded with the greatest interest and were most readily recruited into ERAP. Even when New Left organizers tried other methods of recruitment, they found intensive, interpersonal contact to be absolutely necessary if they hoped to recruit neighborhood residents into the projects.

Recruitment was a difficult, tiring, and slow process. Tom Hayden estimated that one out of every fifteen residents contacted through canvassing responded with interest in the community project. At that rate, an organizer needed to talk with 150 people to get a respectable attendance of fifteen or twenty for a meeting. "Recruitment is a drag, man," Jeffrey wrote wearily from Cleveland. "I go out every so often," Jeffrey's colleague Evan Metcalf reported, "and listen to people complain and say that they don't have time to do anything and that you can't do anything and that they are moving, and that the neighbors and the kids are bastards. Shit."[45]

Even residents who consistently welcomed ERAP canvassers to their door did not necessarily become project participants. In Chicago, Jean Tepperman paired up for canvassing with Marilyn Katz. "We did an experiment one day," Katz remembers.

> We went to this old lady whose house we had gone to with the *JOIN Community Newsletter*. . . . And she would invite us in every week and give us lemonade or tea or whatever. This day we said, "How you doin'?" She says, "How you doin'?" And we say, "Fine, we're planning on blowing up three banks and robbing some shoe stores." She said, "Good things you kids are doing." It was clear that content of what we were saying had no meaning to her but she liked the company.[46]

Organizers tried to approach this frustrating, time-consuming process with spirit and a sense of humor; they even wrote song lyrics, as did NCUP. "You go back to the block and you talk some more / You're knocking on a door . . . / Lady says who's there and who you looking for / I ain't got time, slip it under the door."[47] Nevertheless, they persisted in the face of disappointing encounters and relatively few successes, because canvassing recruited community members often enough.

It brought Lillian Craig into the Cleveland Community Project (CCP), for example. "Sharon Jeffrey knocked on my door and asked me if I was registered to vote. I asked her in, and after awhile I told her I was on welfare. That's how our friendship began." Born in 1937 of Czech heritage,

Craig had grown up in the city. When her mother died, her alcoholic, violent father could not care for her and her two sisters, and they were separated. At age twelve, Craig was placed in foster care. Upon her graduation from high school, she won a college scholarship, but because it failed to cover living expenses she could not take advantage of it. She worked and eventually married. In the early 1960s, Craig was a divorced, full-time mother of three children, trying to make ends meet on Ohio's inadequate welfare benefits. So ashamed of living as a single mother and receiving welfare, she told people her husband was in the service. Yet she also had a strong streak. Her mother used to tell her, "I will never raise a doormat," and Craig once lost a job attempting to organize a union. She also had been a member of the Inner-City Protestant Parish's welfare rights group and remained dedicated to community activism.[48] She immediately became a crucial participant in the CCP.

Although New Left organizers primarily used canvassing door to door to recruit participants, they also developed alternative methods to attract specific constituencies. Members of the Hoboken project, established in the summer of 1965, found jobs and attempted to recruit people through work. Nick Egleson worked in a box factory. "I made the boxes that stored the Constant Comet tea." Helen Garvy, a Harvard graduate and recent assistant national secretary for SDS, held jobs in a radio parts factory and later as a welfare caseworker. They were not attempting workplace or union organizing but rather "trying to meet people and find out what the issues were and learn something about them."[49] Building on the original Chicago JOIN project's leafletting at unemployment compensation offices to meet the unemployed, organizers in Cleveland and Chicago canvassed and leafletted at local welfare benefit offices to recruit welfare recipients. "Here every Tuesday was a long line of people," Jeffrey recalled, and "they *loved* having someone to talk to." Hazel Williams met an organizer as she left a food stamp office in Cleveland. "As I walked up the walk, a lady asked me, 'do you want more money?' I gazed at her shocked. It seemed to me she was reading my mind." Williams later joined the Cleveland project's welfare rights group.[50]

Dovie Thurman, a resident of Chicago's Uptown, "was organized by Rennie Davis" outside a welfare office as well. "I'm a black woman who grew up in poverty and on a welfare roll. I was raised in the Pruitt-Igoe Projects in St. Louis. They blew them up, they were so bad. I moved to Chicago when I was eighteen with three kids. My husband was in Vietnam at the time." She joined her aunt, "Big" Dovie Coleman, when she arrived in the city in the mid-1960s. She struggled to support herself and her children on welfare, and her situation dovetailed with a history of struggle with the inequities and indignities of the welfare system. "As a child growing up, I hated the welfare system." When Davis introduced himself and handed her a leaflet that said, "Are you tired of late checks, no checks, midnight raids, caseworkers' harassment? Come to a meeting," she "couldn't believe they were saying this openly. My aunt said, 'Oh, we need to go there. I'm tired of all this.'"[51] Thurman and Coleman came to that meeting, and they both quickly became leaders of JOIN.

As the cases of Bessie Smith, Craig, Williams, Thurman, and Coleman suggest, community women proved most receptive to ERAP—ironically, given the privileging of men as a constituency and the low priority assigned to women's organizing in the original strategy.[52] In this way, ERAP contributed to a twentieth-century tradition of women as the mainstays of community organization. From settlement work and the voluntarism of black and white clubwomen in the Progressive Era to tenant and community organizing in the 1970s through the 1990s, women constituted the majority of activists.[53] Women, according to one ERAP canvasser, were "open to the intrusion of the organizer." They were ready to discuss and organize around community problems—problems that particularly concerned them as the caretakers of households and families. "The women dominate household decisions, the upbringing of the children, and frequently the dispersing of the finances," Cathy Wilkerson wrote.[54] For many, a lack of community resources hindered their ability to carry out domestic responsibilities. They also saw such problems as theirs to solve, viewing community improvement as a logical extension of their obligations to home and family. Women's past community activism also stemmed from this sexual division of labor that gave women primary responsibility for family, household, and community maintenance. By improving their neighborhoods through ERAP, women residents believed they could both meet their obligations and ease their own burdens.[55]

Already existing networks among neighborhood women aided the organizing process. Women created many of the social ties that existed among community residents, as ERAP organizers discovered. "The first door I knocked on," Casey Hayden described, "I asked the lady . . . if she knew any people who were having trouble with Welfare. She said the lady across the hall was trying to get on. So I met the lady across the hall who turned out to be a very strong person. . . . Through her I met a lot of other people in the building." ERAP organizers were able to build on such networks of daily life. In Cleveland, Charlotte Phillips worked with a friendship group of women welfare recipients who were "living close to each other" and "visiting each other on a day-to-day basis."[56] These networks greatly facilitated women's activism: personal connections brought women into organizing and provided practical support. As did NCUP organizer Carol Glassman, Helen Garvy found such connections in Hoboken among black but not white women, who "were much more isolated." "It was the black women who were the community. 'A meeting? Oh, the lady up the stairs will watch the kids. No problem.' They had a lot more freedom."[57] Even so, it was generally women, not only in ERAP, who established the social interdependence that historically formed the basis for community organization in neighborhoods, civil rights activism, and labor struggles.[58] They became the projects' first and largest constituency.

Further contributing to this development was the fact that community, as opposed to workplace, organizing never favored men's participation and leadership. When organizers leafleted unemployment compensation offices and focused on the issue of unemployment, they did attract more men than women. Similarly, the issue of police brutality would later draw "[l]ots of men, youngish men" to the projects.[59] The emphasis on neighborhood canvassing as a means of recruitment changed that. Not only was a man less likely to be home during the day when organizers stopped by, he also was less interested than women in discussing problems with "the realities of his domestic life," as Cathy Wilkerson found in Chester.[60]

Not everyone was entirely pleased with this situation, and efforts were made to bring more men into the projects. Something needed to be done, Kim Moody warned from Baltimore, because the projects were starting to develop "a special constituency, housewives." Organizers in Chester started recruiting on a street that appeared to have a concentration of men. "This is an experiment for block organization since in every previous group there has been a predominance of women."[61] Male organizers in Chicago also experimented with recruiting men by lounging on a street corner in Uptown's tavern district and talking to anyone who showed up. Glenn Thureson reported that these "newly discovered techniques" met with "surprising success . . . [and]

convinced us to continue in the future—on the corner as long as the Indian summer lasts, and in the bars when it gets cold." These techniques had an unexpected side effect. "I was virtually drunk all week," Rennie Davis recounted. "The fellows drink all day on that corner."[62] This method of canvassing represented a direct and masculinist counterpoint to door-to-door canvassing and the recruitment of community women. But, with a few exceptions, ERAP failed to develop stable constituencies of men.[63]

Recruitment involved much more than just meeting and chatting with potential ERAP participants, however. Organizers needed to spur low-income residents to come together to change the conditions of their lives and communities. This effort was easier where ERAP could capitalize on already existing struggles, as in Chester, and with individuals, like Chicago's Peggy Terry and Newark's Louise Patterson and Jesse Allen, who brought organizational experience from church, union, and other activities into the projects. Others, such as Boston resident Gertrude Nickerson, also needed little persuading. "I think it's my temperament. When I don't like certain things I have to sound off my mouth and see if I can possibly change them." In Newark, Daisy Ash and Marian Kidd came to NCUP to set up a welfare project. They were "very entrepreneurial," notes Eric Mann, and were "looking for a better vehicle."[64]

But most residents, especially in white neighborhoods, simply "saw no value in banding together." In Hoboken, Helen Garvy found welfare recipients willing to "gripe and . . . talk—but action is hard for people to think about." Of those interested in organizing, like residents attracted to settlement houses early last century, a certain proportion tended to be the most marginal in the community: needy, alcoholic, disorganized.[65] During ERAP's first summer, Bob Ross and other organizers in Chicago held a meeting for unemployed workers at Hull House, the settlement cofounded by Jane Addams. "Five or six people came, and they were literally plastered. They must've all been partying together in an alley and rolled on into the meeting. We stayed with it, . . . but I remembered thinking at the time, 'Jane Addams must have had evenings like this.'"[66] In theory, ERAP organizers intended to go into communities already in motion and give radical direction, but most often in practice they found themselves in quiescent neighborhoods trying to "stir things up"—a far more difficult task.

As a consequence, organizers needed to convince most residents of the power and positive outcomes of working together, of the efficacy of solidarity and organization. The problems plaguing individuals needed to be linked to a broader set of concerns and collectively targeted. Organizers asked questions and shared insights with residents to prompt such realizations. "An organizer can spend two or more hours with a single individual," Rennie Davis noted, and residents can "go round and round on their personal troubles." This one-on-one, discursive, even "psychoanalytic" way of organizing was slow, time-consuming, and necessary. "[L]istening, listening to peoples' problems, their ideas, their fears, their aspirations" was a crucial way both to allow community residents to "speak out" and for organizers to provide a new perspective.[67] This tactic, too, mirrored the Alinsky method, whereby organizers recruited individuals "by convincing them that only through neighborhood collective action" could local improvements be achieved. As Alinsky himself put it, the organizer's "biggest job is to give people the feeling that they can do something."[68] New Left organizers were learning that bottom-up participation in ERAP necessitated supplying a measure of top-down direction. Yet at the same time they were realizing that direction could inspire confidence and action among community residents; it could be empowering, about challenging and changing power relationships, rather than about giving and taking orders.[69]

Organization Building

ERAP sought to build organizations in the communities that provided a political base for an interracial movement of the poor, maximized the democratic participation of residents, and minimized the role of New Left organizers. Like Alinsky and SNCC, organizers expected the community constituencies to participate in and eventually take over management of the projects. In the words of Stan Nadel, "You go in, stir things up, you create an organization, local people take it over, and you leave."[70] To this end, they introduced into the neighborhood projects a decentralized, nonhierarchical structure and shared leadership with decision making by consensus.

Drawing on criticisms of bureaucracy, traditional leadership, and top-down decision making articulated by the veteran civil rights activists Ella Baker and Septima Clark and the founder of Highlander Folk School in Tennessee, Myles Horton, SNCC and SDS utilized this model of organization as a way to deal with specific conditions of civil rights activism in the South and to prevent hierarchy and inequality in their own organizations.[71] According to SNCC veteran Casey Hayden, student activists were viewed by southern blacks "as an elite educated group which should be expected to provide leadership." To develop indigenous leadership, then, student activists needed to counter that expectation, and, where there was local leadership able to withstand physical and economic reprisals, they should "only be used as auxiliary help."[72] This model also, as the sociologist Wini Breines argues, explicitly rejected prevailing styles of bureaucratic organization found in contemporary politics and the authoritarianism of Marxism-Leninism.[73] And it stood at odds with the structure of community organization utilized by Alinsky. His "organization of organizations" brought together existing neighborhood institutions, such as church groups, local unions, and block clubs, and put a premium on strong leadership and centralized decision making.[74] Although the New Left model emphasized equality and bottom-up participation while eschewing hierarchy and top-down leadership, it had been developed within SDS and SNCC, in small meetings and face-to-face encounters among members with common interests and fairly homogeneous experiences. In the ERAP context, however, it did not always work as expected.[75]

ERAP's decentralized structure aimed to maximize community participation in ERAP. Organizers focused on mobilizing individuals at the grassroots into decentralized structures ranging from block organizations, or "communities of place," to individual issue groups, or "communities of interest," around concerns like welfare and housing.[76] NCUP established block organizations that brought together residents of a specific area (not always a geographical "block") and focused on any issues of concern to them, while the Boston and Cleveland projects established issue groups from the start, including Mothers for Adequate Welfare (MAW) in Boston and Citizens United for Adequate Welfare (CUFAW) in Cleveland.[77] In each project, a community union served as an umbrella structure to represent the interests of the community as a whole. In the absence of a formal, coordinating body, however, organizers found themselves serving as the main conduits of information and connection among community participants working on different issues, which gave them, according to Rich Rothstein, "inordinate power."[78] Newark and Chicago organizers moved to correct this problem by adding program or executive committees to their organizational structures in 1964 and 1965.

Composed of organizers and residents, these more centralized and hierarchical bodies made decisions and developed a program for the entire organization; around the same time, SNCC established a coordinating committee to make policy decisions.[79]

Similarly, the New Left concept of leadership did not play out as intended in the community projects. Highly critical of, even opposed to, traditional leadership, organizers believed that centralizing power and authority in only a few individuals was incompatible with the goal of democracy and open to potential corruption. "We," Newark organizers declared, "do not believe in leadership because so many organizations have been sold out by leaders." John Bancroft, a red-diaper baby ("although I didn't know it until I was seventeen"), New Yorker, and Swarthmore student, participated in the Chester protests. He remembers criticisms of Stanley Branche, a local, "kind of charismatic" black leader. "We didn't want to create a mass organization with a leader; we wanted to have something more grassroots."[80] Yet, as it turned out, community people often wanted leaders. Evan Metcalf felt that the Cleveland Community Union in fact had suppressed organization-minded people who wanted to elect leaders. In Chicago, Casey Hayden believed that residents were interested in having one of themselves "heading up the organization, as a leader . . . [who can] express their class and ethnic group in [a] positive way." These insights spurred organizers to foster indigenous leadership but still in a way that avoided leaders as "titular heads and spokesmen."[81]

Consequently, organizers dedicated themselves to helping others realize their own potential. Like SNCC and Alinsky, ERAP assumed that everyone could be a leader, motivate others to participate in actions and in decision making, and take on project responsibilities, but their leadership qualities and talents needed to be recognized and developed.[82] Training varied from learning how to run meetings and how to research and write about topics relevant to organizing, like the War on Poverty and urban renewal, to developing personal confidence. What they called "leadership development" owed much to the Alinsky model of community organization, and Nicholas von Hoffman, of the IAF, presented a paper, "Finding and Making Leaders," at an ERAP conference. In ERAP, however, this was a more difficult process than Alinsky's search for "local opinion shapers," such as ministers and priests or local union officials, because organizers could not rely on an existing leadership structure. It also meant overcoming the resistance of community people who did not believe they had the capacity to be leaders. "They feel that you want to be a big shot or you want to be an authority," one member complained. "I'm certainly not going to go up there and try to lead nobody myself if I feel incapable."[83] To change this and "make" leaders, most projects relied on informal means—for example, one-on-one interactions between organizers and community members—rather than formal mechanisms, such as workshops, training programs, or, in the case of Chicago, the JOIN School initiated by Rich Rothstein.[84]

As part of their critical view toward traditional leadership, New Left organizers also resisted providing guidance or direction to the projects themselves. In the South, civil rights activists were "cautioned to give 'considerable weight' to the opinions of local residents" as to what should be done in their communities.[85] After all, residents were far more familiar with the political dynamics of their localities than were outside organizers. This situation existed in ERAP and other SDS projects as well and led to meetings like that described by Steve Max, who participated in the joint SDS–Committee for Miners project in Hazard during the summer of 1964. "The idea was that the organizer called the meeting and found the place to hold it and turned on the lights, and the people would find the solution." But "nobody had a clue as to what to do," and at numerous meetings "people would look at us and say, 'What should we do?' And we would say, 'You tell us!' And they would say, 'Well, what should we do?'" After going through three or four rounds of this at one meeting with no resolution, Max decided that organizers needed to have a plan, something to offer local people.[86]

Of how the commitment to hold back, not impose their ideas on residents, and "let the people decide" played out in a different context—in the Chicago JOIN project—Rich Rothstein was far more critical. He charged that this commitment unwittingly contributed to less honest relationships in the projects. It led "organizers to pretend (at the time even to themselves) that 'the people' were deciding issues that only organizers knew about, let alone understood."[87] Contributing to this situation were the profound social barriers existing between organizers and residents. Only over time, when, as Rothstein wrote, "we had been there long enough for a truly honest recognition of the legitimacy of the knowledge and experience of both resident and student," were organizers more forthright about offering their political views and strategic and tactical suggestions in a given situation. By the time Eric Mann got to Newark in the fall of 1965, "all this kind of hokey . . . there are no leaders here, we didn't hide behind, we didn't use that. Tom [Hayden] was a very aggressive leader."[88] Indeed, leadership development itself—deciding which residents demonstrated leadership qualities and providing them with the training and skills to represent their own interests—required direction from organizers. Meanwhile, SNCC activists too were in the process of rethinking their avoidance of leadership roles.[89]

In addition to developing leaders, ERAP directly involved community members in the running of the projects. Entire areas of practice and decision making remained under the purview of organizers by virtue of their staff positions; they were far more knowledgeable than community leaders about the day-to-day running of the projects, especially fund-raising and financial realities. Community leaders, then, needed to be brought on staff. In this way, ERAP began to break down the distinction between "organizers" and "leaders," between "staff" and "active membership," and, most important, between those from outside and those from inside the community. This development indicated a growing awareness on the part of New Left organizers of the limits of the "outsider" as organizer. As Kim Moody argues, "Outsiders can play an important role," but "social movements don't happen that way."[90] The motive force needed to come from community "insiders." But bringing neighborhood people on staff meant increasing fund-raising efforts, because they needed to be paid directly by the projects—in contrast to New Left organizers who supported themselves with full- and part-time jobs or parental largesse.[91]

New Left organizers also had to adjust to the fact that, given the greater prominence of neighborhood women in ERAP, most community staff members were mothers with children at home.[92] Women's responsibility for home and family could motivate and justify but also bar participation in community activism. Because many were women living apart from men, they did not confront resistance to their involvement from husbands or partners, as is often the case.[93] Even so, the Cleveland project early on feared that few neighborhood women could make "the kind of ongoing commitment to the organization required from a leadership person." The projects tried to ease the double burden of domestic and community work by providing babysitters and holding meetings in people's homes, as later happened in the welfare rights movement.[94] Even so, New Left organizers did not always understand or respect the double burden or very different life situations of community staff, something that appears to have changed little with later community organizing efforts. "This is more important than her ironing," one male organizer commented about Louise Patterson missing a meeting of NCUP, not recognizing the economic or cultural value of her housework or that how one dressed and kept the house mattered very much in Clinton Hill.[95]

In the end, ERAP did see the emergence of new community leader-organizers, especially among women. Although a community location and the recruitment of women contributed most to this development, ERAP's rejection of more traditional forms of organization also made it more structurally open to women's participation and leadership, as happened in SNCC.[96] Take Dovie Thurman, for example. At the first JOIN meeting she attended, she was asked whether she had anything to add to the discussion about welfare:

> I stood up and made a couple of statements. "I'm sick and tired of this welfare system. I don't know what to do about it, but I want to fight, too. It's doing the same to all of us." It was my first encounter speaking to a group of people, and I got a big hand. . . . At the next meeting I was nominated to be chairperson. Just that quick. What was most exciting was somebody wanted me. I didn't even know what a chairperson was. I had a lot inside of me that I always wanted to say, but I never knew how to get it out. I didn't use to be a person that would speak out a lot. 'Cause I was angry that night, it just came out real easy.[97]

Similarly, Cleveland community leader Lillian Craig discovered that "it was important that I was in the spotlight. . . . I needed to feel that I was *somebody*. I hadn't been sure I was anybody." This "sense of somebodiness"—a sense Martin Luther King, Jr., used to talk about—conveyed her growing self-respect and self-confidence.[98] Testimony like that of Thurman and Craig demonstrated the value and importance of people representing and speaking for themselves, one of the aims of building grassroots leadership in ERAP.

Decision making by consensus—seen by organizers as basic to shared leadership and participatory democracy—also did not always meet the needs of ERAP's constituency. To achieve consensus, ERAP members initially organized meetings that were unstructured, without rules of procedure, and open-ended until the last person had the last word. But unstructured meetings demanded much time, a commodity in short supply for community members, especially women with domestic and child care responsibilities.[99] In Cleveland Mrs. Ellis, a CUFAW member, complained about a meeting where she felt "nothing had been decided—everybody had just talked about their own problems." "ERAP organizers would sit around and jawbone interminably," Paul Booth notes, "and they'd wonder why people didn't want to come back to the meetings."[100] Even organizers themselves were affected. "Not everyone wants to go to meetings all the time," Carol Glassman said during the summer of 1965. "I myself have just come to a point where I can't bear the thought of another meeting."[101]

New Left organizers further discovered that consensus decision making could actually undermine grassroots participation in ERAP. Decisions arrived at by consensus ostensibly ensured the participation and agreement of everyone in attendance. A more inefficient process than "one man, one vote," it involved people in sharing ideas and options and prepared them to act collectively. But this method assumed that participants had some experience with meetings and the confidence to speak whenever they wished, and for many community members ERAP meetings were the first they had attended in their lives. As a consequence, apparent consensus could hide disagreement and even misunderstanding. On one occasion, CUFAW decided to act on the suggestion of Don Armstrong, a minister with the Inner-City Protestant Parish, and conduct a "steal-in" as a way to demonstrate the inadequacy of their welfare budgets. Members planned to enter a local department store and pretend to steal school clothing for their children. Only after the meeting did organizers discover that many of the women had not grasped the symbolism of the tactic and thought they really were going to steal clothing. These women did not want to take part but had been intimidated into silence by "the vocal elements" at the meeting.[102] In situations of unequal power, the costs of participating and the ability to participate were not distributed equally. In ERAP, consensus decision making could yield inaccurate and unfair results.

To ensure accountability, organizers reconsidered how they ran meetings and made decisions. In 1964 the Cleveland project put together a manual on how to hold a meeting, added a written agenda, and formalized decision-making procedures, while by 1967 Chicago organizers chose to use parliamentary procedure and make decisions through majority vote. Both projects wrote rules and regulations for membership rather than defining anyone who attended meetings as a member, and by the spring of 1965 required those members who could do so to pay dues on a monthly basis.[103] When the Newark project encountered difficulties reaching consensus in large meetings, in the absence of alternatives to secure the participation of all members, they reconsidered returning to voting and parliamentary procedure. In the ERAP context, parliamentary procedure could in fact be more democratic than decision making by consensus.[104]

The unexpected and contradictory outcomes stemming from the implementation of the original ERAP model of organization had the most dramatic, as well as best documented, impact on JOIN, due to Rich Rothstein, who emerged as a strong critic of informal and decentralized organization in both SDS and ERAP.[105] In the fall of 1965 the project formed an organizing committee, which was open only to "organizers," defined as those who actually performed tasks. A chair, elected from among community residents, appointed the committee and held formal veto power on project activities. A year and a half later, in 1967, the project reorganized again. They set up an executive committee (or JOIN council) charged with making all project decisions and composed of only community residents elected by "dues-paying, card-carrying JOIN members," with one representative for every ten members.[106] From ERAP's collective, consensual model, the Chicago project had adopted an organizational form based on the principles of representative democracy, with accountable leadership and clear membership criteria.

For ERAP, this was an ironic but also rare development. The original model of organization garnered much criticism from Alinsky and members of the Old Left for its lack of structure, and the Chicago project came to agree with this criticism.[107] But the original model also expressed values and goals important to the New Left, and the rest of ERAP declined to follow Chicago's example. Many organizers, for example, had no desire to form program committees or boards to oversee the community unions, because "[t]he whole idea of a board . . . is alien to a dynamic, community movement." Over time, the Newark program committee disappeared as a functioning body, as participants began to "feel a way into something more organic."[108] ERAP as a whole remained strongly committed to decentralization and, in the spring of 1965, disbanded as a national SDS project. Due to this commitment, former activists and scholars argue, ERAP failed to build permanent community organizations and "unleashed" these "centrifugal forces" in SDS itself.[109]

Even so, ERAP organizers as a whole learned that no one organizational model guaranteed grassroots democracy and participation or prevented hierarchical authority and control in every situation. Instead, to be truly open to the participation and concerns of community residents, they realized they needed to commit themselves to taking a flexible, experimental approach in the projects, especially in the absence of an agreed-upon "organizing technology," and even if it required the exercise of a measure of top-down leadership and control. They continued with this approach as they sought to balance the "nitty-gritty" of everyday organizing from the bottom up with their larger aim of building an interracial movement of the poor. This balancing act pushed ERAP organizers to rethink and revise their original strategy once the community projects were under way.

Chicago JOIN protest against slum housing, summer 1966. (Courtesy of Nancy Hollander.)

5

Strategic Revisions

As they negotiated the dilemma between top-down and bottom-up organizing in ERAP, New Left organizers confronted a disjuncture between their strategic assumptions about how to build an interracial movement of the poor and the concerns of neighborhood participants. Consistent with their commitment to participatory democracy and bottom-up organizing, they needed to take seriously and act on the requests and responses of community constituents. This need pushed organizers to continue to take a flexible, experimental approach to their work in the neighborhoods, an approach that over time came to substitute for the original, more definitive ERAP strategy as laid out by Carl Wittman and Tom Hayden in An *Interracial Movement of the Poor?*

Yet, in the process, organizers questioned the political content of their new approach, specifically the issues for organizing, service demands, and bases for solidarity suggested by residents, mostly women. Were issues such as children's welfare and housing, strategies of service provision, and identities other than "the poor" legitimate elements of politics? Would they contribute to building a social movement of poor Americans? In revising the original ERAP strategy, organizers began to rethink their understanding of politics and social movements and contributed to the expanded definition of "the political" for which the New Left is known. Importantly, the larger attempt to redefine the accepted boundaries of politics during the 1960s proceeded from the Old Left's early politicization of economic issues. SDS and ERAP activists could build on the Marxist revision of classical liberalism's strict division between public and private sectors, between the political and the economic.[1] ERAP's contribution to the decade's transformation of the categories and meanings of politics happened through a series of encounters, negotiations, and conflicts between New Left organizers and community residents.

Politicizing Issues

While organizing from the bottom up, New Left organizers learned that what they had defined as the primary organizing issue for ERAP—jobs—was only one of a constellation of concerns articulated by low-income community residents. Taken together, residents voiced problems with welfare, housing, urban renewal, children's welfare, police brutality, as well as jobs. Not only that, the issue of jobs failed to mobilize significant numbers of neighborhood residents, prompting a major debate about whether the projects should remain focused on unemployment or shift to the concerns articulated by community residents. The question at the center of this controversy was whether distribution- or consumption-based issues, like housing and welfare, were as political as unemployment—a production-based issue.

During the summer of 1964 ERAP organizers were forced to admit that the strategic focus on employment issues was not working. In Cleveland the project's unemployment committee never achieved even a consistent membership; from one weekly meeting in August to the next, for example, there was almost a complete turnover in attendance. Philadelphia organizers sought to win a retraining program for unemployed longshoremen and organize "the unorganized": migrant farmworkers, mostly African American, bussed from the city to pick blueberries in southern New Jersey. After several months, they announced they had "reached a dead end" and were discontinuing their jobs committee.[2] The Baltimore project worked with UAW members at a local Martin Marietta defense plant and unemployed workers in the building trades. "These were people who had discovered the limitations of what they could get in the unions," Kim Moody notes. "Our idea was to have a rally at the end of the summer to draw attention to the issue" of unemployment, but "the rally was pretty much a flop, not very many people showed up." By the fall, even JOIN conceded defeat, after a year of trying to organize unemployed men in Chicago on a citywide basis. That is when they decided to relocate to Uptown and to widen the project's scope to encompass a range of community constituencies and concerns.[3]

Organizers arrived at no single explanation for this failure. Some felt that poor organizing was responsible. Those in the Philadelphia project admitted they "had run out of ideas and had no faith in what we were doing." Others believed that the unemployed did not form a solid, stable constituency. George Graham, an organizer with the Cairo, Illinois, project, felt there was "no community of interest among the poor." Also hindering mobilization was the fact that, as Mike Zweig found in Newark, "the unemployed don't like to talk about their unemployment."[4] To be sure, ERAP had taken on a difficult task. "Organizing the unemployed is so tough that even seasoned union organizers shrink from it," lamented one journalist writing on the ERAP projects.[5] Moreover, the rate of unemployment was on the decline; it averaged just above 5 percent over the decade. The economist Ray Brown's prediction of rising unemployment did not materialize until the 1970s, in part due to the Vietnam War. "Just as we got to Chicago," Lee Webb remembered, "lines at the unemployment compensation center started to get shorter." Although employment problems nevertheless existed throughout the country and in ERAP's project locations, organizers "were not met by armies of the white unemployed."[6]

Over time, increasing numbers of New Left organizers found fault with the basic strategy. "The strategy of organizing the unemployed to demand jobs or income always sounded right, but it never felt right," recalls Connie Brown, who worked in both the Philadelphia and Newark projects. As early as the fall of 1963, Joe Chabot, the first ERAP organizer, discovered that "people have trouble relating directly to unemployment," whereas they "believe something can be done" about smaller issues, like bureaucratic problems and "red tape." And, in fact, JOIN's first demonstration occurred around cuts in welfare benefits.[7] The problem of structural unemployment was too abstract and too distant from people's everyday lives, and later suggestions for ERAP campaigns around unemployment—for example, supporting the so-called Clark bill, designed to implement the Full Employment Act of 1946, and lobbying for government-supported job creation—were too national in emphasis.[8] Moreover, the "radical separation" between what the sociologist Ira Katznelson has called "the politics of work from the politics of community" in U.S. political culture made ERAP's community location a difficult place from which to organize around residents' identities as workers. For Tom Hayden, the "neighborhood process did not lend itself to organizing around jobs issues."[9]

Even if ERAP had managed to develop a large constituency and a strong campaign for "jobs or income now," its efforts were unlikely to succeed. The Clark bill and later full employment legislation languished in Congress during the 1960s. Institutional reform did not even result in 1968, when the SCLC's Poor People's Campaign demanded full

employment and public jobs, the Kerner Commission made a similar rec-
ommendation after investigating the causes of black urban riots, and 79
percent of those polled by Gallup favored the idea of the government
guaranteeing a job to all Americans.[10] Full employment and public job
creation were too costly and required government planning and direction,
something that had been rejected by the late 1940s. They also stood at the
intersection of economic and poverty policy, at a point when economic
policy increasingly was viewed as unconnected to, and kept bureaucrati-
cally separate from, the nation's poverty policy.[11] Such social democratic
proposals were untenable in the U.S. political economy of the 1960s.

In the summer of 1964, as the failure of unemployment organizing became increasingly clear, New Left activists debated whether they should
change their strategy and shift to organizing around the issues raised by
community residents. The "JOIN-GROIN" debate, as it came to be
called, pitted activists not only in the Chicago project but all those still interested in the original ERAP strategy and unemployment organizing—
labeled "Jobs or Income Now (JOIN)"—against those urging a focus on
community concerns—derisively dubbed "Garbage Removal or Income
Now (GROIN)."[12] The "JOIN-GROIN" debate continued the strategic
criticisms of ERAP that arose in the spring of 1964. In general, "JOIN"
advocates were more oriented toward Marxism and committed to the
labor metaphysic than were "GROIN" advocates. Kim Moody, who
"pretty much had a Marxist, class outlook" at the time, characterized it
as a "fairly sharp debate" but not a "nasty debate."[13]

The central question in the debate was whether the organizing issues
proposed by community residents had political content and could contribute to social change. Such issues as welfare, housing, and children's
recreation—in keeping with ERAP's location in the community, and not
the workplace—generally emerged from inequalities in the areas of economic distribution and consumption and often were defined as private
concerns that fell outside the domain of politics and social movements.
As did the Old Left, ERAP organizers on both sides of the debate considered unemployment a political issue because it connected to fundamental
inequalities in American society and challenged entrenched power relations. "Unemployment is a political problem," argued SDS leader Richard Flacks. "Major centers of power in our society support policies which
prevent full employment and actively favor a high rate of unemployment."[14] They questioned whether the new issues posed the same radical
challenge or would translate into bringing about social change.

Shaping the "JOIN" position was its definition of ERAP's constituency. Although both "the poor" and "the unemployed" were mentioned in the original ERAP strategy, "JOIN" advocates aimed to organize the unemployed, not the poor, a term they took to mean people whose economic role was marginal or insecure and defined as "the lumpenproletariat."[15] Michigan student Stan Nadel volunteered for the Chicago JOIN project, because he sought to reach "not the lumpen[proletariat] but the proletariat, the temporarily unemployed, . . . those who were capable, in a position to carry out real change, as opposed to those who were essentially defined as surplus elements in society and had no leverage." Nadel grew up in the Jewish Left in New York and had been a member of the Young Socialist Alliance as a teenager. "As a socialist, I thought it was real important to reach workers."[16] The issue of unemployment and the goal of "jobs or income now," the "JOIN" contingent believed, were more likely to do that.

Was the "GROIN" focus on "immediate grievances" and "non-radical issues," then, politically "a step or more backwards" for ERAP, as Chicago organizer Rich Rothstein asked?[17] With this question, "JOIN" supporters articulated a fundamental dilemma for ERAP and community organizing efforts generally, that is, can fights for incremental changes contain or lead to larger structural change? The danger of concentrating on "GROIN" concerns was that they would fail to get to the root of the problem. For Steve Max, successful "non-political community work"—by which he meant neighborhood organizing not oriented toward electoral politics—most likely would result in small and temporary improvements in neighborhood conditions. In the course of a rent strike, for example, a landlord may paint apartments or provide more garbage cans. However, "once the demands are met and the pressure dies down, the situation tends to revert to its former state," because the "ghetto-producing forces of exploitation" had not been targeted.[18]

Part of the problem was that community issues reflected the concerns of ERAP's largest constituency: neighborhood women. For "JOIN" advocate Kim Moody, it was "difficult to see how an organization of women built on neighborhood concerns will lead to anything else."[19] Changing ERAP's organizing focus necessitated opening up putatively apolitical spaces and activities to politics, and defining concerns associated with women's responsibilities for home, family, and community as legitimate elements of a social movement. In ERAP, as was true historically, women's community activism challenged dominant understanding of the scope and definition of politics.[20] Even so, the problem remained of how to make each project "something more than a neighborhood improvement association" and fulfill the original purpose of building a social movement of poor Americans.[21]

Supporters of ERAP's shift to distribution- and consumption-based "GROIN" issues answered critics by beginning to formulate such issues as political, a process that continued throughout the lives of the projects. The Cleveland project set out to do "more thinking about how [community issues] might lead to broader problems [and] might be turned into a 'radicalizing' experience." When they first took up welfare organizing, they did not consider the goal of achieving an adequate standard of welfare benefits a "radical" demand. How could they "translate the . . . bread-and-butter demands of a welfare constituency into demands with political content?"[22] They started by connecting community issues to fundamental social, economic, and political inequalities. Inadequate city services, for example, revealed the blatant discrimination against, and the lack of political power in, low-income neighborhoods. And issues like children's welfare and, yes, garbage removal were "the tangible manifestations of people's alienation," Carl Wittman argued from Newark, and, in fact, could "fit together into a radical program of demands."[23]

As a consequence, when community residents expressed concern about children's safety, recreation, and education, New Left organizers began to frame these issues in political terms. Threats to the safety and well-being of children formed, as is true today, the most reliable reasons for neighborhood activism, and ERAP recruited sizable constituencies to campaign for changes necessary to guard children from danger, secure safe locations for play, and improve conditions in local schools.[24] "I used to think such issues were 'superficial,' they didn't deal with root problems, etc.," Tom Hayden wrote in his daily journal in 1965, "but I've felt my thinking shift bit by bit this year. I had to learn that *real* children are killed, all the time. What the city fails to do about such 'minor' ills . . . is a clear measure of the callousness of the officials."[25]

ERAP held the state, in the form of local government, responsible for ensuring children's welfare. Participants in various projects, including Newark, Trenton, Chicago, and Cleveland, wrote letters to municipal authorities, circulated petitions, sent delegations downtown, and held demonstrations to have condemned houses and abandoned cars removed, traffic lights and playgrounds installed, and school overcrowding and cruel treatment of children ended.[26] All the projects confronted municipal intransigence and met with little success, but participants understood children's welfare as a public responsibility and, therefore, political.

As with children's issues, "GROIN" advocates asserted the political content of resident concerns by focusing on how they emerged from within or near the domain of the state, an assertion made more feasible by increased postwar state intervention in the economy.[27] This politicization process happened with housing, when poor conditions and high rents made housing a primary concern for community constituents in all the ERAP locations. During the summer of 1964, when the CCP catalyzed a major confrontation with Cleveland officials by organizing tenants in a public housing project, organizer Paul Potter concluded that "GROIN" issues directly confronted state institutions and occurred within "a framework of action that challenges the power structure."[28]

Public housing, therefore, was political; could the same be said of private housing? Historically, housing activists—especially during the 1930s—enjoyed success not with landlords but with the state and establishing and improving public housing.[29] In the summer of 1964, Newark organizers hesitated to target landlords for fear it would "perpetuate the myth that private enterprise could provide good housing for everyone." Focusing on the city, by contrast, would "push solutions into public sector."[30] But Clinton Hill residents preferred to take on landlords, for concessions from a landlord would yield concrete, if short-run, results. Building on the efforts of Jesse Gray and other organizers of the Harlem rent strikes to shift focus from landlords to the city administration, NCUP activists resolved to pursue private landlords but use the regulatory power of city government, such as housing code enforcement, to buttress their efforts. Projects in Chester and Chicago followed suit. "Contrary to the views of some," NCUP reported when a series of rent strikes in August sparked conflict with the city, "we find ourselves in a situation that is intrinsically political."[31]

Over time, ERAP started to consider all sorts of connections between public institutions and recipients as political relationships. If political power and social movement issues existed in a variety of institutional settings—not just economics or elections—then interactions between recipients and the state became political encounters. This insight meant that problems emerging from such encounters were political issues.[32] Casey Hayden expressed this idea when she wrote about her work with women welfare recipients in Chicago. "They are tied to the state through the welfare system, and thus their gripes are easily politicized."[33] Cleveland organizer Evan Metcalf expanded this insight. "[W]e are trying to change these institutions, [because] it is through these institutions that many forms of social oppression take place (. . . urban renewal, the welfare system, all the little points [where] politics touches people's lives—city services, all sorts of red tape registrations—cops, etc.)."[34] By continuing to emphasize public institutions as the crucial loci of political contestation, ERAP organizers failed to go much beyond a traditional public sphere conception of politics. Still, they began to develop an understanding of power relations that could be extended to practices and interactions operating beyond the state—in personal life, for example.

In addition to challenging the definition of nonproduction issues as private problems without political content, "GROIN" supporters asserted that these issues had solid constituencies and organizing potential. They had been proposed, after all, by residents themselves. In contrast to the small, irregular groups involved in unemployment organizing, the constituencies for welfare, housing, and children's issues were larger and more stable. The "GROIN" contingent did not address the concern of "JOIN" advocates that these constituencies were primarily the lumpenproletariat, but they did point out that community women were interested and ready for organizing. In Newark's Clinton Hill, "mothers and kids [were] clearly the most vocal elements in the Negro community," while Casey Hayden insisted that "there is a real potential for organizing welfare women."[35] The presence of these constituencies demonstrated the soundness, relative to the original ERAP strategy, of embracing a range of community concerns and capitalizing on the sources of strength and activism that existed in the different neighborhoods.

What further justified the "GROIN" focus was its consistency with ERAP's dedication to mobilizing communities from the bottom up. New Left organizers began to see that "the search for a radical lever"—the search for an issue that would propel poor Americans into a social movement—should be undertaken together with community residents. "Where the energy was, was where we went," Carol Glassman recalls.[36] Selecting the "correct" issue became less important than involving residents in the process of selecting and organizing around issues, defining and solving problems. The process became the political content. The crucial question for Casey Hayden was "how we organize people to make demands." This perspective was in keeping with that of

Ella Baker, Septima Clark, and Myles Horton—and therefore SNCC—
to "start where the people are," to enable people "to see themselves as
having the right and the capacity to have some say-so in their own
lives."[37] "GROIN" organizing contested the original ERAP strategy's
top-down mandate of unemployment as the privileged organizing issue, and resulted, according to two researchers in Chicago, in "a grad-
ual playing down of the elitist role of the student staff."[38]

The concerns of community residents pushed ERAP beyond the con-
fines of the productionist bias of the Old Left and labor and toward
greater strategic flexibility. Paralleling the development of the U.S. Communist Party in the early years of the Great Depression, New Left organizers came to see consumption and distribution as arenas for organizing
and just as politically legitimate as organizing in the sphere of production.
This development also created a crucial opening for women and their interests in the projects.[39] "[W]e have . . . refined our ideas about what constitutes a 'radical' issue," Cleveland organizer Dickie Magidoff claimed in
the fall of 1964, "and have developed a more flexible position on this
(that is jobs is not the only one)."[40] Organizers continued with such
strategic flexibility when they took on service provision in the projects.

The Politics of Service Organizing

In all the projects, ERAP organizers received consistent requests for
service work from community residents. Residents asked for aid with
bureaucratic procedures, such as dealing with caseworkers, correcting
the arbitrary elimination of recipient names from benefit rolls or reduction in benefit amounts, tracking down late or lost checks, and filling
out forms. A reduced, delayed, or missing payment could cause tremendous hardship for poor people living on a minimum budget and from
check to check. Even so, many organizers feared that helping people
with services neither constituted a political activity nor contributed to
building a social movement. Could they deliver services in a way that
empowered residents and generated political challenges?

ERAP's service work began in the fall of 1963 with the initial Chicago
JOIN project, but during the summer of 1964 objections to service activity began to emerge from other projects. By locating their office near an
unemployment compensation center, early Chicago organizers—including Joe Chabot and Danny Max—provided services. While one passed

out leaflets and spoke with recipients standing in line at the center, the other ran the office and offered free coffee, help with problems related to unemployment compensation, and information about job openings.[41] They found service work to be a political necessity in the city of Chicago, where Mayor Richard Daley's powerful political machine provided assistance and a range of services and city residents expected them.[42] As more projects got under way and residents in other neighborhood locations requested services, organizers began to express concern about the tensions between service work and political organizing.

ERAP's doubts reflected the dominant view that politics and services were, or should be, separate activities. At the time, both political activists and social work professionals believed that an opposition existed between "making change" and "helping people."[43] As Carl Wittman urged, ERAP needed "to strike at the heart (rather than the periphery, which the service idea hits at) of the problems." Service provision, critics contended, targeted only the symptoms and not the causes of poverty and, if successful, merely advanced small-scale reforms. Receiving help with services did not guarantee that community residents would "develop radical consciousness" and move toward political organization and social protest.[44]

Providing services also could sidetrack ERAP from the broader political program of building a social movement. The Trenton project found service activity to be wholly consuming and counterproductive, and, when organizers decided to disband after the first summer, their final project evaluation included a section entitled "In Which We Wasted Time with Service Programs." Women organizers in Cleveland also worried about falling into "the we-can-help-you trap" and being unable to expand a service-based welfare recipient group into politically challenging the welfare system.[45] Reflecting these concerns, "The Role and Function of Service" was on the agenda at the 1964 summer ERAP conference; one question to be discussed was how service could "be used to mobilize the community around economic, political, and social issues?" Boston organizers believed this could not be done and, to keep their focus on gaining political power, decided to provide no direct, personal services.[46]

Most important, organizers felt that providing services contradicted ERAP's goal of building community organizations based on equality and democracy. More often than not, service work was a top-down activity, and they understood this activity in both gender and class terms.

Historically, service provision was linked to both the private nurturing and public activism of middle- and upper-class women, and popular images of service providers, such as "Lady Bountiful," were usually female and class-based.[47] When organizers warned of the dangers of a "social work conception" in ERAP or the impossibility of delivering services "without becoming a social worker," they referred to a field dominated not only by women but what they perceived as professional, middle-class women. Whether JOIN could "be known as an organization that 'helps people' or fights for people" expressed a difference between feminized "helping" and masculinized "fighting."[48] Service work also required providers to define the needs of recipients, and, according to Cleveland community leader Lillian Craig, "The local poor people feel very sensitive to people . . . coming in to 'help' them. . . . [and] tell[ing] them how to live."[49]

But as SNCC found working in the rural South, needs were great in these communities, and organizers became intimately aware of how often residents lacked basic necessities and facilities. While canvassing in Chicago in 1964, Bob Ross "vividly" recalls visiting one woman's home:

> This was an apartment that had almost nothing in it. A card table in the kitchen and a metal chair, and a mattress in a bedroom, and no furniture in the whole living room and maybe some seltzer in the refrigerator. And I'm giving the standard rap, you know, poor people have to get organized. . . . She looked at me and she said, "You can't help me." I said, "Well, we are going to help each other." And she said, "No, you don't know what I mean. I understand about politics. You can't help me today. I need groceries today." And it was true, I couldn't help her today. . . . I remember having this feeling of deep inadequacy.[50]

Such experiences repeated throughout ERAP and spurred organizers to think through how to integrate services—concrete, practical ways to meet the immediate, felt needs of low-income residents, often for essential items such as food, clothing, and shelter—and politics.

They decided that engaging in service work, in keeping with bottom-up organizing, permitted residents to define ERAP's issues and activities. The projects mostly provided help with welfare and other public aid grievances. During the summer of 1964, for example, a community woman came into JOIN. She had been laid off weeks before at a factory and felt she had gotten the "run around" at the state unemployment compensation office. An organizer accompanied her back to the office, met with a supervisor, and then sent a typed letter of grievances to the director of the city division. She received her compensation in a matter of days. Paul Millman was known as JOIN's "best-qualified Comp System challenger." "One day it hit me that I had responsibility for people, . . . this was very important to them in their lives."[51] In addition to providing this type of aid, projects offered a range of services. In Chicago, for a while at least, a lawyer and a hairdresser volunteered one day a week at the project office, and by the winter of 1965 Baltimore became "the home of a massive 'kiddies' program."[52] In Hazard organizers not only helped people get back on welfare and into the hospital but also built at least one outhouse, while Chester organizers sponsored a "rat day." "[L]aden with rat poison, mouse poison, and roach spray [they] went around door-to-door to every house on the block." Such services, like those provided by black clubwomen to their own communities at the turn of the twentieth century, were "necessary but unspectacular" efforts that improved the health and environment of neighborhood residents.[53]

Over time, organizers decided that service activity was part of ERAP's broader political program. It built a neighborhood base and reputation for the projects. "People know JOIN's there," Uptown resident Bobby Joe Wright noted. "And if they have any problem they try to get in touch with JOIN."[54] At a minimum, as Stanley Aronowitz and others pointed out, low-income residents were not going to put their faith or futures in the hands of youthful, New Left organizers over the long term, if they could not help with, or solve, immediate problems. SNCC, too, had realized the importance of being known among rural black southerners as providing "direct aid," such as food, medicine, and clothing, not just "agitation."[55] By doing so, services created ties and established trust between organizers and residents and brought community people into the projects. Margaret McCarty encountered the Baltimore project when it offered low-cost coal for winter fuel. "These people cared when I really needed help. I told them when I got straightened out I would come and work for them—really work." McCarty later became chair of the project's welfare rights group. New Left organizers came to see service work, or "person-to-person" work, as "building the movement one-by-one."[56]

Even so, ERAP organizers still feared that service provision was paternalistic and reinforced powerlessness and dependency among poor community residents, and they sought alternative methods of service delivery. Cleveland organizers were the first in 1964 to criticize ERAP's failure to train community residents to participate in, or to assume any responsibility for, service work. Rather than being sole service providers, they sought to make services more of an exchange between equals or peers, and other projects soon followed Cleveland's lead. By 1966 the Chicago project presented service provision as a "give-and-take," whereby a "person who receives help from JOIN is explicitly expected to help the community in return."[57] In this way, services would bring residents together, break down isolation, and translate individual problems into collective, community concerns, a development that occurred for women welfare recipients in ERAP and later welfare rights organizing as well. In Cleveland, Elaine Maramick worked with the project's Welfare Grievance Committee, CUFAW's successor, formed in the fall of 1966. "Whenever a complaint comes in we follow it up by going to the case worker and finding out what is wrong." Boston welfare recipient Gertrude Nickerson reported on her experience with grievance work as well. "You sort of stagnate on aid. Now you have other people to help, share problems and get together. It's a fine feeling."[58] As did other contemporary critics of "the expert-client relation typical of existing service efforts," ERAP organizers hoped to connect "the 'service approach' with a truly democratic movement" by involving residents in service provision.[59]

Along these lines, ERAP sponsored community experiments in self-help. This traditional method of community support appealed greatly to neighborhood residents, and they proposed a range of activities. Consistent with ERAP's location in the community and constituency of women, who made the majority of family purchases, most self-help activities oriented around consumer issues. In Cleveland, women welfare recipients suggested a day care exchange and food stamp pool and eventually set up a "Buyer's Cooperative" to purchase items excluded from the food stamp program, such as soap powder, toilet tissue, toothpaste, and sanitary napkins.[60] JOIN formed a food cooperative for purchasing staples in bulk at cheaper prices, and community members were involved in all phases of the project, from taking orders to packaging and selling the products. They also opened a "charity store," staffed by Uptown residents, which sold secondhand clothing. For participant Jim "Skipper" Sisk, these activities meant that JOIN members were "people who like to help people."[61] As in the Seattle cooperative movement in the 1920s, such efforts increased ERAP participants' "purchasing power" and strengthened community ties, creating a sense of cohesion and mutualism in the projects.[62]

In addition to consumer cooperatives, ERAP's dedication to service and self-help spawned community schools as alternative institutions. As the decade continued, poor conditions in public education prompted projects in Cleveland, New Haven, and Boston to establish neighborhood "freedom schools," similar to those of the Civil Rights Movement. The Cleveland Children's Community, located on the city's East Side, involved parents as teachers and built its curriculum around black history and the struggle for civil rights. Delores Maxwell, a neighborhood mother and teacher in the school, praised it for allowing students to "progress and learn at their own rate of speed . . . without feeling imposed upon or ashamed."[63] "Freedom school is a place to learn about your own kind," New Haven student Calvin West, Jr., wrote, "and that's black." Members of the Boston project began to design an elementary school organized and directed by community residents as well. The Roxbury Community School would be small, racially integrated, and committed to education that "expressed the values of the community."[64] By establishing schools outside the public school system, participants, such as Cleveland organizer Bill Ayers, hoped to provide needed social services and advance a critical, alternative vision of what children's education could be, at a time when the War on Poverty made education a policy priority and launched Head Start, the federally funded preschool program for low-income children.[65]

Resident participation in service delivery also provided a crucial basis for collective action. During the summer of 1964, a Newark landlord threatened to evict a woman who had recently applied for welfare benefits and was waiting for her first check. Some twenty people attended the hearing for her eviction case, which was dismissed after she explained her situation. They then proceeded to the welfare office and obtained an emergency check for her. This particular service strategy was reflected in a stanza from an NCUP song. "Now one of our ladies on Hunterdon / Went to the Welfare and couldn't get in / Rachel and Ethyl Sloan said what the heck / They went down with her and she got her check."[66] Collective action not only often yielded results where individual efforts had failed but also could benefit more than the one individual involved. In June 1965, JOIN conducted a sit-in at a welfare office after officials refused to show Dorothy Perez the regulation they claimed was the reason for holding up her check. Perez and three organizers were arrested and later fined. On the following day, with a large picket line of Uptown residents outside, welfare officials admitted to having made a mistake. They also acknowledged that recipients had the right to see the rules that applied in their cases and bring an advocate with them to appointments with caseworkers.[67] Such successes demonstrated the power and positive outcomes of working together and acting collectively against injustices.

For neighborhood residents, working to achieve self-help goals and struggling against public agencies contributed to a greater sense of personal competence, control, and, most important, political efficacy. Although low-income residents, especially women, already interacted and negotiated with community-based services and state institutions, with ERAP's service organizing the balance of power shifted.[68] As Elvie Jordan, a member of Cleveland's Welfare Grievance Committee, stated,

> Before I started working with the Welfare Grievance Committee I had the feeling that any time I would attempt to go to the Welfare Department for anything I would be embarrassed and insulted before I could get over to them why I was there or why I called. . . . [With the Welfare Grievance Committee] you learn how to gain the respect of the Welfare Department. And as long as we have this respect we can work with the Welfare Department to make this a better welfare system.[69]

In ERAP, community members began to confront and demand respect from public institutions and officials that formerly deemed them undeserving of aid and worthy of contempt. By gaining some measure of control over such interactions, they redefined their relationship to the state as one of citizenship and entitlement and challenged the power relations basic to the welfare system.[70]

Propelled by the demands of constituents, service work provided the ERAP projects with their most consistent, albeit small, victories. JOIN, for example, claimed to have handled some 250 welfare grievances between 1965 and 1966, with all but two resolved in favor of the recipient.[71] By handling and resolving grievances, participants helped to ensure that recipients obtained the benefits to which they were entitled by right. Difficult forms, complicated procedures, and intransigent caseworkers could keep people from receiving the social benefits and services they deserved. "Micropolitical" encounters—such as Elvie Jordan's—involved "macropolitical" conflicts and concerns and could be an entree to wider, systemic problems, as the Communist Party had found in the early years of the Great Depression.[72]

ERAP's service achievements should not be exaggerated, however. The consumer cooperatives and community schools did not become permanent institutions, and to what extent community members were involved in service provision is difficult to gauge. Like service providers in the War on Poverty, organizers surely found the balance between helping residents and residents helping themselves "difficult and delicate to maintain" and spent a great deal of time directly providing services themselves.[73] Nonetheless, the cumulative impact of service activity in the projects led New Left organizers to recognize services as political. Even Boston organizers, who had pledged not to provide services in favor of political mobilization, worked on grievances with their welfare rights group, Mothers for Adequate Welfare. ERAP thus contributed to the larger politicization of service delivery that occurred during the 1960s.[74]

Identity Politics

The "central issue of the development of a radical movement," Newark organizer Connie Brown observed, was "the forging of a new identity."[75] Along with service organizing, ERAP used political education to forge solidarity and what social movement scholars later would call "a collective identity" among project participants. The projects initially sought to build solidarity by drawing on community members' shared status as poor Americans, in keeping with the aim of sparking an interracial movement of the poor. Like the planners for the War on Poverty, New Left organizers utilized the category of "the poor" to construct a constituency for the projects. In the process, ERAP sought to define poor Americans across differences of race, geography, age, and economic background as a single group with common problems, interests, and political potential as the poor, a definition that community members resisted.[76]

To create a constituency of the poor that would claim and act on this identity, organizers needed to counter the common association of stigma and shame with being poor in the United States. One Cleveland woman welfare recipient movingly expressed this perspective. "At times you lose your identity and feelings of worthiness as a human being. There is a feeling of depression and defeat . . . because [you] know there is no way out."[77] Low-income residents also tended to blame themselves for their economic situation, although organizers found this tendency more commonly among white than black residents, who looked first to racial discrimination and a lack of available jobs as the reasons for their economic situations. "There can be no poor people's movement in any form," Tom Hayden recognized, "unless the poor can overcome their fear and embarrassment."[78] To this end, organizers set out to show that economic problems "were not personal but rather systemic and historical" and to redefine the identity of poor Americans without negative connotations such as laziness or stupidity. "We," Cleveland organizer Bob Smiddie declared for the entire project, "are not a lot of ignorant poor people who don't know the score."[79] New Left efforts in this direction indicated the beginning of an understanding of identity as both a source of oppression for groups and communities and one of strength and resistance for challenges to oppression.

Organizers also wanted black, white, and Latino community residents to identify collectively as the poor. Transcending divisions of race and ethnicity that obscured common problems and experiences and prevented poor Americans from uniting to form an interracial constituency was not an easy task. Although blacks in the various ERAP locations did not necessarily see the economic problems they shared with poor whites, racial divisions were sharpest in the ethnically heterogeneous, yet predominantly Appalachian white, neighborhoods, such as Chicago's Uptown and Cleveland's Near West Side. The culture and heritage of these residents, observed Kim Moody, were "shot through with individualism, . . . anti-laborism, and racism." Cleveland organizers reported hearing "derogatory comments [about] the 'colored'" on nearly a daily basis, and in Uptown Judith Bernstein recalls how difficult it was even "to walk in an integrated group in that neighborhood. It was not done."[80] Despite such overt forms of white prejudice against blacks, organizers still believed that an interracial movement of the poor could be built.[81]

Through political education, ERAP attempted to change residents' ideas about the causes of their poverty and encouraged them to come together despite racial differences. Conversation, project newsletters, leadership development sessions, community conferences, and cultural activities, organizers hoped, would allow neighborhood members to air their grievances about poverty and race and put them within a larger context. This concerted effort at discussion and consciousness raising would enable residents to realize they were not alone in their various difficulties, nor should they feel ashamed or keep silent about their "personal" problems. And, hopefully, it would overcome the racism of white residents. To this end, ERAP endeavored to create an environment in which residents of different backgrounds and experiences could meet and learn about one another. Fran Ansley hoped that JOIN's experiment in community theater would work in this way. "We'll put on skits about welfare with Negroes and Puerto Ricans in them. The white migrants see their problems are the same as these people; it changes them like magic."[82] Although idealistic, naive, and not always successful, ERAP's political education rested "on the assumption that . . . consciousness and imagination can be broadened by structured discussion with people . . . doing similar work."[83]

This assumption fit with "the belief that the oppressed themselves, collectively, already have much of the knowledge needed to produce change," a belief advocated by Myles Horton at Highlander Folk School and adopted by civil rights activists like Ella Baker.[84] It also underlay ERAP's two community conferences, in Cleveland in February 1965 and in Newark in August 1965, which gathered together guests, such as the SNCC activist Fannie Lou Hamer and participants from CORE and NSM projects, and activists from all the ERAP projects.[85] In Newark, Eric Mann noticed that community members often used project meetings to share their experiences and troubles. At one meeting, they spent much time reporting on negative or hostile encounters they had experienced recently, reports that inevitably ended with "and so I told the motherfucker . . ." Frustrated after an hour and a half of "and so I told the motherfucker," Mann wanted to get on with the meeting, but, as he remembers it, Tom Hayden argued that this exchange was necessary. "If they don't get it out of their system, we're never going to have an effective meeting, because they are so enraged by daily life."[86] ERAP gatherings could provide a place for reflection and exchange about "everyday life experiences of injustice, inequality, and abuse" that helped to open "spaces for oppositional consciousness and activism."[87]

ERAP's political education around inequalities of class and race encouraged the development of a broader political vocabulary and new categories of analysis among community participants. In Chicago, Virginia Bowers believed she "got a lot of education through organizing and stuff with JOIN." Dovie Thurman's involvement prompted her "to look at the system: 'Who is the culprit?' . . . I was using the word 'system' instead of the word 'you.' . . . I wasn't thinking on the race side. My thoughts were on the poor versus the rich. I began to learn about class."[88] When Cleveland's Lillian Craig wrote about her confrontation with county commissioners about restoring free school lunches for children of welfare parents in early 1965, she sounded like an SDS activist. "I stood up and blasted the whole power structure sitting up on the platform in front of the room."[89]

Positive results emerged from political education particularly around race, although ERAP's strong interracial commitment probably kept the most avid racists away. "That's one of the things I liked about the group," Thurman remembered. "I found out that poor white people ate like poor black people. They eat greens, they eat chitlins, they eat grits. We found out they were living in some worse apartments than we were."[90] Seeing John Howard, a "very hard-drinking, hard-fighting guy, who was fairly racist when we first got to know him," become an interracial leader in Chicago convinced Bob Ross that "if there's going to be political change people have to change and they do, they do. People really can change." JOIN member and former Tennessean Ralph Thurman certainly did. "We were raised that way," he noted of hating blacks, "and it made us feel bigger." But he "learned that if we're ever going to stop being poor, it's going to take Negroes and whites together to do it."[91] Residents often expressed their commonality with all impoverished Americans, black, white, or Latino, in religious terms. "[R]egardless of color, race, or creed we all can live together as one," declared Newark resident Barbara Jackson after the Cleveland Community Conference. "Just as God intended it to be." Others spoke of the need for "interracial [and] interfaith organizations of the poor," revealing faith as an important source of their strength.[92] Going beyond Alinsky's reliance on shared economic interests as a basis for consensus, ERAP showed, in small ways, how solidarity could be created and broadened through interaction and activism.[93]

Yet, for community members, solidarity in ERAP was not necessarily based on the category "the poor." Uptown residents, according to one commentator, resented "characterizations of themselves which stressed their dependency, poverty and oppression." Indeed, federal policy makers, concerned about such resentment, tried to avoid using "poverty" in the title for the War on Poverty, but no euphemism worked.[94] In ERAP, community members only rarely chose to represent themselves as "the poor" or as "poor people." They used "people" most often to refer to themselves and their fellow participants. JOIN, according to Jean Brown, was "an organization of working and non-working people, who are fighting for equal jobs and income for all." Cleveland's Lillian Craig remembered taking over the offices of the welfare department and answering the phones with "This is the People's Welfare Department. Come on down and join us!"[95] Organizers, in contrast, more often modified "people" with "poor." When Chicago participant Dorothy Perez dictated an article, she used "we" and "us" to refer to residents; the organizer typing her article then parenthetically inserted "(the poor)" after every occurrence.[96]

Why did so many community residents tend to reject "the poor" as an identity? Renouncing this identity did not necessarily mean they did not recognize the structural causes of poverty, or did not seek to create a group identity for themselves. More accurately, the label of "the poor" still held negative connotations for them. Phyllis Jackson, an active member in the Cleveland project, responded angrily to a local editorial that had labeled "us poor, as bumbling idiots at best."[97] Many differentiated between themselves and other residents, whom they really saw as "poor." The early Chicago project, members later noted, "helped poor people (although we didn't think of ourselves as poor— like poor people are winos on Wilson Avenue)."[98] This rejection also reflected their hopes for a future without poverty. "[P]overty is imperfectly permanent," argued an ERAP critic, and residents saw themselves as people who happened "to be poor now."[99] After all, project participants were a self-selected, motivated group. They aspired to a higher standard of living and considered ERAP organizing to be an opportunity for social mobility and uplift. In Cleveland, Lillian Craig described CUFAW as a group of "A.D.C. mothers who are concerned with their lives and want to better themselves." "I've met plenty of welfare mothers who really want to strive," reported Baltimore's Margaret McCarty.[100] Finally, poverty was not a homogeneous experience, and "the poor" failed to encompass the multifaceted identities of community members.

Instead of identifying as "the poor," community residents considered other aspects of identity more salient for organizing. During these years, 1964 to 1966, as was true later in the decade, a combination of choice and oppression propelled residents to identify along the lines of race and ethnicity. The experience of racism and the Civil Rights Movement's politicization and redefinition of black racial identity contributed directly to this outcome for blacks.[101] Whites, too, shared a consciousness based on whiteness, but the white identity of southern and Appalachian migrants in the ERAP locations was complicated by class, and they were seen as "white trash" and "dumb hillbillies." In fact, well before JOIN arrived in Uptown, residents had carried signs declaring "hillbilly power" at a local protest.[102] Community participants, one SDS member wrote, did not think of themselves as "poor," but "as a Negro who is poor or a Hillbilly who is poor."[103]

ERAP organizers were aware of these sensibilities and geared their newsletters and events toward their racialized constituencies. The *Mothers for Adequate Welfare Newsletter*, written primarily by and for African American women in Boston's Roxbury–North Dorchester, included notices about lectures on black arts and discussion groups on African history. In Chicago's Uptown, project songs had, according to Todd Gitlin, "a hillbilly cast . . . reflecting the dominant population and culture."[104] ERAP also fit fund-raising events into the cultural life of the community, as did Saul Alinsky. NCUP sponsored cocktail "sips" and rent parties, two traditional means of fund-raising in black communities, while JOIN held a dance with a bluegrass band.[105]

In the main, however, New Left organizers remained committed to organizing on an interracial basis. Activating identities based on race and ethnicity within relatively segregated communities, such as Chicago's Uptown and Newark's Clinton Hill, would only lead to a segregated movement of poor Americans. Moreover, as organizers argued, policies like urban renewal, or "Negro removal," were motivated as much by economic as racial discrimination, and the poverty of African Americans could not be attributed to racial discrimination alone. Blacks "simply don't understand the concept of non-racial economic problems," Trenton organizer Walt Popper commented.[106] By emphasizing the commonalities of poverty and class, while downplaying or ignoring racial differences, ERAP's initial emphasis challenged white racism and avoided refueling prejudices in white and heterogeneous areas. But it worked against collective racial consciousness in black locations. In Newark, Tom Hayden declared, "we are trying to organize, first, around the feeling of being poor and powerless, rather than being black." "I wanted to prove in action that an integrationist perspective stressing common economic interests could still work," he later recalled.[107]

ERAP's integrationist or assimilationist stance on race, in fact, was out of step with changing ideas about race and politics in the mid-1960s. In this view, race was inseparable from racism and could only signify stigma. When racism was eliminated as a social problem, race as a category or concept would wither away, leaving the promised "color-blind" society.[108] "The thinking was that class is more powerful than race, that old argument," Dave Strauss recalls. "So that if we could get people acting in their class interest race would sort of dissolve as such an issue." And ERAP was not alone. "Race is becoming unimportant," a progressive journalist observed about ERAP's interracial organizing, "and may finally be eliminated as a factor."[109] With the rise of Black Power, however, racial integration declined as a civil rights priority, interracial organizing came to be viewed as an inappropriate goal for radical organizers, and the role of white organizers in black neighborhoods became increasingly contested. Unfairly accused of "tracing everyone's problems solely to economics" and refusing to "differentiate black from white," the ERAP projects did come to endorse race as a repository of cultural pride and political opposition for blacks as the decade progressed.[110]

In the end, however, a common citizenship, or identity as "the people" or Americans, provided the most consistent basis for solidarity in the ERAP projects. This populist basis best fit the slogan of New Left organizers, "Let the People Decide," and the political knowledge and experience of community residents. Project participants were able "to reach into the ample, preexisting vocabulary of politics to seize a word and press it into new service."[111] The rich history of the language of populism conveyed community members' understanding of the conflict between the powerless and the powerful. For community member George Fontaine, NCUP was "the 'small people,' at the grass-roots." "The people should make the decisions, not the big bosses," Cleveland's Jean Joachin reported.[112] Moreover, "the people" could be inflected with class, race, gender, and geographical meaning for use in a variety of situations. Given ERAP's aims of forging interracial solidarity, participants used it to bind rather than divide. "As citizens of America we should fight for decent communities," Mrs. Alcantar of JOIN declared. "Just because we are poor, we should not have to live in slums and be pushed around because we are Puerto Rican, Mexican, hillbillies or colored."[113] By using the identities of "the people" and citizen interchangeably, community members drew upon the concepts of both democracy and rights, exhibiting a growing, popular rights consciousness that owed a great deal to the Civil Rights Movement. In this way, they claimed for themselves the status, often denied them, of full and equal citizenship.[114]

Citizenship linked to motherhood fueled community women's political action in ERAP. "The mothers are now demanding their rights as citizens," Cleveland welfare recipient Sandra Echols proclaimed.[115] Although the welfare state already recognized and politicized the motherhood of poor women receiving Aid to Families with Dependent Children, this identity was a stigmatized one, revealing how both the public perception and personal experience of motherhood varied by class and race. "[W]e have been called lazy, incompetent, negligent," Dorothy Hammer, a member of the Cleveland's CUFAW, asserted.[116] Women welfare recipients in ERAP claimed for themselves the positive and powerful aspects of motherhood, by emphasizing their devotion to children and work as mothers. "Remember," Cleveland organizer Joan Bradbury noted, "nothing besides the FBI is so sacred as American Motherhood."[117] This emphasis on "motherwork" dovetailed with the community activism of women past and present. It also may have been part of their rejection of "the poor" as an identity, as it was later on for women volunteers in Head Start, who saw "the poor" as deficient in a work ethic that included mothering. Their insistence on being seen as "good" mothers also refuted the accusations of immorality often directed at single mothers, especially black single mothers, and gave community women a "sense of collective power, entitlement, and moral authority."[118]

Due to the perspective of residents, ERAP's search for solidarity did not culminate in one, all-encompassing solidarity. Instead, it indicated an emerging "identity politics" within the ERAP projects, whereby community activists began to privilege and organize politically around specific group identities. By articulating a range of identities, community members hinted at the fluidity of identity and solidarity in the context of political organizing. For organizers, the acceptance of identities based on citizenship, motherhood, and later race in place of "the poor" alone demonstrated their willingness to revise the original ERAP strategy, as they had with issues and services, in order to achieve the priorities of bottom-up organizing. Spurred by the prominence of community women and their concerns, in particular, New Left organizers expanded their understanding of political organizing and made public matters out of ostensibly private concerns. Because what is defined as political affects what is understood to be important, ERAP's process of politicization contributed to a growing recognition of the significance of women's community-based activism. This revised strategic approach would lead, in turn, to a redefinition of ERAP's goals.

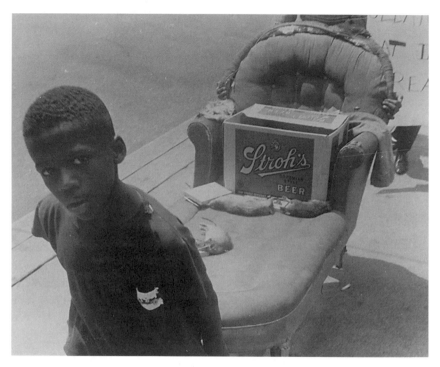

Cleveland "Rat March," August 1965. (Courtesy of John Bancroft.)

6

Redefining Goals

The Newark project for jobs, income, freedom, and stop signs is
underway.   —"Newark Project Report," 1964

When Newark organizers began their project in the summer
of 1964, it was already clear that ERAP's initial, concrete goals of
achieving full and fair employment or guaranteed annual income, and
democratic, national planning were changing.[1] Organizers still wanted
an interracial movement of the poor to end poverty, achieve racial
justice, and extend democracy. But now, in keeping with organizing
from the bottom up, they undertook to define ERAP's immediate,
short-term goals together with community participants. Consequently,
project aims multiplied to meet the range of needs in ERAP's low-income neighborhoods. What remained consistent, and resonated with
community members, was the commitment to connecting "bad housing
and urban renewal programs, unemployment and token retraining programs, rotten educational systems, police brutality, [and] inadequate
welfare systems" to "the lack of democracy in American society."[2] The
projects argued for and attempted to realize participatory democracy
on the neighborhood level, believing that only in this way could the
array of problems associated with poverty and inequality be successfully targeted.

Through campaigns around elections, the War on Poverty, urban renewal, police brutality, and welfare, ERAP activists demanded and
sought to enlarge openings for greater political participation, to develop new ways community residents could voice their needs and interests. Occurring during a decade in which citizen participation gained
greater national currency and legitimacy due to the grassroots organizing of civil rights and community activists, this effort continued an
American historical tradition that sought to augment representative

government with forms of direct democracy.[3] It also meant that ERAP
participants did not just view the state as simply co-optive at best or es-
chew any engagement with the state as futile. Instead, they made the
state a primary arena of struggle, as was true for community activists
generally.[4] In pursuing their goals, they acted on and advocated an expanded definition of political "participation" beyond that of voting
alone. As it turned out, welfare organizing, dominated by New Left
and community women, gave ERAP its greatest, tangible successes,
particularly around what can be understood as a new form of political
participation: the right to be treated with dignity and respect in face-to-
face encounters with public employees.

Political Influence

Electoral politics constituted an obvious arena for political participation and avenue to state power, but ERAP organizers never considered
electoral politics a desirable means of achieving their goals. Periodic
voting for representatives was no substitute for genuine democratic
participation—as earlier Progressive Era political thinkers and activists
had known—and, at the most, provided a means of political influence,
not decision-making power.[5] Yet enough community members, women
and men, were interested in electoral politics to prompt ERAP's participation. Following their lead, organizers decided that elections could be
used for political mobilization and education, for making connections
between politics and poverty.

During the decade, there existed within SDS a critique of electoral
participation. Many believed that ERAP needed to remain outside established political institutions to keep its original vision and change society. For Paul Booth, who headed up the Oakland project during the
summer of 1965, "real social change comes only when ordinary people
get organized. . . . [Y]ou must have some kind of thrust, an independent thrust from the grassroots."[6] Electoral campaigning not only
would take energy away from community organizing and sidetrack
ERAP into working with "the Liberal Establishment," it also would le-
gitimize the political system and make local projects vulnerable to co-
optation. The problem, according to Cleveland organizer Dickie
Magidoff, was "how to participate in electoral politics without getting
sucked into party machinery or supporting fink candidates."[7] Reinforc-

ing this anti–electoral politics position were the strong, entrenched political—usually Democratic—machines ERAP encountered in nearly
every city, which provided few political opportunities and little access
to city government for low-income and minority residents.[8]

Other New Left organizers, however, stressed direct political involvement as, very simply, ERAP's only means to gaining power. According to Steve Max, those who eschewed electioneering believed that
"Politics is dirty! Power corrupts! Leaders sell out!" He favored using
ERAP to build grassroots party organizations, as he had done organizing in East Harlem, because electoral politics could wrest "from the
hands of the exploiters the power through which they exploit—that is,
the political power of . . . governmen[t]."[9] For those open to electoral
participation, the community projects should have the flexibility to
pursue activities as participants saw fit, believing there would be times
and places where local activists would wish to work in liberal coalitions.[10] They questioned, too, the equation of political participation
with co-optation, arguing that involvement in mainstream politics need
not blunt ERAP's radical edge. As SDS leader Carl Oglesby succinctly
put it, "You are coopted when the adversary puts his goals on your
power; you are *not* co-opted when your power allows you to exploit
his means (or contradictions) in behalf of your goals."[11]

Regarding electoral politics as an important arena in which to claim
and exercise their citizenship rights, community members felt that providing a voice for low-income residents within mainstream politics
should be one of ERAP's priorities. "After all," Newark resident Barbara
Jackson pointed out, "the power of the government is divided among the
nation, states and the people. Most of all, all of the people which is best
illustrated by the Preamble to our Constitution."[12] Taking part in elections allowed residents to make political claims on government officials
and hold them responsible for representing their interests. Betty Moore
felt this way about Newark mayor Hugh J. Addonizio. "I voted for the
man to get where he is; I work hard in the school and on the post [getting
the vote out]."[13] Members strongly believed they had a right to accountable political leadership and were motivated to participate in electoral
politics as a way to keep or secure this right.

Contributing to this grassroots motivation in black neighborhoods in
cities like Newark and Boston were the electoral and voter registration
campaigns of civil rights activists in the South. In 1963 SNCC organized
a "freedom vote" in Mississippi to protest political disenfranchisement

and the next year, as part of Mississippi Freedom Summer, registered voters and held elections for a counter-delegation to the Democratic Party convention in Atlantic City as a challenge to official party delegates elected in white-only primaries.[14] The voting rights situation for blacks in the North, although certainly not southern-style disenfranchisement, hardly resulted in equal political representation, particularly due to the political machines they faced. Norm Fruchter, an SDS member who made a film, *The Troublemakers,* about the Newark project, considered the city government "a Democratic Party fiefdom . . . dependent to a certain extent upon black votes but treating the black neighborhoods of the city as essentially colonial neighborhoods." As late as 1964, Newark had only one black elected official: city councilman Irvine Turner.[15] Meeting Fannie Lou Hamer at the Cleveland Community Conference in February 1965 and hearing about the activities of the Mississippi Freedom Democratic Party convinced Newark resident George Fontaine that "organizing has to be political." To put pressure on elected officials and make sure they followed through on campaign promises, he called for "our own Freedom Democratic Party."[16]

In response and in keeping with bottom-up organizing, the ERAP projects took up electoral politics. Eric Mann of the Newark project at first strongly opposed participation, but "community residents saw electoral politics as useful, and I started to listen better to the community."[17] But ERAP's first opportunity to take part in an election, the presidential race of 1964 between President Lyndon Johnson and his Republican challenger, Barry Goldwater, marked a low point in the New Left's attitude toward mainstream politics. They were "heartbroken and bitter" after Johnson and other national Democratic Party leaders, including the UAW's Walter Reuther, chose to seat the entire Mississippi delegation at the Atlantic City convention, offering only two seats to the Freedom Democrats. What party leaders saw as a compromise, New Left activists considered a betrayal of the Mississippi Freedom Democratic Party's just fight against racially based political exclusion. Moral values and party politics were clearly incompatible.[18] In ERAP, widespread interest in the presidential race among neighborhood residents encouraged organizers to launch anti-Goldwater campaigns, but New Left ambivalence about Johnson remained, reflected in their slogan "Part of the Way with LBJ."

As it turned out, organizers found participation in electoral politics to be an important organizing and educational tool. In Cleveland the project integrated anti-Goldwater campaigning into both its welfare rights and unemployment organizing. CUFAW set up a voter registration table at the local food stamp office, registered some four hundred voters while they were waiting in line, and held a political education session to discuss the candidates' views on issues like education, medical care, jobs, nuclear weapons, and welfare. There women welfare recipients learned of Goldwater's support for significant welfare cutbacks and restrictions on eligibility.[19] The Chicago project also informed their constituency of Goldwater's positions on various social issues and distributed leaflets proclaiming, "In Your Heart You Know He's Nuts," a play on Goldwater's campaign slogan. More than an individual act, voting in ERAP, as it had in SNCC, signified the collective involvement and mobilization of community constituents.[20]

ERAP used later electoral campaigns to raise questions about the qualifications of elected officials who failed to understand the lives and problems of poor Americans. In the fall of 1965 JOIN member Carl Lorig proposed running an independent candidate for alderman who would more meaningfully represent Chicago's Uptown population. "I think we should have a representative of *all* the people, for the people, which I don't think we have now."[21] For similar reasons, CUFAW leader Dorothy Hammer decided to run for the Cleveland school board in 1965. "The reason behind my deciding to run for the School Board is because I feel that someone who knows the problems of poor people and their children should be on the Board."[22] Cleveland's school board was chosen in a citywide election, however, a no-win situation for Hammer. Still, like the 1964 presidential election, Hammer's campaign provided an opportunity for education and organizing; her candidacy alone constituted an alternative to mainstream candidates and highlighted the inadequate representation of the poor in city politics.

For the community projects, electoral politics became a site not only for casting a ballot but also for defining an agenda.[23] Campaigns communicated information about the needs and circumstances of low-income residents and what they saw as public responsibilities. Cleveland organizer Evan Metcalf hoped the "publicity and legitimacy" associated with Dorothy Hammer's school board campaign would "make it more possible to raise issues" to a larger audience.[24] In 1965, after much debate, the Newark project endorsed the third-party United Freedom Ticket, as part of a larger electoral coalition of blacks, Puerto Ricans, and white liberal and left activists. "It so smacked of traditional politics," Carol Glassman observes, "but the argument for it was visibility raising, talking to people about issues, . . . and building coalitions with progressive people."[25] On the ticket was George Richardson, an independent candidate for the state assembly. Although some NCUP organizers saw him as "sort of a politician" and "no great prize in his political views," Richardson's commitment to confronting the problems of slum housing and police brutality in Newark, as well as his break with the local Democratic Party over just these issues, meant that his campaign focused on the primary concerns of project participants.[26]

Nevertheless, the Richardson campaign revealed the political limits of ERAP's electoral participation. The Newark project worked hard for the candidate, distributing leaflets calling for "decent housing, more and better jobs, and freedom," registering residents to vote, and using a sound truck to get voters out on election day. A lack of resources meant that the project covered only one-third of the target area, while the Democratic and Republican party organizations saturated the area with canvassers and publicity. In the end, the independent United Freedom Ticket received less than 5 percent of the total vote.[27] NCUP's electoral involvement reinforced how effective political participation necessitated access to economic and social resources and the difficulties of third-party politics, especially of overcoming traditional voter loyalties to the two mainstream parties.[28]

The barriers to electoral participation for low-income neighborhood residents also appeared in other ERAP locations. The Cleveland project was unable to secure enough signatures to place Dorothy Hammer's name on the ballot for the school board election, and, in the face of Mayor Daley's powerful political machine, Chicago participants chose to remain outside electoral politics. Judith Bernstein believed that challenging the corrupt and undemocratic machine would be "the greatest organizing issue." But, she added, "We would be crushed if we tried that."[29] Recent migrants, a significant proportion of ERAP neighborhood populations in all the cities, were unacquainted with the ins and outs of local politics, and this lack of familiarity dampened their political involvement. As a consequence of small numbers and minimal voting power, electoral politics failed to yield any significant victories or political influence for ERAP anywhere.[30]

Despite such barriers and defeats, and in contrast to the perception that ERAP never worked through electoral channels, project participants did work within the political system to further their aims.[31] Low-income, racially diverse neighborhood residents were not as politically uninterested and apathetic as many contemporary observers claimed. True, many expressed great skepticism and even active "antipathy" toward politics generally.[32] But community members involved in ERAP, although certainly a select group, felt they had a right to present and receive consideration for their political views, and when they believed they had something at stake in an election and reform possibilities existed, they took an interest and participated. Hammer demonstrated as much in Cleveland, and in 1974 Jesse Allen ran and was elected a Newark city councilman from the Central Ward.[33] Poor Americans were not wholly marginalized from, and in fact shared important values with, the dominant political culture, and New Left organizers were "willing to confront the necessities of struggling for power."[34] Both were evident in struggles to make decisions about the War on Poverty and urban renewal in the neighborhoods.

Decision-Making Power

At a time of welfare state expansion, the greatest since the New Deal, ERAP sought to redistribute available government funds and resources more equitably by insuring the participation of low-income Americans in the War on Poverty and urban renewal. In these campaigns—which mobilized a mixed constituency of community women and men— ERAP exploited federal mandates for the "maximum feasible participation of the poor" in the poverty war and citizen approval of urban renewal plans. The projects defined these provisions broadly to mean that poor people and neighborhood residents should have real decision-making power over the planning and implementation of all policies and programs. With this expanded definition of participation, ERAP activists demanded both adequate representation for low-income residents on local poverty and urban renewal boards and the acceptance of their own proposals for eradicating poverty and renewing communities.

ERAP's participation in the War on Poverty, in contrast to electoral politics, occurred with little debate. When the Economic Opportunity Act passed in the summer of 1964, the projects aimed to ensure that local poverty programs—run by newly created agencies as a way to bypass city officials and bureaucracies—adhered to the provision mandating that

they be "developed, conducted, and administered with the maximum feasible participation of residents of the areas and members of the groups
served."[35] Without the direction and participation of low-income residents, the poverty war would fail to target the sustaining conditions of
poverty: the political powerlessness and social marginalization felt and
lived by those in poverty. After all, Chicago organizer Rich Rothstein argued, "The demand for an end to poverty, and the demand for participation of the poor in that fight are in reality one."[36] Along with policy makers, ERAP wanted poor Americans "to become not only recipients but
participants."[37] Some SDS members feared co-optation, but most did not
question ERAP involvement. Many believed, as then SDS president Todd
Gitlin contended, "if radicals are not participants in mass movements,
then assuredly the movements *will* be co-opted." Community members,
too, saw the benefits of participation. The participatory possibilities inspired Newark resident Mary Grace. "The future doesn't seem so dark.
Makes you think that democracy is not in vain."[38]

Yet the exact meaning of "maximum feasible participation" was
open to interpretation, and ERAP encountered a range of definitions in
the different cities. While prominent liberals, such as Sargent Shriver,
head of the Office of Economic Opportunity (OEO), and the UAW's
Walter Reuther, believed that the poor must "have a voice" and "genuine representation," this lack of clarity permitted local government
officials great latitude.[39] In Baltimore, Cleveland, and Philadelphia,
poor residents were excluded from the initial planning and decision-
making structures for the local poverty wars. Chicago's War on Poverty, due to the power and control exercised by Mayor Richard Daley,
was notorious for having the most minimal participation of the poor of
any major city. The mayor himself appointed all the members of the
Chicago Commission on Urban Opportunity, which directed the city's
poverty war, and the advisory boards for the neighborhood-based Urban Progress Centers, and at first he included not a single low-income
Chicago resident.[40]

Joining grassroots protests across the country, ERAP activists objected to blatant disregard of the federal mandate. The Philadelphia
project criticized "the real power" remaining with politicians.[41] In Baltimore in early 1965, New Left organizers and community members
testified at a city council hearing, pointing out the lack of involvement
from poor residents in designing the city's so-called Human Renewal
plan, presented a protest petition with some nine hundred signatures,

and signed on to a new Anti-Poverty Action Committee with civil rights organizations. They also proposed their own plan to ensure participation. "The joke we made at the time," according to Kim Moody, was it "was sort of like a Soviet Republic or something completely never going to happen. The idea was the community would elect its representatives who would then be the governing boards in the neighborhoods over the distribution of funds."[42] In the spring, the Chicago project condemned the fact that of seventy-one people on the advisory board for their local Urban Progress Center, all but three were professionals or government officials, most did not live in the Uptown neighborhood, and not one was impoverished. The project picketed the opening of the center, because it failed to incorporate the input of local residents and, subsequently, reflect the needs of the community. They proposed instead that advisory board members live in the neighborhood served by the center, earn less than $5,000 a year or receive public assistance, and collect fifty signatures for a petition of support.[43]

In the fall of 1964 the Cleveland project joined the Citizens' Committee for an Adequate War on Poverty Program in coalition with local church and civil rights organizations to counter that city's plan and demand participation. When the city appointed only one low-income resident to the local board by the following summer, the Citizens' Committee sponsored a "Rat March" in which protesters carried to city hall various symbols of poverty, including rats and roaches caught in slum apartments, torn winter coats, shoes with holes, and broken-down furniture. CUFAW leader Carole King captured the spirit of the "Rat March" in a poem:

> 17 suburbanites—8 people from the city
> This isn't representative of the poor.
> We are protesting this; we want more. . . .
> How can you, OEO Board, say what poverty is like?
> We can, the Poor and Needy; we have the right.[44]

When they decided to leave their symbols of poverty on the steps of city hall—an action repeated the following year in Chicago by CORE —a number of demonstrators were arrested.[45]

In the process of demanding "maximum feasible participation," the community projects challenged society's definition of precisely who was qualified to make decisions. At one meeting of the advisory board for Uptown's Urban Progress Center, JOIN reported, board members argued that "the poor couldn't make their own decisions" and, if low-income residents directed the War on Poverty, "it would be like the blind leading the blind."[46] When the *Cleveland Press* editorialized that the city's "impoverished could hardly care less" about the poverty program, CUFAW member Phyllis Jackson responded, "[W]e could hardly care more." Reminding local officials of the federal mandate, Jackson added, "[W]e are trying to get the voice President Johnson says we should have."[47] Project activists sought "to dispel the notions that the poor and the working class are somehow 'unfit' for exercising political control" and asserted the knowledge, expertise, and decision-making rights of residents based on their personal experience of poverty.[48] Chicago's Dorothy Perez urged greater participation from low-income Americans, because only they "know what it is like to be in need, and to fear hunger." ERAP encouraged, as SNCC leader Stokely Carmichael had urged, "the growth of belief among the unqualified that they are in fact qualified: they can articulate and be responsible and hold power."[49]

In 1965 campaigns for participation in the War on Poverty in Cleveland and Chicago succeeded in catching the attention of federal authorities. The objections of Cleveland's Citizens' Committee prompted OEO authorities to halt federal approval of the city's plan while they investigated, and the House Committee on Labor and Education, under the chairmanship of Adam Clayton Powell, held hearings, at which Phyllis Jackson testified.[50] When Chicago project participants conveyed their criticisms and demands to federal authorities, Sargent Shriver promised that the OEO would investigate to insure "the meaningful participation of the poor." To ensure that Shriver made good on his promise, they joined Alinsky's IAF-initiated Woodlawn Organization, led by Reverend Lynward Stevenson, a strong critic of "maximum feasible participation of the rich," in a demonstration during a visit by Shriver in December.[51] In these ways, ERAP strengthened grassroots pressure on officials at both the local and national levels to fulfill the rhetorical promise of maximum feasible participation in the War on Poverty.

The results were negligible, however. At the prompting of the OEO, Cleveland officials reserved five seats for low-income, inner-city residents—protesters had wanted eleven.[52] In February 1966 elections for the board were held in the city's designated "poverty spots," including the Near West Side and Glenville, and ERAP participants campaigned in the neighborhoods. As happened throughout the country, voter turnout was disappointing, with only 7 percent of those eligible to vote actually casting ballots. The fact that voters had to meet an income requirement, take a "pauper's oath," and identify themselves as poor—all for only token representation—dissuaded many from taking part.[53] In Chicago the OEO intervened in November 1965 and accepted JOIN's proposal that the advisory board be restricted to persons having an annual income of less than $5,000, but only for all future appointments. JOIN reported that its "plans for the Urban Progress Center [were] accepted—sort of."[54] In Chicago and Cleveland, ERAP participants succeeded in winning recognition for the principle of resident involvement in the War on Poverty but had no power over how it was defined and implemented. In Baltimore the Human Renewal plan passed the city council without one dissenting vote; ERAP opposition was simply ignored.[55] For ERAP, these developments made a mockery of "maximum feasible participation."

Of all the ERAP projects, the Newark project gained the most influence in the local War on Poverty. Cyril Tyson, the head of Newark's antipoverty agency, the United Community Corporation, was a strong advocate of participation and developed a relatively open decision-making structure for the program. The city was divided into seven geographical areas, and each had an elected poverty board charged with making decisions about local programs, a structure later advocated by militant poverty war critics in San Francisco.[56] In the early months of 1965, NCUP members became active in Area Board 3, the poverty board that oversaw Clinton Hill and the rest of Newark's South Ward. They thoroughly studied the rules governing the area boards and, with successful grassroots organizing, often constituted a significant proportion—in one instance, twenty out of a hundred—of those in attendance at early meetings. At the first organizational meeting in February, their nominee for chair of the board of directors, NCUP leader Bessie Smith, won; at another meeting, the name proposed by NCUP organizer Jill Hamberg, "People's Action Group," was adopted in place of Area Board 3, signifying a collective identity, democratic participation, and political action. In March, Tom Hayden proposed a motion stipulating that the Area Board/People's Action Group must be composed of a majority of low-income residents, defined as a person earning less than $4,000 a year, receiving welfare or public assistance, or living in substandard housing or in a blighted area. Those in attendance at the meeting passed the motion by the narrow margin of fifty-one to forty-five.[57] In contrast to electoral politics, the War on Poverty provided a smaller, more contained environment in which NCUP could mobilize successfully. "We were maximum feasible participation in living color," Carol Glassman recalls.[58]

In addition to demanding, and enlarging, openings in the state for greater citizen involvement in the War on Poverty, ERAP activists criticized federal and local poverty policies and programs. JOIN objected to the city of Chicago's approach, which—consistent with national policy—focused on providing services aimed at preparing and "urbanizing" Uptown residents to compete in the marketplace. "Presumably the poor are to be relieved of their difficulties through proper counseling." For Baltimore activists, such plans exposed "the inability of liberalism to deal seriously with poverty."[59] Policy makers' understanding of poverty as a product of blocked economic opportunities and personal or psychological handicaps failed to confront underlying structural inequalities. "One thing ought to be clear in any organizer's mind about the War on Poverty: it isn't," observed San Francisco activist Mike Miller.[60]

ERAP, like community organizations elsewhere, offered alternative proposals based on the needs and concerns of local residents. In Baltimore and Chicago, activists demanded jobs. "People like me and millions of others are not being reached by the War on Poverty program," Chicago community leader Dovie Coleman protested. "I'm a Negro woman, 45, needs a job and can't get one. When are you going to start listening to me?"[61] Uptown residents, at a minimum, wanted a public, nonprofit employment agency to replace existing, private day labor agencies.[62] Residents in all the neighborhoods pointed out the inadequacy of existing job training programs; one in Trenton could only find jobs for one-tenth of those registered.[63] Working mothers in ERAP neighborhoods in Philadelphia, Baltimore, and Chicago needed low-cost day care. Because many women in Uptown were employed full-time, mostly managing apartment buildings and working in retail and service industries, the Chicago project petitioned the poverty board for such a center.[64] In 1965 the Boston and Cleveland projects developed detailed recreation proposals and submitted them to local War on Poverty agencies and park commissioners, while JOIN activists began work on a playground after unsuccessfully petitioning their local Urban Progress Center for one. When the city built a playground the next year with poverty war funds, although in a different location, residents dubbed it "the JOIN playground."[65] With control of the People's

Action Group, Newark activists achieved ERAP's only clear poverty war success when they secured funding for a community center and, with other city area boards, for the summer recreation Block Improvement Program.[66]

Despite few tangible victories from such efforts, ERAP activists still participated in the various service programs sponsored by the War on Poverty, seeking to turn them to their own ends. In Cleveland, women organizers and community members participated in Head Start, and NCUP sponsored VISTA volunteers.[67] Chicago organizer Vivian Rothstein in 1966 became an assistant supervisor in the "Girls Streets" program, a summer employment and job training program for teenage girls from low-income families. Rothstein soon involved the girls in an anti–lead poisoning campaign—an effort quite apart from the classes on personal appearance and typing proposed by local poverty officials. The girls went door to door testing Uptown children for lead poisoning and apartments for lead paint.[68] Lead poisoning especially affected children in low-income communities, for slum housing disproportionately contained lead paint, and hungry children were more likely to eat paint chips. Building on Rothstein's efforts, JOIN used the information gathered to improve the health and welfare of children and to force landlords to remove lead paint from their buildings, intertwining health and housing reform, as had the settlement movement earlier in the century. By 1967, Chicago's poverty program had its own lead poisoning testing program.[69]

As with its War on Poverty efforts, ERAP's campaigns aimed at halting urban renewal capitalized on federal provisions mandating citizen participation. The "citizens" usually consulted during the planning stage were real estate agents, developers, and middle-class homeowners. With this kind of "citizen participation," ERAP pointed out, publicly funded urban renewal benefited private businesses. Plans for Newark's Clinton Hill included conversion to a light industrial park, while several private hospitals and schools, with no interest in serving the local, low-income population, planned to expand into areas soon to be cleared on Cleveland's Near West Side.[70] Without the participation of those living in affected areas, renewal and redevelopment came at the expense of poor, urban residents. Chester's urban renewal, or "Negro removal," program required black residents to relocate, sacrifice homes, and leave their communities. White, southern, and Appalachian residents in Uptown also accused the city of Chicago of intentional "people removal." One resident declared, "when they talk about 'IMPROVING UPTOWN' what they really mean is 'CHASING US OUT' into some other area, or back where we came from."[71] As a result, Cleveland activists demanded "that people who live in this neighborhood must have a say in planning Urban Renewal," and in 1967 JOIN demanded representation on Uptown's business-dominated urban renewal board, the Uptown Conservation Council.[72]

If renewal occurred, ERAP participants also wanted it not just to eliminate inner-city slums but also properly house—or rehouse—residents. In Boston, Cleveland, and Chicago, they protested the lack of adequate housing for residents displaced from their homes and neighborhoods, an endemic problem in urban renewal areas. The upscale housing planned for a "renewed" Uptown would make it impossible for residents like Bob Wable to live there. "We cannot afford townhouses, row houses, high-rise efficiencies and luxury one bedrooms."[73]

When demanding replacement housing, activists referred to the Federal Housing Act of 1949, requiring "safe, decent, and sanitary housing . . . adequate to meet the needs" of all those relocated, and began to move from a negative to a more positive definition of participation. It was easier to defend against urban renewal as a threat to "home territory" than to advance an agenda. Yet, as the Cleveland project contended, it was "not enough just to be against something."[74] Consequently ERAP, like community organizations across the country, insisted that new construction meet the needs of residents. In Chester and Chicago most soon-to-be-displaced residents preferred public to private housing and, as generally was the case, low-rise buildings rather than massive high-rises like Chicago's Robert Taylor homes.[75] Like the Woodlawn Organization on Chicago's South Side, the Newark and Cleveland projects designed alternative programs for completely rebuilding Clinton Hill and the Near West Side. In Cleveland participants envisioned new, low- and moderate-income housing, medical clinics, schools, parks, playgrounds, and public swimming pools. Such facilities would allow "people [to] have interesting, happy lives here."[76]

But ERAP's campaigns around the War on Poverty and urban renewal never achieved significant decision-making power for low-income neighborhood residents. Mobilization in Uptown, Clinton Hill, and Roxbury–North Dorchester only helped to slow the process of urban renewal or laid the groundwork for later community organizing to halt urban renewal. The exceptional participation of the poor in Newark's poverty war provoked vociferous criticism from local authorities for being too much participation or even domination and, in fact, was remembered as "a 'deviation from democracy'—i.e., a departure from the normal operating (and, for the poor, disempowering) procedures of local government."[77] Developments in Newark and elsewhere contributed to the 1967 Green Amendment to the Economic Opportunity Act, which allowed local governments to take over poverty agencies and limited representatives of the poor to no more than one-third of board members. For many ERAP participants, these experiences demonstrated the impossibility of achieving genuine decision-making power within the existing political system and confirmed what numerous scholars have argued since: the poverty war preempted social movement activities, integrated leading community activists into the welfare state bureaucracy, and substituted symbolic participation for actual social change.[78]

Still, by taking part in these liberal reform efforts, ERAP could claim some gains. As part of a larger anti-renewal movement that included critics like Jane Jacobs and Herbert Gans, protests helped to bring about an important shift in urban renewal policy. Between 1965 and 1968 the rate of housing demolition and resident displacement sharply declined as cities began to adopt a policy of rehabilitating—rather than clearing—existing buildings and neighborhoods. Moreover, the 1966 Model Cities program adopted a broader definition of citizen participation that involved neighborhood-based organizations in the urban planning process.[79] In addition, over time, the People's Action Group became "indistinguishable" from the Newark project in terms of membership, leadership, office space, and publicity. It also provided a political base, jobs, and funding for a coalition of groups that included not only NCUP but also SNCC and the Black Liberation Center. "They didn't create a revolution," Corinna Fales recalls, "but they moved people into positions of power who had been a totally disenfranchised group of individuals." As neighborhood residents gained access to government funding, "they brought their NCUP mentality with them," according to Carol Glassman. "So there was this sort of proliferation of activity, and available resources and services."[80]

At the time, Derek Winans, an ERAP organizer and native of Newark, believed that the city's War on Poverty "is undoubtedly much less undemocratic than it would be without NCUP pressure." In the end, they "had some success in persuading some people that they have a *right* to power, office and participation, even though they're without money or education."[81] And Winans was right. ERAP's campaigns promoted the "right" of low-income citizens to participate actively in state bureaucracies and programs rather than just offering input. They took an opening for participation in the War on Poverty and sought to make it real, just as they attempted to redefine what "citizen participation" meant in urban renewal planning. At the same time, they challenged the idea of poor people as unorthodox citizens, lacking in the economic independence deemed necessary for full citizenship and participation. Questions about who should hold power and make decisions in society, and on what basis, also appeared in ERAP organizing around police brutality and welfare.

Political Respect/Political Control

ERAP's campaigns around police-community relations and welfare called for new forms of political participation. While community and New Left men dominated efforts around police brutality, and welfare was considered to be "women's organizing," both efforts asserted the right of citizens to function in an oversight capacity with regard to public institutions and bureaucracies as well as to respectful and dignified treatment from public servants.[82] Interactions between citizens and the police-welfare state constituted a face-to-face mode of political participation. For many low-income residents, these interactions shaped their understanding and experience of citizenship; patterns of disrespect needed to be overcome before residents could enjoy more equal participation. The concern with respect and dignity with regard to the police and welfare prompted ERAP activists to go beyond participation as political influence or input to seek a measure of political control and autonomy.

ERAP activists wanted both an end to police brutality and better police protection in the neighborhoods. A factor in race riots in Harlem and Watts in 1964 and 1965, brutality by a virtually all-white police force was considered to be "standard operating procedure in the ghetto" in Newark. In 1965 black resident Lester Long, originally stopped for a loud car muffler, ended up dead after being shot in the back of the head while running away. NCUP protested at City Hall and then took part in a series of marches, sponsored by Newark CORE, against police brutality and intimidation of blacks.[83] In Cleveland, where the police department was characterized in 1967 as "defensive, isolated, parochial, and mistrustful of the public it serves," a group of black and white mothers decried incidents in which police shot and killed two teenage boys, one as he was running away. They asserted that to "punish with death a child for being scared is one of the most INHUMAN things America can be ashamed of."[84] ERAP also urged police officers to live up to their duty "to serve and protect" and called for "police protection not police brutality." Mrs. Heyman of Clinton Hill reported stores being held up "all the time" and wanted "a beefing up of police patrols." Uptown resident Virginia Richardson wanted protection from her abusive husband. "Sometimes it seems to me the law works against the woman. My husband busted up my apartment. You can call the police and they'll turn him loose." "A lot of times," she added, "they don't even want to come."[85] Both men and women registered complaints and participated in protests against local police. However, men more often experienced and objected to brutality, while women more often needed and sought protection; the police in these neighborhoods, thus, were both mistrusted and essential.

Respectful treatment from the police was a priority as well. Residents complained of rudeness, name calling, and harassment from law enforcement officials. J. C. Nichols felt that the Newark police "are fresh . . . and have no idea about respecting people."[86] Young, white southern and Appalachian men dominated the Chicago JOIN project's organizing around police-community relations in Uptown and expressed similar views. Their attraction to street life, congregating on street corners, "raising hell," and other rebellious behavior, and sometime criminal activity brought them into contact and conflict with local police more often than other residents, particularly women. During the summer of 1966 JOIN marched on the police station at Foster Avenue. "We're here to tell the police that they can't treat [us] like dirt . . . they've got to treat us with respect." "It takes people from the south, from Puerto Rico and Mexico, and other poor people to get justice," Mrs. Alcantar reported.[87] Such grievances stemmed from the feeling that they had not been given the rights and dignity owed them as citizens and, for men, the respect their manhood deserved.

To realize these aims, project participants—echoing civil rights activists and the American Civil Liberties Union—campaigned for civilian review boards and greater community oversight. Boards and oversight would check police brutality by investigating complaints and dismissing offenders and improve police-community relations by fostering dialogue about residents' concerns. But low-income residents, rather than distinguished, ostensibly "impartial" citizens, should dominate these boards, according to ERAP; NCUP, for example, wanted "a civilian review board of the people."[88] Deciding not to wait for civilian review, young men and male organizers in JOIN took steps to put the police on notice, as did activists in Watts and in the Black Panther Party. They compiled records and affidavits of violent acts, encouraged victims to remember badge numbers, and launched a radio-car and foot patrol to monitor police behavior in the neighborhood.[89] After the tragic Hough riots in 1966, the Cleveland East project issued a list of demands, which included a civilian review board and racial integration of the police force. Project organizers also demanded that "police show more respect to community people." The demand for racial integration later spurred minority recruitment in municipal police departments and the emergence of community control as a new, more radical solution to police brutality than civilian review.[90] Significant progress on this issue did not occur until the late 1970s, long after the end of ERAP organizing, but the insistence that citizens possessed a right both to oversee public institutions and to receive consideration from public servants was an important political claim and found reinforcement in ERAP's welfare campaigns.

New Left organizers initially expressed uncertainty about welfare organizing. Such activity meant making at least a short-term commitment to the existing, inadequate, and faulty welfare state rather than replacing it completely with "socialism," as Cleveland organizers put it.[91] In their view, the welfare system fostered dependency and political powerlessness among recipients, and such conditions were intentional products of the social control inherent in the system. The welfare system, Nancy Hollander asserted, "stamps one *dependent.*" It created "permanent economic and psychological dependency," the Cleveland project reported.[92] Although policy makers would link welfare to the "problem of dependency" in the late 1960s and 1970s, organizers did not attribute dependency to the fact of receiving welfare benefits but rather to the means- and morals-testing, supervision, and loss of privacy that went along with benefits. ERAP director Rennie Davis summarized this view succinctly when he called for a paper on "the welfare state and how it crushes people." This thinking—that welfare state institutions produced passive, controlled clients and thus contributed to maintaining the impoverished state of poor Americans—was the beginning of what would come to be called the New Left social control model. Yet the successful mobilization of women welfare recipients in the communities indicated that institutional social control was partial and incomplete.[93] While New Left organizers questioned whether they wanted to work to perfect the welfare system or create the conditions to allow impoverished Americans to leave welfare, women recipients in ERAP made demands for both.

Behind these demands was an understanding of assistance from the state as an aspect of citizenship and an entitlement, rather than the dominant conception of welfare as undeserved charity. By transforming their needs and the needs of their children into rights, recipients made political claims on the state. Every project wrote a "Welfare Bill of Rights," which included rights to appeal the decisions of caseworkers, to obtain an adequate education for children, to "control our own lives," and to have "a real future."[94] In claiming welfare rights, recipients emphasized their roles and work as mothers. Mothering was a need of children and an important occupation. "I'm a citizen who has a job to do, instead of a poor forgotten colored woman like some of our people feel," Baltimore recipient Margaret McCarty argued.[95] Boston's Mary Murphy maintained that a welfare mother "insures the country of productive, self-reliant, self-supporting citizens" and by "fulfilling her most important and satisfying role . . . is a more useful and productive citizen herself." Welfare was part of an exchange, as payment for services rendered as the caretakers of children.[96] Recipients also linked welfare to the larger cause of social justice. Carole King, a leading welfare rights activist from Cleveland's East Side, spoke at the "Ohio Walk for Decent Welfare" in 1966, a founding event for the National Welfare Rights Organization (NWRO). "We want equality at all levels for all humans—NOW, and not some day."[97] Legal strategists, including the law professor Charles Reich and the welfare rights innovator Edward Sparer, a former Communist with whom ERAP organizers corresponded, formalized this political argument for welfare rights and sought a constitutional right to welfare. This argument, however, was rejected by the Supreme Court in 1970.[98]

All ERAP's campaigns around welfare aimed to win adequate income for recipients; the names of Cleveland's and Boston's welfare rights groups, Citizens United for Adequate Welfare (CUFAW) and

Mothers for Adequate Welfare (MAW), indicated as much. In Cleveland women began a campaign to raise Ohio's welfare benefits from 70 percent to 100 percent of the state's "minimum standard of need" set in 1959. In 1965 they secured signatures for over four thousand letters to the Ohio Senate and sent a delegation to Columbus to testify before the Senate Finance Committee, where they were told that the welfare budget could not be increased until 1967 at the earliest.[99] Dovie Thurman also testified in 1965 before an Illinois state committee about inadequate public aid payments. "I'm here because of the laws you made about rent ceilings and budget levels, which are impossible to live under." Thurman then detailed the difficulties she encountered as she attempted to manage financially on the monthly budget.[100] In Boston MAW successfully targeted the low rent allowance of sixty-five to eighty dollars included in calculating state welfare benefits. In 1966 they managed to get a bill introduced into the state legislature to execute a rent survey to justify an increase in the allowance. They spent a great deal of time attending hearings, lobbying, and testifying, and were rewarded with the bill's final passage.[101] One of the goals of the later NWRO, adequate income would begin to meet the basic needs of ERAP's welfare constituency, allowing them to maintain at least a minimum standard of living.

Meeting the basic need to live and eat decently also was the goal of revising existing or winning new school lunch, food surplus, and food stamp programs. "Food is the major problem," Sharon Jeffrey reported after an early meeting with welfare recipients in Cleveland. Carole King was "tired of people feeling like they are doing a great thing because they are half-feeding my children because children have the *right* to eat."[102] For low-income families, food was both a basic necessity and, given the high prices charged by the few stores operating in inner cities, the largest expense. Campaigns around school lunches and surplus food gave ERAP its first tangible victories. In the fall of 1964 CUFAW members organized a letter-writing campaign, a demonstration, and a meeting with county commissioners to rescind a new fifteen-cent lunch fee for middle and high school students of welfare parents. School lunches were a fundamental part of their children's diet, especially since family breakfasts generally consisted of oats or cornmeal, and in April 1965 they won their battle.[103] MAW helped bring the federal food surplus program to Boston in 1965, which provided eighty-six pounds of food per month for a family of four, including such items as butter, cheese, canned meats, rice, dried milk and eggs, corn grits, peanut butter, and rolled wheat, and saved a family about twenty-six dollars on their monthly grocery bill.[104]

Project participants preferred the food stamp program, however, because it offered a variety and choice of items. As NCUP organizer Carol Glassman observed, "The power of the consumer is largely taken out of the hands of the welfare woman," but they, like later members of the NWRO, sought to participate more fully in the U.S. consumer economy.[105] Only made permanent in 1964, the food stamp program was valued highly by community welfare recipients. "[T]his is our children's bread and butter," stated Chicago project member Mary V. Hockenberry.[106] Yet, "[t]o be eligible for it," Chicago resident Frank Blalock complained, "you practically have to be starving," and items such as coffee, tea, bananas, toothpaste, and laundry and household cleaning supplies were restricted. The program "is clearly not designed for the poor but for the farmers," explained Dorothy Perez, "since no items are allowed for except those raised by the American farmers."[107] Over 1964 and 1965, activists in Cleveland and Chicago worked to have eligibility requirements loosened and freedom of choice broadened over the types of items they purchased, but to no avail.[108]

Decent clothing, as with food, constituted another basic necessity for recipients and their children. Ohio welfare recipients received five dollars per child monthly for clothes—an amount that would not purchase even one pair of blue jeans. In the fall of 1964, with school and winter approaching, mothers articulated the desire to provide their children with presentable and warm clothes. Under the auspices of CUFAW, they held a demonstration at the office of the county commissioners the following winter.[109] The children's clothing campaign culminated in a "buy-in" at a local department store in August 1966, a direct action also utilized by recipient groups elsewhere. Fifty members of the Welfare Grievance Committee entered the May Company, selected the clothing needed for their children, including pants, shirts, winter coats, and scarves. They had the cashier ring up the total, "charged" it to the Cuyahoga County Welfare Department, and then left the clothing on the counter. Sandra Echols, an East Side resident, helped plan the buy-in "to express how we felt about the $5 allowance." Bertha Rice participated in the buy-in because "my kids have only one pair of pants each without a hole in them to start school with. There's plenty of money in this land. People shouldn't be living like this."[110] The buy-in received much media attention and prompted a meeting between the Welfare Grievance Committee and the director of the county welfare department. But nothing developed until over a year later, when the proceeds from the inaugural ball of the newly elected—and Cleveland's first black—mayor Carl Stokes went toward school clothing for the city's AFDC children.[111]

In addition to demanding adequate benefits, food, and clothing in order to mother their children properly, women welfare recipients in ERAP sought a welfare policy that offered a range of programmatic options—options that supported them as mothers and wage earners. Insisting on the right to choose to work outside the home if they wished, Cleveland's CUFAW and Boston's MAW called for the "right to work to meet needs" without "endangering their welfare payments."[112] It is difficult to ascertain whether community women or New Left organizers first proposed jobs as an aim of welfare organizing. As Cleveland organizers pointed out during ERAP's very first summer, "the welfare mother constituency is primarily interested in more adequate payments, not, let's say, in getting jobs."[113] Moreover, why would these women seek an employment option? After all, they defined mothering as important and responsible work and believed children needed a mother's care, a claim especially significant for black women, whose motherhood historically was seen as irrelevant to employment.

Yet the ability to choose between staying home and wage earning allowed women welfare recipients a measure of control over their lives. "We are sick of being dependent on [case]workers and handouts," exclaimed Boston's Doris Bland and Gertrude Nickerson. They wanted the welfare system to make it "easier for some of us to get jobs."[114] Women in Boston's MAW and Cleveland's Welfare Grievance Committee insisted on the right to choose to work outside the home if recipients wished and criticized welfare policies that penalized recipients by deducting the equivalent of any earned income from their monthly check. Indeed, as happened elsewhere, in the absence of adequate income many women already were working "under the table," cleaning houses and babysitting to augment their meager welfare checks, and they hated the stress of having to keep their employment hidden.[115] At the very least, they needed work experience to prepare for the time when their children reached the age of adulthood and left their homes, because at that point they would no longer be eligible to receive AFDC payments. Already in the projects there were mothers "whose children are now grown up, who are too old (45 or older) to find employment."[116] Finally, activists shared with the dominant culture a commitment to the work ethic, as did welfare recipients across the country. "For me, work is very good," Lillian Craig later noted, after she had left welfare. "[T]he ideal is to have a job you feel good about, and where payday means something."[117]

To enter the paid labor force, however, mothers needed support, including jobs, job training, a higher minimum wage, and day care. Women welfare recipients in ERAP would have agreed with Los Angeles activist Johnnie Tillmon, then emerging as a national welfare rights leader. "Nobody denies, least of all poor women, that there is dignity and satisfaction in being able to support your kids through honest labor. We wish we could do it."[118] But doing it was difficult. One Cleveland woman welfare recipient noted how, once "the mother would find a job, then a new set of problems present themselves. She would need an adequate earning to cover all the expenses, babysitting, carfare to and from work, decent clothing." A contemporary study of Chicago welfare recipients found that, although most wanted to work outside the home, they needed skills and training in order to qualify for good jobs.[119] Carole King in Cleveland felt that if the welfare department "feels people are employable they should help people find jobs," and each ERAP project included the right to a decent job and to job training in its "Welfare Bill of Rights" and called for public, low-cost day care centers. But this effort to improve the conditions and rewards of poor women's workforce participation went nowhere. When welfare reform occurred with the punitive 1967 Work Incentive Program, employment became mandatory—not optional as ERAP activists wanted—and without the support mothers needed, contributing to strong recipient opposition.[120]

For ERAP activists, these problems with the welfare system highlighted the issue of democratic participation, because they were connected to the fact that recipients "have no control over the way Welfare is administered."[121] Clients in the social welfare context were rendered passive and dependent recipients of aid rather than active participants in the welfare system. Consistent with New Left participatory democracy, welfare rights in ERAP were not only to be won but to be exercised, through a process of participation. Anticipating another of the NWRO's goals, that of democracy, project activists demanded that recipients take part in, and thus gain some semblance of autonomy and control within, the welfare system itself. "You can talk about giving welfare recipients bigger budgets," Casey Hayden argued. "But you can't suggest they should control the welfare department."[122] They set out to change this situation.

ERAP first demanded that caseworkers treat recipients with respect and consideration. Since recipients were theoretically the bosses of the caseworkers, they should be treated accordingly, an argument advanced by later welfare rights activists. "From the President of the United States down to the caseworker, they are all servants of the people," noted Princess Redfeather in Chicago.[123] Cleveland participants called for better-qualified caseworkers with some knowledge of "poor people's problems," and in October 1966 began evaluating caseworkers for a monthly Louse List and Honor Roll. The former named "caseworkers who misinform, misuse, and threaten people," while the latter listed "caseworkers who interpret the Welfare laws correctly and are understanding, give respect, and support clients' right to organize."[124] By demanding that caseworkers act according to standards set by recipients, they asserted the right to define a "good" caseworker. This assertion was particularly meaningful, for it was the job of caseworkers to define a welfare recipient as "deserving" of assistance or not.

In addition to respect, the "right to privacy" appeared on every project's "Welfare Bill of Rights." Welfare departments justified their invasions of privacy as a way to determine whether those in need met moral standards of deservingness and whether women's mothering provided a "suitable home" and was in the "best interests" of children.[125] Recipients rejected the welfare department's interference into how they raised and cared for their children and especially to caseworkers' inquiries and incursions into their relationships with men. Chicago recipient Phronie Simpson furiously protested the welfare department's "midnight raid" of her home. "If a woman's by herself and ain't got her husband with her, they never leave you alone and act like it's a sin or something."[126] In Cleveland the police department's Bureau of Special Services cooperated with the welfare department in its interrogation of AFDC children about their mothers' male companions. Cleveland's Lillian Craig responded with an article about the relationship between morality and sex, in which she argued that mistreating others, not sex, should be the "great taboo." And Boston's MAW demanded that the word "illegitimate" not be used in describing their children, refusing the social stigma associated with giving birth and being born out of wedlock.[127]

Toward changing the relationship between recipients and the welfare system, ERAP publicized information about welfare rights and benefits. "On welfare, you don't know your rights," Simpson complained. "You don't know whether you're coming or going."[128] Recipients needed to know when they were underbudgeted or unjustly terminated. In order to put together their own welfare rights manuals, ERAP activists researched the welfare system and, in Cleveland, stole the welfare department's own manual. "We wrote our manual in 'people terms' that anybody could understand," Craig recalled. "When it was finished, our manual was so readable and thorough that caseworkers began to steal it from us!"[129] New Left organizers, like Carol Glassman, Connie Brown, Carole McEldowney, and Helen Garvy, also gathered information by taking jobs as caseworkers. Basic facts about how to apply for welfare, the rights of welfare recipients, and new legislation concerning programs created informed, knowledgeable recipients and prepared them to confront caseworkers and deal with the welfare state bureaucracy. Although MAW failed to get a bill passed requiring the annual publication of local welfare department rules and budgets, activists in Chicago and Cleveland won the right for recipients to see department regulations upon request.[130]

ERAP participants also campaigned for a role for recipients in the administration of the welfare system, because, as Chicago's Dorothy Perez insisted, "recipients have a right to help make the decisions that affect their lives so radically." The Chicago project wanted recipients "to change and run the welfare system."[131] They demanded boards or committees, composed mostly of women welfare recipients, established in every welfare office to set standards and hear grievances. ERAP activists argued that the knowledge and experience gained from service work prepared recipients for such participation in welfare administration. Chicago organizer Judith Bernstein spoke of the woman who had learned "all the rules of the welfare system" and "now knows they can be changed, and can work for her."[132] In Boston these arguments were convincing. "These women are trained for this sort of thing," one official noted when MAW demanded the appointment of a recipient to the State Welfare Board of Appeal. The first appointee to Boston's welfare board was, in fact, a MAW member.[133]

ERAP's welfare organizing coincided with the years preceding "the high point of welfare rights claims," and these campaigns were the community projects' most successful.[134] They combined a mobilized

and motivated constituency with a state bureaucracy open to some reform measures. Women in Newark were "dying to come" to meetings,
notes Connie Brown. "The assumption was that this is a bad system,
and we were organizing to make it deliver what it promises. 'Give me
what you say I'm entitled to' is a comfortable thing to say."[135] Yet
Boston's food surplus program and Cleveland's school lunch victory
were ERAP's only substantive achievements. And eleven other cities in
Massachusetts already had food surplus programs when MAW began
its campaign, while CUFAW defended an existing free school lunch
program rather than winning something new. Both also were "in-
kind," not cash benefit, programs and thus allowed recipients little
control over the exchange. As part of reshaping the political encounter
between poor citizens and the welfare state, winning rights to sit on a
welfare appeal board, see regulations on demand, and have an advocate in face-to-face interactions with caseworkers arguably were more
significant victories.

What is most notable about these efforts is their feminist content. To
be sure, ERAP's welfare activists operated without a conscious feminist
ideology. Instead, maternalism most explicitly shaped these campaigns,
as community women asserted the needs of children for the protection
of the state, for food and clothing, and for a mother's care. Moreover,
they utilized and reinforced the gender ideology—one that deemed men
breadwinners and women dependent caretakers of children—basic to
the welfare state, in policy if not in practice.[136] And women organizers—their own feminist consciousness in process—generally did not
recognize any feminist content at the time, with the important excep-
tion of Casey Hayden, "a feminist from birth." "Working on organizing welfare women was a return to organizing women" for her,
and "feminism was a primary concern."[137] Even so, all these welfare campaigns contested women's subordinate status, whether as citizens, clients, mothers, or wage earners, and asserted women's needs
for respect, self-determination, control, and even autonomy from the
state.[138] In addition, by taking personal interactions between citizens
and representatives of the state to be political encounters—as did
ERAP activists concerned with police-community relations—they were
beginning to see how "the personal" could be "political."

Overall, ERAP's campaigns sought to expand political participation
beyond the influence and input attainable through electoral politics. As
they demanded greater political power, activists also revealed how they

would use that power: to provide jobs and job training, new housing in urban renewal areas, and children's recreation and day care. Yet, despite a few successes mainly around women's welfare organizing, ERAP's direct engagement with the state and attempt to realize full political and social citizenship for poor Americans met with failure. Community participants may have found their voice. But voices needed to be heard, and listening and dialogue were not forthcoming from elected and appointed officials. That such a tremendous amount of energy and effort yielded so little led to a sense of futility in ERAP about trying to achieve gains within the existing political system. Disillusionment and frustration set in and contributed to the disbanding of the community projects.

Cleveland "Rat March," August 1965. (Courtesy of John Bancroft.)

7

Disbanding Projects, Gathering Movements

For Cleveland community leader Lillian Craig, the late 1960s, after New Left and other progressive organizers had left the Near West Side, was "a difficult time." "When they left . . . I felt disillusioned. 'How *could* they—they get me all involved, and then they go.' I resented their mobility."[1] By 1967 and 1968, it became clear to ERAP organizers that they would never create an interracial movement of the poor, or even establish strong neighborhood projects. Sharon Jeffrey left Cleveland in 1967 to direct the Hyde Park–Kenwood Community Conference, a prominent community organization in Chicago. Others, such as Carol McEldowney and Kathy Boudin, headed east, later joining, respectively, the burgeoning women's liberation movement and the revolutionary cadre known as Weatherman. Dave Strauss, who won conscientious objector status after being drafted for the Vietnam War, volunteered for an internship with the American Friends Service Committee in Dayton, and Dickie Magidoff began teaching in Boston and involving himself in the counterculture. Although Oliver Fein and Charlotte Phillips were still in Cleveland, they focused on integrating their medical training into their activism and participated in the new Radicals in the Professions. As New Left organizers drifted away from the project, Craig recalled thinking, "'Why should I stay involved? Why should I even bother?' But then," she added, "something good would always happen."[2]

Similar developments also affected other ERAP projects, as New Left organizers disbanded projects and left communities in the late 1960s. Organizers departed because of their failures and frustrations with community organizing, but they also were drawn to emerging new social movements and other forms of political action. Moving on, they left behind neighborhood residents like Lillian Craig in the process. These developments prompted project activists—organizers and residents alike—to assess the impact and outcome of ERAP. What had they accomplished? What contributions had they made and what legacy had they left? As Lillian Craig's recollections indicated, feelings of disappointment and defeat certainly loomed large and strengthened negative evaluations of ERAP organizing. Yet, as Craig noted, positive events and circumstances often inspired former participants to continue their social and political activism. As they did, they took with them important lessons and commitments from their ERAP experience.

ERAP's End

In 1967 and 1968 the last community projects disbanded. A combination of conflicts and pressures inside and outside the projects brought to an end the attempt to build an interracial movement of the poor. Internal developments, such as heightened tensions around class and race differences and the growing feminism of New Left women, were connected to larger social and political trends, as elements of what the historian Allen Matusow has called "the unraveling of America" in the late 1960s played out within these projects and communities. Internal problems are often emphasized over external events in accounts of the closing of the neighborhood projects. But in fighting inner-city poverty, "we were resisting large demographic and economic forces that proved too strong to withstand," Stanley Aronowitz later noted, with the broader, historical perspective necessary to understand ERAP's fate.[3]

Part of ERAP's problem was that organizers worked without a strategy. Strategic flexibility went a long way toward making ERAP truly open to the participation and concerns of community residents, but without an overall "metastrategy," disagreements emerged among participants about organizing issues, tactics, and goals. For Boston organizer Marya Levenson, the lack of strategy was a primary reason for ERAP's failure. "[W]e didn't know what the hell we were trying to do and that always caught up with us."[4] Without a strategy, ERAP also had no means by which to evaluate the success or failure of the community projects. "One of the reasons for frustration is not knowing if we are getting anywhere," Sharon Jeffrey noted from Cleveland.[5] The lack of criteria for assessment meant that many projects continued long after they should have been abandoned. In his journal Tom Hayden recorded a conversation with Carl Wittman, then with the Hoboken project, about whether Wittman would continue organizing. Although Wittman admitted things were not going well, he had decided to carry on his work there. "Out of enthusiasm, or from doggedness?" Hayden asked. "Doggedness, for sure," Wittman replied.[6] Unsure of what they were trying to accomplish or how to proceed, many organizers found it emotionally difficult to live with and manage such uncertainties over the years.

The lack of an overall strategy meant that, as JOIN organizer Rich Rothstein noted, "political programs could change as quickly and as irresponsibly as the whims of the organizers."[7] And indeed they did. In Newark residents complained that organizers were involved in too many things. "[W]e start something and it seems like we are going off into something else," Carol Glassman related. "[W]e start out talking about housing" and then somehow end up "talking about recreation and then police."[8] Similarly, Chicago organizers often abandoned campaigns in midcourse. In the case of housing, for example, they established "tenant unions" in rental units to negotiate collective bargaining agreements with landlords. Functioning much like a traditional trade union, the tenant unions signed housing contracts that provided for collective bargaining, outlined grievance procedures and binding arbitration for handling disputes, and even specified repairs to be made. Although this was an innovative effort to shift conceptions of tenant-landlord relations, organizers failed to follow through on what they had begun, to nurture the tenant unions, and to oversee the implementation of the housing contracts. They instead decided to move on to other issues and priorities.[9] As a result, ERAP participants rarely felt they had achieved anything.

In the absence of a strategy, organizers defined their approach as "Let the People Decide." According to Bill Ayers, who worked in the Cleveland project's alternative preschool, the intention was that "we would live with the poor, cast our lot with the poor, and that the wisdom of the people themselves would lead to whatever political direction we took."[10] This position was strongly criticized by SDS members outside ERAP. For SDS leader Clark Kissinger, letting "the poor decide for themselves . . . exempts SDS from the necessity of developing concrete economic, political, or social programs." In an article listing sixteen humorous "plagues" afflicting the New Left in late 1966, one targeted ERAP organizers specifically: "Victim clings to a mystical belief that the Truth will be discovered by the unerring actions of the Poor."[11] ERAP organizers, too, raised doubts about this approach. If ERAP was about allowing residents to determine ERAP's course, "what did they need us for?" Jean Tepperman asked. Over time, ERAP's aim shifted from organizing a national social movement with a specific purpose and clear goals to the more diffuse aim of "building independent bases of insurgency, and hopefully of power, in the ghettoes."[12]

Yet ERAP failed to accomplish even this aim. ERAP never recruited large numbers of people. While NCUP claimed a core group of from fifty to two hundred community members and contact with about seven hundred Clinton Hill residents, Newark was a situation in which, as Carol Glassman describes, "history was moving in a particular direction of black empowerment and civil rights and we were riding that train." Other projects, like Chicago, "didn't have that kind of momentum."[13] In Chicago the recruitment process "was very organizer-intensive and it took a lot to maintain it," Rennie Davis recalls. Casey Hayden "figured it would take five years to create a solid organization. I hadn't the heart for it."[14] Residential transiency also hindered the projects. "One woman moved out—up to Skokie and another moved down South," Chicago organizer Judith Bernstein stated. "And the program I was working on with them fell through."[15] Leaders like Lillian Craig in Cleveland and Jesse Allen in Newark remained dedicated to the projects, but much was demanded of them. In NCUP, Glassman noted, "we ask people to spend seven nights a week going to meetings. That's enough to destroy any organization."[16] Tragically, Bessie Smith died in her sleep the night after she won a position on Newark's citywide War on Poverty board. Her involvement in NCUP, Tom Hayden recalled guiltily, "brought pressure, stress, and death."[17] In the end, the projects never became established community organizations with stable memberships.

The difficulty of establishing strong neighborhood organizations among poor residents prompted New Left organizers to question a central element of the original ERAP strategy: the agency of the poor. Todd Gitlin came to see this belief as "romantic," while Sharon Jeffrey later considered it "stupid." Residents on Cleveland's Near West Side "were basically disorganized people," she remembered. For Vivian Rothstein, Uptown residents' "lives were in such distress they were almost too poor to organize."[18] At the time, some organizers understood this group to be the "lumpenproleteriat" and the attempt to organize them wrongheaded. In contrast, NCUP community leadership was provided not by the poor but by lower-middle- and working-class residents like Thurman and Bessie Smith. And on Cleveland's East Side, according to Dave Strauss, "there were a lot of skilled people who were going off to jobs and coming to a meeting at night. What the theory says is accurate. People that are working feel a lot more powerful."[19]

Even among those residents ERAP successfully mobilized, dissension and conflict existed. This finding contrasted with the New Left's romantic expectations that solidarity and neighborliness characterized poor communities, especially of blacks and Appalachians, who were assumed to have strong "folk" cultures and ties. But as Cathy Wilkerson wrote of organizing in Chester, a "host of personal antagonisms" could create an "atmosphere of defensive distrust." Organizers in Uptown were struck by the high levels of alcoholism, violence, and abuse of women in the neighborhood.[20] Conflicts arose over individual workloads, and as in any organization, those who felt they were working hard resented those they felt were not. At one meeting, Lillian Craig "began by screaming out at those who claim to belong to CUFAW but who do no work. She blasted away for about a half an hour."[21] Moreover, community members often represented different—even conflicting—segments of the neighborhood populations, with different goals and concerns. In Uptown, older and women participants viewed the young Appalachian men protesting police brutality as "Hillbilly punks" and looked with disfavor on their drag-racing, tire-squealing, disorderly behavior. Homeowners and renters in Clinton Hill were "hard to bring together," as the former tended to blame the latter for the neighborhood's deterioration. And employed residents in all of projects often disdained and stigmatized welfare recipients.[22] ERAP organizers did not encounter nor could they create "a community of poverty" after all.[23]

In addition to conflicts among community residents in ERAP, class and racial tensions between residents and organizers heightened. Community activists always differentiated between themselves as older and less educated than "the students" (in Chicago) or "SDS kids" (in Cleveland). "No matter how much we emulated the life style of the people in the community," Kathy Boudin notes, "there was always a giant difference that they understood better than we: we could leave whenever we wanted and go back to our old lives. They could not."[24] Over time, anger and resentment increasingly characterized these differences, a development most apparent in JOIN. In 1966 and 1967 many of the young Appalachian men reported being "peeved with the way the students were running JOIN" and warned residents interested in the project to be prepared to "put up with some of their college bullshit."[25] Community leader Peggy Terry defined interactions between women organizers and welfare recipients as "mother-henning." JOIN's welfare rights group "was never able to keep strong women in the group for very long," she contended. "Any woman strong enough to successfully fight the Welfare Department is too strong to submit to mother-henning." In the spring of 1967 community women left JOIN to form Welfare Recipients Demand Action, which required greater participation from recipients. Finally, in January 1968, community participants voted to ask organizers to pull out of the project altogether, arguing that now a group of grassroots leaders existed to take control.[26]

Racial differences between white New Left organizers and black community residents also became more contested with the rise of Black Power and militant separatism after 1965. "We would never fit in," Elaine Plaisance remembered feeling about organizing in Boston's Roxbury–North Dorchester, and a growing black nationalism and militancy among the predominantly African American MAW began to limit the role of white organizers in the group.[27] Similar developments in Newark and elsewhere prompted ERAP organizers to question what direction their activities should take, and Chester CORE director Donald W. Jackson—who earlier had worked with Chester ERAP—responded. "What is the answer for the white ERAPer in the ghetto? Pack the hell up. Get out. Go to work in your own communities."[28] Then, in the spring of 1966, SNCC leader Stokely Carmichael publicized the slogan "Black Power," insisted that only black Americans should organize in black communities, and called on white organizers to remove themselves from black neighborhoods. Finally, riots in Cleveland in 1966 and Newark in 1967 signaled the end of ERAP's efforts in African American communities. Rooted in conflicts around police brutality, urban renewal, and political power—all issues around which NCUP and the CCP had campaigned—the riots indicated to New Left organizers that everything had changed. The riots "exhausted the dreams of the early sixties," as Tom Hayden put it, and signaled it was time to go.[29]

By 1967 it was clear that ERAP's experiment in cross-class and interracial organizing had run its course. New Left organizers in all the projects found themselves charged with "elitism" and "manipulation." In retrospect, Kim Moody agrees. "I think there was a kind of unconsciously elitist idea here that we the veterans of this student movement of the early '60s could mobilize the poor." Meanwhile, solidarity among community activists was increasingly defined in terms of race. At a 1967 meeting of Chicago's predominantly white ERAP and black West Side Organization to plan a demonstration against police brutality, members of the latter

made comments about "white trash" and "kill the white man." JOIN decided there would be no future cooperation between the two organizations.[30] The reality of de facto residential segregation in urban America
and the employment advantages enjoyed by white southern migrants relative to blacks militated against a common consciousness or political
coalition among low-income whites and blacks. ERAP's interracial movement of the poor certainly was not materializing—and appeared unlikely
to do so in the near future.[31]

As community residents contested class and racial hierarchies, women
began to challenge gender hierarchies in ERAP. There were women who
complained about a sexual division of labor in the projects, in which they
were "relegated to 'female' types of work—dishwashing, cooking, cleaning, clerical work, etc." and in which their organizing, around welfare for
example, carried less status and value.[32] Although there were exceptions
to this division of labor—Steve Goldsmith, a JOIN organizer, worked on
welfare issues and many men performed clerical tasks in the projects—it
was true that men generally provided the leadership and engaged in the
most visible organizing. They also maintained their intellectual hegemony
in ERAP. When Rennie Davis called for papers on ERAP organizing in
early 1965, only two of twenty-three suggested paper topics were considered appropriate for women authors: organizing welfare and public
housing campaigns.[33] For women, as the historian Sara Evans argues,
"there was the contradiction of doing most of the concrete long-term organizing work and remaining invisible," a contradiction that grew more
pronounced as the decade progressed.[34]

These generalizations held most true in JOIN. As early as the summer
of 1964 women in JOIN, according to Toni Helstein, "got very fed up.
We wrote up a flyer that was modeled on the flyers we had passed out to
unemployed workers, invited the men to a meeting at our apartment to
discuss this . . . and we called it ROW: Revolt of the Women."[35] Years
later, Jean Tepperman recalls a meeting where one male organizer

> ordered all the women to leave. "Because," he said, "we got serious
> things to talk about here and we can't have women with all their legs all
> hanging out over the place." The concept was . . . having all these sex ob-
> jects around was so distracting that they couldn't have their serious dis-
> cussion. And we left. We all left.[36]

Male organizers, like Rennie Davis and Michael James, also considered
their constituency of young men, particularly in the campaigns against

police brutality, to be the "potential revolutionary force" for change in Uptown. Of her work with young women, Vivian Rothstein remembered being asked why she thought "teen-age girls had anything to do with the revolution."[37] Organizing a constituency of women or girls constituted a feminist challenge to such sexism within JOIN. Indeed, Casey Hayden's summer in Chicago prompted her to collaborate with Mary King in writing "Sex and Caste: A Kind of Memo" in the fall of 1965. "That memo grew directly out of the conflicts I experienced working to organize women with the Chicago JOIN project. On the basis of that experience it was clear to me that a consciousness of feminism had to be developed on the left."[38] Women began questioning male domination in society in general and raising the "woman question" at official SDS and ERAP gatherings.

High staff turnover and conflict also contributed to fissures in the community projects. Large staffs—forty-five in Newark and thirty in Chicago during the summer of 1965—presented difficulties of coordination and decision making, and the integration of new staff and constant staff turnover, especially at summer's end when student volunteers returned to campus, created problems. New staff members often joined a project in the middle of an organizing campaign and, lacking familiarity with the background, strategy, and community participants, could not really be expected to "have the same intensity that the old staff had," Carol Glassman observed. Newcomers, too, faced an "in-groupism" among staff members that made it difficult to break into existing circles of friends.[39] In some projects, personality conflicts among staff members "paralyzed their operation" or caused organizers to leave to avoid working with a particular person. Rich Rothstein minced no words upon hearing that an organizer he considered "incompetent" was joining the Chicago project. "I am contemplating suicide," he wrote.[40]

Heavy workloads and the stresses of communal living on a tight budget further undermined the appeal of ERAP's "new way of living." "We worked *seven days a week*," Sharon Jeffrey recalled, while Chicago organizers reported eighteen-hour workdays.[41] Even the most committed organizers commented on the constant pressure to work all the time. "I'm working like a son-of-a-bitch," Rennie Davis noted, "feeling the importance of every hour, but frustrated because I don't feel strong enough to sustain the intensity and pace forever." "I can't really say I'm unhappy," he added. "Just overworked." When organizers slept late or avoided going out into "the field" in order to rest, they often felt terribly guilty and engaged in "self-flagellation" afterwards.[42] Adding to these pressures was the lack of privacy in the projects. Only a few organizers had their own bedrooms; many slept on couches and on floors. And low project budgets and a lack of funding made food items like meat and juice luxuries and paying even for the basics, such as rent and utilities, a regular challenge. Although they handled the situation with a sense of humor— "There is . . . an indigenous, grassroots type movement developing for orange juice in the morning," Nick Egleson reported dryly from Philadelphia—it was wearying. "Our spartan life-style," Tom Hayden believed in the end, "was too demanding of people."[43]

Matters of sex and sexuality took their toll as well, eroding the foundation of interdependence and trust among organizers. During this time of "sexual revolution," many organizers, straight and gay, were questioning traditional sexual norms. Yet they also were unsure about what their own sexual attitudes and behavior should be, and this uncertainty contributed to "the reality of painful personal relationships" in ERAP.[44] "[A]s women," one woman recalled, "none of us were very sophisticated sexually." In the absence of a feminist critique, heterosexuality continued to be a male-dominated experience; sexual "liberation" made women free to have sex on men's terms. As a consequence, many young women—"19Fs," nineteen-year-old females—who came through the projects were sexually vulnerable.[45] For gay men and lesbians the situation was difficult as well, but in a different way. Because they were "beyond the pale," according to the historian Martin Duberman, most gay men and lesbians remained in the closet while working in the movement during the 1960s. But homophobia contributed to at least one division in ERAP: the end of the collaboration between Tom Hayden and Carl Wittman. Wittman later reported that "a dignitary of SDS" (Hayden) actually prohibited homosexuality at the initial meeting of the Newark project during the summer of 1964. "Upon discovering that Carl Wittman was gay," Hayden remembered, "I noticed a tendency in myself to withdraw from him."[46] Eventually, Wittman left NCUP and launched the ERAP project in Hoboken, New Jersey.

Taken together, these conditions and conflicts led to emotional fatigue and "burnout" among ERAP organizers. "By 1967, some of the original ERAP people made decisions to leave," Kathy Boudin says about the Cleveland project. "They felt that the goals of ERAP could not be met; they did not feel successful in their work. By now we were living in different houses and the communal aspect of our work slowly came apart." Steve Goldsmith was in Chicago, where organizers early on lived in separate apartments scattered throughout the neighborhood. He believes more emphasis needed to be put into keeping "people together, happy, and organized."[47] Community organizing on its own was already an extremely emotionally demanding activity, but the combination of hard work, close living, tight budgets, and sexual tensions only made it more so. Over time, ERAP's attempt to realize its vision of community could not sustain itself.

The decentralization of ERAP further fostered a sense of futility on the local level. In the spring of 1965, with little debate, the Economic Research and Action Project disbanded as a national organization. The aim, in keeping with the New Left model of organization, was to combat bureaucracy, allow each project to set its own course and make its own decisions, and foster greater involvement from community people. Because every community was different, a central office or even another project could not know what the community organizing experience was like in another location. In this context, John Bancroft decided to edit the *ERAP Newsletter*. "Although it was great that everyone was immersing themselves in their local community, it was important for people to be exchanging ideas about what was working and what wasn't working and what direction we are going in."[48] Later on, various people proposed setting up a second national ERAP office to handle staff recruitment and training, research, and strategic development—functions for which individual projects had little time. Such proposals came to naught, however, and, after only a year and a half as a separate project of SDS, national ERAP ceased to exist. Without a connection to a national movement, each isolated project "acted as though it bore the burden of history on its shoulders alone," Rich Rothstein observed.[49]

ERAP's failures also were intensified by the isolation of the community projects from the student movement and SDS's campus-based organizing. In the middle years of the decade, campus travelers like Ken McEldowney, Dickie Magidoff, and Jack Kittredge, who had worked as ERAP organizers, linked the campus and community. "My sense was," Kittredge recalls, "that it gave a lot of legitimacy" to SDS to be "reaching out to others and trying to . . . get a coalition, an alliance going."[50] But others felt the divisions between campus and community sharpening with time. On the one hand, campus-based activists accused ERAP participants of taking little interest in what they called "students' concerns" and dominated SDS meetings with their own organizing issues and problems.[51] On the other hand, the valorization of "organizing" within ERAP assumed, according to Paul Potter, that "if you couldn't make [it as an organizer], then you just couldn't make it." "We were self-righteous," Vivian Rothstein believes. "We felt we were making sacrifices."[52] Divisions between campus and community were exacerbated by a "generation gap" within SDS by 1965–66, wherein most of the "old guard" remained immersed in the community projects while younger leaders from the Midwest and Southwest—the so-called prairie power—dominated SDS. A number of the younger generation, who had not been part of the organization when it made the decision to move into communities, questioned whether SDS even should have left campus to organize the poor in the first place.[53]

Developments outside the New Left compounded these internal difficulties and eroded the mood of possibility and optimism that had fueled ERAP in 1963 and 1964. All the projects were harassed by opponents who sought to "run them out of town" by whatever means. In Newark supporters of city councilman Lee Bernstein circulated rumors that residents who attended meetings or signed petitions could be thrown off welfare or out of their homes. Pressures—in the form of extra city inspectors and repair bills—were placed on one landlord to evict the project.[54] In both Chicago and Newark counterfeit leaflets and newsletters, with headlines such as "Communists Welcome" and "Headquarters for Hillbilly Winos," were circulated to discredit the projects.[55] Offices were ransacked, windows broken, and mysterious fires started. After having marijuana planted in the JOIN office, police in Uptown raided the place and arrested a number of ERAP organizers and visitors. The charges were later dropped.[56] The Federal Bureau of Investigation assigned undercover agents to investigate NCUP and sent agents to visit the Philadelphia project. When Newark organizers discovered that their office was bugged, Jill Hamberg concluded that having "the police station . . . right next door [was] sort of a mistake."[57]

ERAP projects were red-baited as well. After finding himself the target of a rent strike sponsored by JOIN in Chicago, landlord Jacob Sampson claimed he was the victim of "a communist conspiracy." "In my personal opinion JOIN is financed by a foreign government to upset harmonious life in the United States."[58] To such claims, organizers responded with good humor, as when the custodian of a slum building accused Cleveland organizers of being communists. Connie Smiddie rejoined, "Communists? But I voted for Eisenhower!" Jim Williams recounts an incident in

Louisville when "the FBI came knocking on our door and confronted my mother. And they said, 'Miz Williams are you aware that your boy is associating with people that are trying to overthrow the government by force of violence?' And she just sort of waved dismissedly and says, 'Oh, he never finishes anything he starts.'"[59] Nevertheless, ERAP organizers felt the impact of red-baiting. It personally affected those red-diaper babies, like Dave Strauss, whose parents had been victims of McCarthyism; "I feared I would be outed." Politically, it "scared" and "confused" community people and put projects "on the defensive."[60] It forced Cleveland organizers, including Strauss, to abandon their work with the tenants' council at the Lakeview Terrace public housing project. And it was used to deny the legitimate grievances and anger of local residents when the Newark police department charged "outside, Communist agitators" in NCUP with instigating the city's riots in July 1967.[61]

What proved most frustrating and disillusioning was the sharp contrast between ERAP's initial, wide-ranging goals and the projects' few victories. "We just couldn't get anything," Vivian Rothstein comments about organizing in Chicago.[62] The intransigence of city officials—even over minimal demands like a stoplight in Newark—revealed how officials did not want to give even a small victory to project participants, thus encouraging or strengthening their activism. As Corinna Fales remembers, "We had hundreds of people demonstrate in the streets, sign petitions, go to city hall. We worked for months to get that traffic light, and we were stonewalled. . . . Tremendous, tremendous involvement and no success."[63] Even the projects' few victories—from food surplus and school lunch programs in Boston and Cleveland to NCUP's community center—felt meager in content and value. ERAP organizing certainly never led to the "revolutionary trajectory" where "day to day reforms can lead to revolution" that Tom Hayden had called for in the 1963 Hayden-Haber debate. "The most we could achieve—and it was something—was the control of certain services flowing into our neighborhoods," he later recalled.[64]

Shifting national political sentiment during the second half of the decade made any future victories unlikely. After achieving the Civil Rights and Voting Rights Acts in 1964 and 1965, the Civil Rights Movement in the North and South encountered difficulties and setbacks. According to the historian Harvard Sitkoff, "the leading organizations of the movement . . . floundered in their search for new programs" and "none developed a viable strategy for solving the complex problems of inadequate housing, dead-end jobs, no jobs, and inferior schooling." This later phase of the movement confronted, as did ERAP, the issues of racial inequality that have proved most persistent and pernicious.[65] In 1966, Martin Luther King, Jr., and the Southern Christian Leadership Conference made Chicago and open housing the focus of their first northern protest, which ended in failure. Northern whites would support campaigns against disenfranchisement and segregation in public accommodations in the South, but not integration of their own neighborhoods.[66] That same year, a civil rights bill went down to defeat in Congress. Although Cleveland would elect a black mayor the next year, and Newark would soon follow, the interracial, nonviolent phase of the Civil Rights Movement that had inspired SDS's move into community organizing appeared to be over.[67]

So, too, was the War on Poverty. In hindsight, the "window of opportunity" for the poverty war was very brief; the historian Charles Noble estimates it at about twenty months, from early 1964 to late 1965. Identification with African Americans and with racial conflict and upheaval made the poverty war a target for growing white backlash. Accusations that liberal policies and programs fomented black rebellion, at worst, and were unappreciated by blacks, at best, eroded support for the poverty war among white Americans.[68] More significant, the escalation of the Vietnam War rendered domestic issues less important and took resources away from domestic programs. From 1965 to 1973, for example, the Community Action Program—the best known and most criticized poverty program—received $2.8 billion in federal funds, the equivalent of one month's spending on the Vietnam War.[69] "The bombs in Vietnam explode at home," Martin Luther King, Jr., declared in 1968. In Newark, federal antipoverty monies were cut nearly in half between 1966 and 1967. At the same time, the war was heating up the economy; by 1966 the unemployment rate had dropped to 3.8 percent, the lowest rate since the Korean War.[70] Still, hard-core poverty persisted, and, as optimism about abolishing it vanished along with program budgets, ERAP activists concluded that political leaders such as President Johnson and OEO director Shriver had failed to follow through on their promises: the War on Poverty had been declared but never fought. ERAP's true war on poverty no longer seemed possible.

The Vietnam War hindered ERAP organizing in other ways as well. The draft made it difficult for some men to dedicate themselves full-time to ERAP. In August 1964, Dickie Magidoff had to leave Cleveland and return to school to maintain his student deferment. "I'd rather stay . . . fuck the draft!"[71] And of course the war drew the New Left into antiwar activism. Much has been made of the opposition of ERAP representatives—most prominently Tom Hayden—to SDS's first antiwar march in April 1965. Although it is true some saw the march as "too national" in focus, once the march was decided on, organizers considered it a collective responsibility and supported the march on the local level.[72] Many saw both community and antiwar activism as necessary. "The government could not both wage war and meet people's domestic needs," the argument went, according to Marilyn Katz. "By increasing domestic demand, you would force the government to stop the war because they couldn't fight on both fronts."[73] With the slogan "Welfare not Warfare," community members, like Doris Bland of Boston's MAW and Iva Pearce of Cleveland's CUFAW, also connected domestic and foreign concerns when they took part in SDS-sponsored antiwar demonstrations.[74] But others, both within and outside ERAP, considered the goals of community organizing far less urgent than that of ending the war in Vietnam. "You were not going to strike a blow against the war by organizing welfare mothers," SDS leader Carl Oglesby contended. "You only thought you were."[75]

In response to these developments external to ERAP, activists experienced both demoralization and radicalization. For a significant number, the alliance with liberal-labor forces and attempt to target and transform the welfare state not only appeared mistaken but also reflected political co-optation. As early as 1965, Paul Potter worried that Tom Hayden was "moving closer and closer to a position that the liberal establishment (if not all liberals) constitutes the most dangerous enemy we confront." Potter's concern clearly indicated that this position was not universally held in the New Left at this early point. By 1969, however, Rich Rothstein could say of those who had been in ERAP, "We are now enemies of welfare state capitalism."[76] A range of experiences, including frustration with the pace of social change, encounters with intransigent local governments, and confrontations with police repression, combined with SDS's critique of corporate liberalism contributed to this development.[77] The willingness to consider ERAP's goals as something more complex than "reformist" eroded in the more pessimistic and contentious political climate of the late 1960s, a process also occurring within SNCC.[78]

Within this polarized atmosphere, responses varied. Some participants became alienated from politics completely, while others increasingly viewed alternative, counter-institutions where people could "live according to new values while attempting to build bases of power" as the answer. But this perspective also involved an acknowledgment of political defeat, a suspension of the early commitment to hold the state responsible for improving citizens' lives that initially sparked ERAP.[79] And there were those, like Eric Mann, who looked to more "radical mechanisms." "Most of us became Communists, Socialists, something to the left of where we were, because we felt like we had done such a good job that we were supposed to have won." By 1969 an SDS member concluded that ERAP's major political contribution was that of a failed liberal reform effort that had pushed SDS "to develop radicalism."[80]

ERAP's Impact

As the decade of the 1960s progressed, and as "the movement" became many movements, former ERAP activists took part in this new "kaleidoscope of activity."[81] "I don't remember being discouraged," Nick Egleson says. "It felt at the time as if we were a part of history, that even if things weren't working out in a particular place, that there clearly was a political ferment, and we were part of it."[82] By analyzing both what was mistaken about and what could be salvaged from the ERAP approach, they were able to utilize their organizing experiences in their new efforts and have an impact on emerging forms of social and political activism.

For African Americans, leaving ERAP involved a critique of interracialism within a single movement, and they became involved in civil rights organizing and black identity politics. Before he joined NCUP, Phil Hutchings (one of the project's few black organizers) had been a member of the SNCC affiliate at Howard University. In 1966 he established a branch of SNCC in Newark, and two years later he was elected program secretary of the national organization and emerged as a spokesman of SNCC in its final days, when the organization was a stronghold of Black Power.[83] Dovie Thurman met Martin Luther King, Jr., while she was a leader of the Chicago project, and she and her aunt Dovie Coleman soon became welfare rights organizers for SCLC. They established welfare rights groups on Chicago's South Side, and then Thurman traveled to Birmingham, Alabama, where she initiated the city's first welfare rights march. She also started to express her black cultural identity in her appearance, dress, and hairstyle. "By then I had converted to my Afro and my dashiki and my wire-rimmed glasses. I was Right On, Sister, all the way there. [*Laughs.*] I am a little different now, but I had to get my black identification then."[84] For black participants in ERAP—people who had been discriminated against precisely because of their group identity—the process of redefining and affirming that identity constituted an important, even essential, part of the struggle for political power.[85]

White community activists from JOIN felt similarly and rejected ERAP's commitment to building interracial—as well as cross-class—organizations. Self-consciously identifying as white and working-class, they formed the National Community Union (NCU) shortly after ejecting New Left organizers from the project. NCU members considered themselves part of a larger "White Movement" that included student and rural organizing, and they insisted that all NCU leaders have a working-class background. "[T]he organizing of working class and poor whites can best be done by organizers from that background," they insisted. In fact, Peggy Terry had long believed the directive, "White people, go organize your own."[86] To mobilize their chosen constituency of young, working-class whites, NCU members sought to locate themselves in factories, neighborhoods, prisons, high schools, day labor agencies, and the army.[87]

Meanwhile, seeing the limits of their efforts on the local level, ERAP welfare activists concluded that a national focus would make their organizing more effective and helped to establish the NWRO. They were in attendance at the initial planning meetings for the NWRO organized by the civil rights leader George Wiley in May 1966.[88] The next month, they participated in national coordinated protests designed to advance the formation of the NWRO. Cleveland activists took part in the "Ohio Walk for Decent Welfare," a 150-mile, 10-day march to the state capital, Columbus, to dramatize Ohio's inadequate welfare program. On the day marchers arrived in Columbus, June 30, thousands of sympathizers demonstrated in sixteen cities across the country, including ERAP participants in Chicago and Newark.[89] At the first meeting of the National Coordinating Committee of Welfare Rights Groups in Chicago on August 6–7, 1966, 26 of some 140 delegates represented ERAP community organizing projects and welfare rights groups affiliated with projects.[90] By 1968 Dovie Coleman, a longtime Chicago community leader and a founder of Welfare Recipients Demand Action, served as the financial secretary for the NWRO; Marian Kidd, chair of Newark's People's Action Group Welfare Committee, became treasurer; and Boston's Doris Bland and Baltimore's Margaret McCarty sat on the NWRO's National Coordinating Committee.[91] In 1969 the NWRO had a membership of twenty-two thousand active in over five hundred welfare rights groups. In this way, ERAP contributed to building an interracial movement of the poor, specifically, a mass movement of poor *women*.[92]

Even as the ERAP projects were disbanding in 1967 and 1968, women organizers came to see as necessary a separate movement for women's liberation. From discussing the "woman question" and challenging male domination within the New Left, they began to set up their own, autonomous groups. Feminist groups formed at "an astounding rate" as word swept through the preexisting networks. Vivian Rothstein joined with other women to form the Chicago Women's Liberation Union, Jean Tepperman became a member of Boston's Bread and Roses, and Mimi Feingold and Judith Bernstein, who had been in Cleveland and Chicago, started groups in San Francisco and Canada, respectively. For Tepperman, "the women's movement seemed to offer opportunities to accept one's own needs as legitimate."[93] As part of the larger feminist movement, these women revolutionized the role of American women, creating greater equality and opportunity.

After struggling personally for years over how to deal with his own homosexuality and the homophobia of others within the movement, Carl Wittman became an advocate for gay liberation.[94] Once he was able to be "out" and open about his sexual orientation and identity, he was no longer simply an organizer of others; he became his own advocate. As an activist for the personal liberation and political empowerment of all gay Americans, Wittman is credited with writing the New Left's first manifesto of Gay Liberation, in which he strongly criticized white radical groups for "their anti-gay and male chauvinist patterns" and called on gays to build an identity-based movement. "To be a free territory, we must govern ourselves, set up our own institutions, defend ourselves, and use our own energies to improve our lives," he argued.[95]

For a number of organizers, the ERAP experience prompted a return to labor and working-class organizing. Although increasingly disillusioned with their allies in the labor movement following Walter Reuther's role in stymieing the Mississippi Democratic Freedom Party's challenge in Atlantic City in 1964 and the UAW's early support of Johnson's Vietnam policy, they saw merit in the focus on workers repudiated by the original ERAP strategy.[96] For Steve Goldsmith, the greater stability and bargaining power of workers and union members compared favorably to that of poor and unemployed Americans. According to Kim Moody, the contrast between community and labor organizing "was stark." In the workplace "you've got a leadership structure there," whereas "in the community there was no obvious set of leaders to go to." Jim Williams felt that trade unionism had more of a "payoff," a beginning and an end, an organizing drive, and a contract. With community organizing "it was so hard to define whether you were winning or not, so hard to get a handle on it."[97] At the same time, they could be inspired by the resurgence of black labor activity in the late 1960s, such as that of the Dodge Revolutionary Union Movement.[98]

The ERAP experience prompted others to organize around their own identities as students or college-educated professionals, an effort that explicitly rejected ERAP's understanding of organizers as only "catalysts" among the poor. Now middle-class college students were legitimate political actors in their own right. In SDS, "new working-class theory"—a theory that defined professionals in a service economy as the new working class and, therefore, granted social agency to them—rose to prominence. What one needed to be an agent of social change was radical consciousness; one need not necessarily "be hungry or unemployed or discriminated against to participate in radical political action."[99] In 1967 former ERAP activists helped to establish Radicals in the Professions, an organization dedicated to expanding the base of the New Left by defining a role for and building ties among professionals in the movement, much as Al Haber had wanted to do back in 1963. A primary aim was to bring together radicals working in the "helping professions," such as medicine, social work, and teaching.[100] Charlotte Phillips found that her participation as a doctor in Radicals in the Professions reflected "less of a missionary zeal to do what we thought was right" and "more of a long-range notion" of how to incorporate activism into one's lifespan.[101]

New political priorities led many ERAP organizers back to the student or into the antiwar movements. In the fall of 1964, while Paul Millman was in the Chicago JOIN project, "Berkeley erupted. All of a sudden, something clicked in my head that students had real issues, . . . that we didn't have to go to the communities to be involved with issues, that we had issues too." After dropping out of Antioch in 1967 and later enrolling in the New School for Social Research, he worked in the SDS regional office in New York and helped start the counterculture newspaper *RAT*.[102] Tom Hayden still was organizing in Newark when he traveled to Hanoi in December 1965. His post-Vietnam writings led to a speaking tour of college campuses, and he soon became a movement and media "star." He and Chicago organizer Rennie Davis planned and participated in the most militant antiwar demonstrations of the decade: the March on the Pentagon in 1967 and the Chicago demonstrations at the Democratic National Convention in 1968. For their involvement in the latter, the two were indicted—along with the rest of the "Chicago Eight"—on charges of conspiracy to incite a riot.[103] For some women, SDS's adoption of draft resistance as its primary antiwar strategy (along with the slogan "Girls Say Yes to Guys Who Say No") in 1966 encouraged sexism and proved alienating. Yet others, such as Vivian Rothstein, became important spokespeople in the movement, contributing to mass, popular opposition to the Vietnam War, which influenced the foreign policies of both Presidents Johnson and Richard M. Nixon.[104]

Solidarity with black and other national liberation struggles led a few former ERAP organizers to help form the revolutionary cadre Weatherman. Named after a Bob Dylan lyric about not needing "a weatherman to know which way the wind blows," Weatherman emerged in June 1969, when SDS split into rival revolutionary factions. Four leaders of Weatherman had participated in ERAP: Bill Ayers, Kathy Boudin, and Terry Robbins, all in Cleveland, and Eric Mann, from NCUP. Cathy Wilkerson had worked in Chester pre-ERAP.[105] Mann argues that what happened in NCUP "raise[d] a fundamental challenge about whether or not black people can be liberated under capitalism." "That [challenge] led a lot of us, not to the classic Marxism, but to anti-imperialist, anti racist Marxism in which . . . the interracial movement of the poor got transformed into what I call the national question."[106]

Other former organizers retreated to rural communes or found their way into the counterculture, in part as a way to meet needs unfulfilled in ERAP. "I left the movement and became a part of a commune in Vermont," David Palmer says. Feeling "overwhelmed" by political developments on the Left in the late 1960s, he spent the next "ten years outside of political activity" until the presidency of Ronald Reagan in the 1980s, when a "new Vietnam-like intervention" in Central America threatened.[107] After spending the summer of 1968 working in two factories in Chicago, Jean Tepperman returned to Boston "tired of the constraint" and "respectable look" required of organizers so they would not alienate community people. "I wasn't very politically active for a year. My goal for that year was to learn to be a hippie." Dickie Magidoff, too, found himself "sinking into the counterculture" after moving to Boston. "I had been very anti-drug, as taking away from political energy," but now "I had this vision that you build or you continue to expand and deepen a radical political culture." Although "the burnout factor" contributed, the counterculture helped Magidoff see a new way of creating social change and redefine what being a "radical" meant; it no longer only meant being a full-time organizer.[108]

While the projects' many difficulties, defeats, and conflicts shaped the later activism of participants, so, too, did more positive aspects of the ERAP experience. For many women organizers, feminist consciousness evolved less from awareness of sexist treatment by men in the projects than from how they had benefited from their work in ERAP. In Cleveland, Charlotte Phillips "didn't feel [such sexism] personally."[109] Carol Glassman did not think "the men in NCUP were by design oppressing us. . . . I think they supported us a lot when we had ideas. The welfare rights stuff was pretty much done by the women, and they were very supportive of that."[110] Even in Chicago, men worked to counter sexism and empower women in the movement. When Rich Rothstein was offered the opportunity to travel to Vietnam, he encouraged his wife, Vivian, to go instead, knowing that the trip would establish her "legitimacy" as an antiwar activist.[111] The considerable confidence, organizing skills, and "intellectual ammunition" women gained in ERAP were also a positive legacy that underlay the formation of the women's liberation movement.[112]

Interacting with community women further shaped the consciousness of at least some women organizers. "We . . . were fundamentally transformed by that experience," Marilyn Katz says. It was less that they saw community women as strong or as role models, however; "I never identified with those women," Leni Zeiger Wildflower recalls. Rather it was what they, their lives, and experiences said about women's unequal position in society, although at the time not all New Left women understood this position in feminist terms. Judith Bernstein remembers, "We saw abuse, we saw beatings of women by the men . . . and we never went to that next step of seeing that as something that needed collective response." For Fran Ansley, this was the "time when I was beginning to think about this stuff." "I think there were a lot of things I didn't know yet, that the Dovies [Coleman and Thurman] knew and that Peggy [Terry] knew in their gut, in some way." In hindsight, Katz, too, believes that Uptown community women involved in JOIN had feminist insights. "They saw early on that every issue was a women's issue. Birth control was a woman's issue, that health care was a woman's issue, that food price and quality was a woman's issue."[113] Such ERAP experiences complicate the ostensible wholly middle-class origins of the women's liberation movement.

Both mindful of and seeking to transcend the divisions of race and class, former activists also sought to develop a coalition politics. As a leader of SNCC, Phil Hutchings kept his ties to the white New Left and believed in coalition building across race. In the fall of 1968 he proposed to SDS that white student organizers on college campuses forge working relationships with neighboring black communities and, together, fight the expansionist urban renewal policies of universities. Similarly, in her welfare rights organizing in Chicago with Welfare Recipients Demand Action, Dovie Thurman reached out to whites, blacks, and Native Americans.[114] As part of the National Community Union, white activists in Uptown advocated building coalitions based on common concerns, such as class inequality. "The way I see it," Doug Blakely, a.k.a. Youngblood, asserted, "the movement is like a wheel, with lots of different groups being the spokes."[115] Terry illustrated this commitment when she ran for vice president, together with presidential candidate Black Panther Eldridge Cleaver, on the Peace and Freedom Party ticket during the 1968 presidential elections. Her message during the campaign was that "the real struggle in the country is not a racial thing, but a class struggle, a fight by the poor to lift themselves out of poverty, by the powerless to get power."[116]

Feminists who came out of ERAP committed themselves to coalition as well. Best known for Jane, the underground feminist abortion service, the Chicago Women's Liberation Union (CWLU) supported women's strike actions in local factories and the efforts of African American "janitresses" to improve pay and working conditions at city hall. They also successfully organized a cross-class and multiracial coalition, the Action Coalition for Decent Childcare, which targeted the state to reform licensing and increase funding for day care centers in the city; they eventually secured $1,000,000 in state funding for child care.[117] Boston's Bread and Roses provided support to the Black Panthers, and member Jean Tepperman linked the women's and labor movements in her call for the "liberation" of wage-earning women in factory settings. "Those of us who had been in ERAP were anxious to find ways of organizing women that truly engaged and represented working-class women, not just middle-class women," she recalls.[118] Marilyn Katz agrees. "Those of us who worked in the ERAP projects became a different kind of feminists. . . . We always had a working-class content to the equation."[119]

Relationships forged in ERAP connected women's liberation to the welfare rights movement. The NWRO only "trumpeted [its] status as a women's movement" in 1973.[120] But a full three years before, Carol Glassman wrote an important article on women and the welfare system for the feminist anthology *Sisterhood Is Powerful*. Based on her experiences in NCUP—and as a caseworker for the Bureau of Children Services—Glassman called for feminist analysis and action around welfare. She linked the welfare system to the "larger problem of women's oppression" and saw a "potential base" for women's liberation among "welfare-rights women." Feminist activists, including ex-Cleveland organizer Carol McEldowney, also ran workshops on child care, birth control, and feminism at national NWRO conventions.[121] In addition, women welfare recipients, formerly of ERAP, raised feminist issues and asserted that "the personal is political" within the welfare rights movement. Doris Bland, a leader of Boston's MAW, asserted her right to control her sexuality and reproduction in a piece for the NWRO newspaper *NOW!* in 1966. "Ain't nobody in the world going to tell me what to do with my body," she argued, "'cause this is mine, and I treasure it."[122] Although later attempts at collaboration between feminists in the National Organization for Women and activists in NWRO, as documented by the legal historian Martha F. Davis, "foundered on the divides of class [and] race," these early efforts at coalition building mattered, reminding us that the struggle for welfare rights *was* a movement for women's liberation.[123]

In addition to commitments to coalition politics, former ERAP participants brought lessons about organization building into other social movements. In Boston in 1968, MAW members resisted the efforts of NWRO organizer Bill Pastreich to form an affiliate, the Massachusetts Welfare Rights Organization. They were reluctant to join, or to collect dues for, the NWRO, because of what they considered to be the top-down approach of both the NWRO, headed by George Wiley, and the new Massachusetts organization. "I don't understand why there are all guys running it. Wiley and Pastreich," one MAW activist stated. "Why aren't mothers running their own organization?" According to the scholar Lawrence Neil Bailis, MAW "reflected the SDS biases against hierarchy and in favor of participatory democracy."[124] Taking a different lesson about organization from ERAP, members of the CWLU developed an organizational structure unique among women's liberation groups, which incorporated changes made over time by JOIN toward accountable leadership, structured democratic participation, and well-defined criteria for membership. In a women's liberation movement wary of authoritarianism and, consequently, falling under the sway of "the tyranny of structurelessness," the CWLU was dedicated to formal structure. The CWLU's organizational structure contributed to its eight-year existence, one longer than any other women's union with similar politics.[125] That participants drew different conclusions about organization building in the projects reinforced the later utility of organizational experimentation in ERAP.

ERAP activists also incorporated community strategies into their later organizing. In 1965, during a discussion of what direction SDS's antiwar activism should take, ERAP organizers suggested, naturally, moving off campus and into communities, to "ERAPize the war." Vietnam Summer 1967, an effort modeled upon Mississippi Freedom Summer as well as ERAP, called on antiwar activists to leave campus and to organize in poor, working-class, and middle-class communities.[126] By 1967 and 1968 Nick Egleson, a veteran of the Philadelphia and Hoboken projects, was counseling potential draft resisters in Boston, Rennie Davis was encouraging community organizing around the draft, and a number of former ERAP organizers, including Davis, participated in establishing coffeehouses near military bases where GIs could gather to learn about and mobilize against the war. "Coffeehouse organizing very much borrowed from ERAP and a lot of the same people were doing it," Bill Ayers observes.[127] The student movement, too, borrowed from ERAP. In 1968, when Eric Mann became involved in the student strike at Columbia University "as an outside agitator," he contributed a new tactic: organizing the dorms door to door rather than just leafleting students on the campus quadrangle. Steve Goldsmith found that labor organizing used the same techniques. "It wasn't going door to door but now locker to locker." And Weatherman launched a number of "action projects" à la ERAP designed to organize urban working-class youth.[128]

Many New Left organizers continued with their community organizing and service after the ERAP projects disbanded. ERAP and other SDS activists, cognizant of the need for more formalized training for community organizers, established a School of Community Organization in Chicago in 1967, although it lasted only briefly.[129] In 1973 former Hazard organizer Steve Max joined the staff of the Midwest Academy, a training institution for community and citizen action organizers founded by former SDS member Heather Booth that continues to exist today. "The Midwest Academy was a coming together of," according to Max, "the politics of the New Left with the science of organizing from Alinsky."[130] After NCUP ended, several white organizers, including Carol Glassman, moved to Ironbound, a white, ethnic neighborhood in Newark's East Ward, where they continued their community organizing and established an alternative school.[131] Junius Williams also stayed on in Newark to run the Model Cities program, where he focused on building low-income housing.[132] In Chicago, Rich and Vivian Rothstein moved to Maywood, a working- and lower-middle-class neighborhood, to focus on consumer organizing, while Stan Nadel, who had been in JOIN the first summer, worked for New York's Housing Development Administration as a community organizer after graduating from college in 1966.[133]

Community leaders and residents also continued to pursue grassroots organizing in their localities as well. The Young Patriots, which grew out of the Chicago project's police brutality campaigns, briefly ran a public health clinic and a free breakfast program, and the Uptown People's Planning Coalition (UPPC), with its base of support in the low-income, Appalachian community, mobilized against urban renewal. At the time, a Chicago journalist attributed the "organizing expertise" of UPPC leaders to their work with JOIN.[134] Dovie Coleman and Dovie Thurman became involved in Voice of the People, an organization that became a redevelopment force in Uptown by rehabilitating old and building new housing. JOIN participants were credited with helping to make Uptown a stronghold of support for Mayor Harold Washington in the 1980s. "It was the coalition forged in the late '60s and early '70s that . . . brought Harold ultimately to power," argues Marilyn Katz, who was the media and press manager for the campaign.[135] Similarly, Tom Hayden believed that NCUP helped to pave the way for the election of that city's first black mayor, Kenneth Gibson.[136]

As ERAP ended, project leaders found their way into, or were hired by, local social and community agencies. Cleveland's Lillian Craig, after attracting controversy for grabbing the microphone from Sargent Shriver at a 1966 national meeting of the United Automobile Workers–sponsored Citizens' Crusade Against Poverty in protest of the event's top-down nature, initially found steady employment difficult to secure. She held a series of community-based, social service jobs until she was chosen to direct the new Near West Side Multi-Service Center in 1976. "Phenomenal" was the description applied to her accomplishments in this position.[137] Louise Gaston later worked with the Glenville Legal Aid Office, where she assisted welfare recipients and organized around welfare rights; she also sat on Mayor Carl Stokes's much-heralded Welfare Crisis Commission. By 1969 Carole King held a job as a coordinator of the Health and Welfare Task Force under the auspices of the Council of Churches of Christ of Greater Cleveland.[138] And Newark community leader Thurman Smith became director of a minority contractor's program in the city, while the Bessie Smith Community Center honored the remarkable organizing efforts of his wife during the 1960s.[139]

ERAP participants in all the cities left a community organizing legacy that lasted well beyond the decade of the 1960s. ERAP's commitment to local participatory democracy and "Let the People Decide" constituted the projects' greatest contribution. This commitment inspired and left its mark on "the backyard revolution" of the 1970s and 1980s and helped to develop a national "vocabulary" to defend local neighborhoods. "It added to the stew, the mix of American politics in mid-1960s, a rejuvenation of the idea of democracy," Bob Ross maintains.[140] Additionally, a 1976 national survey of thirty-two community organizations found that one-fifth of the organizers and leaders traced their roots to SDS and ERAP and another one-fifth to the NWRO. Along with the Civil Rights Movement and the efforts of Saul Alinsky, most prominently, these organizations provided a training ground for activists in the major community organizing networks.[141] Finally, building on Alinsky's example of organizing as a lifelong career and profession, ERAP contributed to establishing community organizing as the radical vocation ERAP planners originally had envisioned. "We created a model for how you could live your life as a full-time organizer," Vivian Rothstein says. New Left organizers, the scholar David Bouchier has commented, "now seem more and more like the unheralded vanguard of a new wave of social protest."[142]

ERAP's failures were decisive. But in the process of attempting, yet failing, to design a strategy for and build an interracial movement of the poor, and confronting, albeit unsuccessfully, differences of race, class, gender, and sexuality among themselves, New Left organizers and community members gained an awareness and a set of skills that they brought into their later activism. In this way, the participants, ideas, and lessons of ERAP "spilled over" the projects' boundaries to affect other social movements and forms of political action.[143] As a distinct, self-contained effort, ERAP was undoubtedly a failure, but the projects' effects on subsequent movements demonstrated ERAP's larger continuity and impact.

ERAP ephemera. (Courtesy of Helen Garvy.)

Conclusion

[A]lthough in retrospect the ERAP program seems to have missed
the mark very widely, it might be an even greater mistake to reject
the positive elements of that failure.　　　—Paul Potter, 1971

To follow Paul Potter's lead in assessing the meaning and
legacy of SDS's community organizing fits with the "silver-lining school"
of history, to seek out a measure of "success" in what was a clear failure.
The "common fate" of the projects was "failure by any reasonable criteria," the historian James Weinstein concludes; the sociologist Wini
Breines agrees. "ERAP was, on balance, a failure."[1] This failure raises
other questions, however. What kind of failure was it? What did it yield?
And what would have constituted success? Certainly, building a social
movement, ending poverty, achieving racial justice, or creating the new
society SDS envisioned would have meant success. But as the social movement scholars Frances Fox Piven and Richard A. Cloward contend,
"What was won must be judged by what was possible."[2] The story of
ERAP, then, is one of large defeats and small victories.

This assessment of ERAP fits with the larger history of twentieth-
century neighborhood organizing. According to the historians Neil Betten and Michael J. Austin, limited achievements have always been the
"rule" for community organizing efforts. Few resources for organizers,
conflicting interests among community residents, and external pressures created persistent difficulties, and as a result, most community
organizations were short-lived.[3] These problems were exacerbated further when community organizing involved "outsiders" coming into a
neighborhood, as had ERAP, rather than "insiders" mobilizing their
own. Given these obstacles, Saul Alinsky believed that involving even
5 percent of the population in any neighborhood was "a tremendous
democratic phenomenon." Moreover, past community struggles never

followed a linear path toward success, but instead experienced small victories and defeats along the way.[4] From this perspective, then, ERAP's failures were not unusual, nor were its accomplishments minor.

Comparing ERAP with the efforts of earlier community organizers also reminds us that New Left activists never saw community organizing as an end in itself. They entered the neighborhoods in 1963 and 1964 primarily not to ameliorate local conditions or to organize residents in their own interests, but to spark a social movement of poor Americans. In keeping with the original ERAP strategy and goals, community organizing was a means to the end of influencing politics on the national level, as part of achieving thoroughgoing social and structural change over the long run. What underlay this, as it turned out, inaccurate vision of social change was what Paul Booth called the "tidal wave theory," the belief that "the actions of a few people, due to their dramatic or radical quality, would unleash a tidal wave of supportive and sympathetic action, eventually forcing adjustments and change when the waves reached the centers of power."[5]

As a consequence, not enough New Left organizers understood or appreciated community organizing on its own terms, as the slow, undramatic, and long-term process of helping people develop their powers—even when that was exactly what they were doing.[6] Leni Zeiger Wildflower pinpoints "the discrepancy between the metatheory and what you did every day" as the aspect of organizing that "tore you up. Had we just gone in there saying we were going to help poor people, we'd have been a hell of a lot better off." They needed the broader, long-term perspective of organizers like Alinsky and the civil rights activist Ella Baker. In the end, the difficulty of reconciling what they achieved with what they had envisioned, and lack of appreciation for what community organizing is and what accomplishments it can yield contributed most to New Left organizers' sense of failure and frustration. Only later in life, looking back, did they truly recognize what had been gained from their organizing in ERAP, "because," as Zeiger Wildflower notes, "we did help poor people."[7]

The tidal wave theory of community organizing also meant that New Left participants failed to adopt a model for lifelong organizing. Most followed SNCC's example of young people "dropping out" from school or careers for a few years of full-time organizing. For those who stayed, the sense of urgency that sparked ERAP in the first place encouraged them to take on heavy workloads, labor for long hours, and demand a lot from themselves and others. Inadequate, stressful living conditions further took their toll. Jim Williams remembers, "They just kept blowing off about taking care of people's needs and stuff and I'd say, 'Look, you got to look at the long haul.' But there was none of that kind of thinking."[8] They were young, of course, but by making it difficult to integrate their work with other needs and responsibilities, ERAP failed to develop a model of organizing, like those of the settlement worker Jane Addams or Saul Alinsky, they could sustain over the long haul. Instead, their approach led to exhaustion and "burnout."

The American Left, former SDS leader Richard Flacks has argued, needed to mix "history-making" goals with everyday activities, to allow the expression of individual needs in the context of collective political action.[9] In fact, Eric Mann learned this lesson one day in Newark.

> I was going door to door, and it was Saturday, 110 degrees, . . . and I'm going to these people who are sitting out, drinking rum and Coke. And I go, "Well, you know, there's rent strikes and rats and roaches and racism." And the woman looks up and says, "Child, do you ever take a day off?" . . . It like was such an insight: you were allowed to take a day off. . . . It was realizing the long-distance runner thing, if you like this kind of work and want to do it, lighten up a little bit.[10]

Over time, other former ERAP organizers joined Mann in such realizations, as they created the lifelong radical vocations they had hoped ERAP would provide.

Yet ERAP can be credited with some successes. Like community organizing efforts before and since, the neighborhood projects concretely improved people's lives in small ways through service and welfare organizing. They also provided a set of experiences for participants—both New Left organizers and community members—that had the more intangible benefits of political and personal growth and development. As noted by none other than Karl Marx, and many others since, those who try to create social change are certain at least to change themselves.[11]

Politically, ERAP organizing confirmed the importance of having a multiplicity of visions and strategies for social change. "I no longer believe in the catechism of 'what is the right way to effect social change,'" Tom Hayden later stated, "because it usually happens in surprising ways, unexpected ways."[12] This understanding represented a rejection of the more deterministic elements of Carl Wittman and Hayden's initial strategy for ERAP and a return to the experimentation of the early

New Left. It also built on the flexibility and creativity ERAP organizers pursued in the interests of organizing from the bottom up and meeting the needs of community members. What most prompted this change in the projects' strategic direction was women's organizing. The work, insights, and demands of community and New Left women fell within a tradition of women's community organizing in the twentieth century. By doing, as had women before them, "just what needed to be done" to advance and protect the interests of their communities and families, they contributed to what was understood at the time—despite resonating with historical precedent—to be new, expanded definitions of politics and social movements that continued on past ERAP's demise.

ERAP also made its personal impact on participants. The "positive, life-altering experiences" reported by SNCC volunteers also occurred among New Left organizers. It was "a Bildungsroman-type experience for people," Oliver Fein believes.[13] By taking part in ERAP, a core group of radical activists not only gained training and experience as organizers but also an irreplaceable perspective and lasting understanding of poverty. "I don't think that we could ever forget about poverty," Vivian Rothstein noted. "It was just so profound compared to our upbringing." "You see on a daily level what people's lives are like," Corinna Fales says. "I don't think you can get it from any book, from any theory, from any schooling. I don't think you can get it any other way. And that's what I feel grateful for."[14]

For most community members, life improved in only small ways, but for a few, participation in ERAP was a transformational experience. As in SNCC, the local people in ERAP were "empowered personalities" before they even met a New Left organizer, but there is no doubt that ERAP activism "took their empowerment to another level."[15] The projects created a context in which they developed confidence, skills, and experience, and these attributes, in turn, provided a spur to political activism and a means for upward mobility. Jesse Allen, Thurman Smith, Marian Kidd, Louise Gaston, Carole King, Dovie Coleman, Dovie Thurman, Peggy Terry, and Doris Bland all continued in their work after ERAP. "You have skills that you don't know about," Lillian Craig later contended. "You can get involved in your immediate community, and then go from there." Dovie Coleman wrote of finding "freedom of mind" through organizing. "When I began to organize other people for the first time in my life I began to feel free. . . . I want other people to feel the way I do."[16]

As project leaders continued in their political and community activism, they articulated philosophies that underlay their lives and activism. Lillian Craig believed she had lived according to the maxim "We are all responsible for other people's lives. We hold their lives in our hands." She tried to be a "friend to people." "If I hadn't lived like that, I would not have meant anything to myself."[17] Dovie Thurman's myriad political experiences and strong Christian faith shaped her fundamental outlook.

> I don't even look at race anymore. Color of skin doesn't make a person good or bad. Dr. King saw that. I'm looking for the inner, not the outer. In the end we are all going to be together one way or the other. We will all be in heaven together or in hell. How are you going to get separated then? At the end, people won't win when they're separated here on earth or up there. Or down there.[18]

After the end of ERAP, Dovie Thurman and Lillian Craig remained committed to their philosophical and activist convictions. That commitment is part of ERAP's legacy.

ERAP left another legacy: a vision of political community and personal relationships based on a foundation of interdependence and trust. After the projects disbanded, New Left activists still considered ERAP to be the place where this sense of community was achieved. At one ERAP meeting, Tony Kronman, a JOIN organizer, "began to feel that I was a part of the group, and party to the spirit that developed. Whatever that spirit was (community?) it was beautiful." For David Palmer, "the most important friendship group of my life" was the organizers he worked with in Cleveland.[19] There is also a continuity in political beliefs and activities among former organizers that reveals the enduring impact of the commitment to ERAP. "The people who went through that experience, unlike people who might have passed through SDS as students, are almost all still active," Kim Moody remarks. "Maybe it's self-selecting that if you're dedicated enough to go do something kind of crazy like then you're going to stick around." "Emotionally I have faith in people if they were in ERAP," Jean Tepperman says. "I believe they're really still there."[20] Community, friendship, and shared political discovery occurred not only among New Left organizers, however. When asked what summed up "the sixties" for her, Lillian Craig responded, "Excitement. And a sense of belonging. The country music song 'May the Circle Be Unbroken' reminds me of those years."[21]

Notes

NOTES TO THE INTRODUCTION

1. Dave Strauss, interview with author, November 29, 1999.

2. Lillian Craig, "Welfare Mothers Hold Vigil against Rhodes," *Cleveland Community Project Newsletter* (November 1964), and Beulah Neal, "Rummage! Rummage!" *Cleveland Community Project Newsletter* (February 1965), SDS Records, series 2B [hereafter SDS-2B], box 24, folder 12; "This Week's Activities of Grievance Committee Members," *Welfare Grievance Committee Newsletter* (June 28, 1966), Carol McEldowney Papers, 1964–1968 [hereafter McEldowney Papers].

3. Strauss interview.

4. Payne, *I've Got the Light of Freedom.*

5. Staples, "Blaming Nixon"; Ellis, *The Dark Side of the Left*, 110.

6. On the campus New Left as a homogeneous environment, see Sara M. Evans, "Women's History and Political Theory: Toward a Feminist Approach to Public Life," in Hewitt and Lebsock, eds., *Visible Women*, 124. Andrew Barlow discusses the white student movement as being isolated from communities in "The Student Movement of the 1960s."

7. Evans, *Personal Politics*, 148–49, 154–55.

8. Simmons, *Organizing in Hard Times*, 29.

9. O'Neil, *SDS 101: From the Inside*, 6.

10. For more negative assessments of ERAP, see Isserman, *If I Had a Hammer*; Isserman, "The Not-So-Dark and Bloody Ground"; Weinstein, *Ambiguous Legacy*. For those who see ERAP mainly in a positive light, see Evans, *Personal Politics*; Wini Breines, *Community and Organization*; O'Brien, "The Development of a New Left." Other authors see community organizing as an important experiment, but do not consider it to be a good move for SDS. See, for example, Sale, *SDS*; Calvert, *Democracy from the Heart*; Potter, *A Name for Ourselves.*

NOTES TO CHAPTER 1

1. Paul Booth and Edward Greer, "A New Left Manifesto," January 28, 1968, 2, Paul Booth Papers, 1956–1970 [hereafter Booth Papers], box 1, folder 9.

2. Richard Flacks, quoted in Miller, *"Democracy Is in the Streets,"* 182.

3. Lee Webb, "National Secretary's Report, 12/63," 1, SDS Records, series 2A [hereafter SDS-2A], box 3, folder 9.

4. "Hayden Priority Proposal," [December 1963], 1, SDS-2A, box 3, folder 9.

5. Al Haber to SDS National Council, "Report of the Economic Research and Action Project, October 1 to December 15," [1963], 3, and Al Haber, paraphrased in "National Council Meeting Notes," December 1963 (handwritten), 3, SDS-2A, box 3, folder 9.

6. Bill Strickland, paraphrased in "National Council Minutes," December 1963, 2, SDS-2A, box 3, folder 9.

7. Al Haber, quoted in Miller, *"Democracy Is in the Streets,"* 34.

8. Tom Hayden, *Revolution in Mississippi,* SDS pamphlet (1962), 21; Evans, *Personal Politics,* 111.

9. Sale, *SDS,* 36.

10. Kim Moody, interview with author, November 18, 1999.

11. Carson, *In Struggle,* 27.

12. Carson, *In Struggle,* 82.

13. Payne, *I've Got the Light of Freedom,* 68.

14. Morris, *The Origins of the Civil Rights Movement,* 222–23; Miller, *"Democracy Is in the Streets,"* 103; Calvert, *Democracy from the Heart,* 282 n. 1.

15. Tom Hayden, editor's note, *SDS Bulletin* [1] (March–April 1963), 16.

16. Danny Schechter, interview with author, November 14, 1999; Miller, *"Democracy Is in the Streets,"* 186–87.

17. William Strickland to "Dear Friend," January 2, 1964, Booth Papers, box 1, folder 3.

18. Carl Wittman, "Cambridge: A Report," *SDS Bulletin* 2 (November 1963), 1, 12–13; Carson, *In Struggle,* 72, 90.

19. Nick Egleson, interview with author, November 13, 1993; Fraser, ed., *1968,* 64.

20. Hamilton and Hamilton, *The Dual Agenda,* 122–23.

21. Kelley, "Birmingham's Untouchables," 87.

22. Hamilton and Hamilton, *The Dual Agenda,* 122–23.

23. Burns, *Social Movements of the 1960s,* 19–23; Farber, *The Age of Great Dreams,* 88–89.

24. Richard Rothstein, quoted in "Chicago: JOIN Project," *Studies on the Left* 5 (summer 1965), 108; Bacciocco, *The New Left in America,* 136; Carson, *In Struggle,* 93.

25. Paul Booth and Edward Greer, "A New Left Manifesto," January 28, 1968, 3, Booth Papers, box 1, folder 9; SDS Economic Research and Action Project, "An Introductory Statement," [fall 1963], 2, SDS-2B, box 15, folder 5.

26. Sale, *SDS,* 102.

27. Miller, *"Democracy Is in the Streets,"* 28–29 and chapter 7.

28. "National Council Minutes," August 30–September 1, 1963, 10, SDS-2A, box 3, folder 8; Robb Burlage to Rennie Davis, July 21, 1964, SDS-2B, box 18, folder 3.

29. Irving Bluestone to Walter P. Reuther, January 8, 1963, Walter P. Reuther Collection [hereafter Reuther Collection], UAW President's Office, box 523, folder 13; Tom Hayden to Todd Gitlin, August 2, [1963], SDS-2B, box 16, folder 1; Levy, *The New Left and Labor in the 1960s,* 11–12, 14, 20–25; Nina Helstein and Toni Helstein, interviews with author, September 17, 2000.

30. Lichtenstein, *The Most Dangerous Man in Detroit,* 387.

31. Evans, *Personal Politics,* 112.

32. "Summarized National Council Minutes," September 1963, SDS-2A, box 3, folder 8.

33. Sharon Jeffrey, quoted in Miller, *"Democracy Is in the Streets,"* 31–32, 38, 144.

34. "National Council Minutes," August 30–September 1, 1963, 2, SDS-2A, box 3, folder 8.

35. Carl Wittman, *Students and Economic Action,* SDS pamphlet (1963), reprinted in Teodori, ed., *The New Left,* 128; Carl Wittman, "Swarthmore College," *SDS Bulletin* 2 (November 1963), 3–4, John Bancroft, interview with author, November 7, 1999.

36. Egleson interview; Carl Wittman, *Students and Economic Action,* SDS pamphlet (1963), reprinted in Teodori, ed., *The New Left,* 132–33.

37. Sale, *SDS,* 118.

38. Lee Webb, "National Secretary's Report, 12/63," 1, SDS-2A, box 3, folder 9.

39. "National Council Minutes," December 1963, 2–3, SDS-2A, box 3, folder 9.

40. Nada Chandler, "University Reform Project—Progress Report," [December 1963], 2, SDS-2A, box 3, folder 9.

41. Paul Potter, quoted in Sale, *SDS,* 84–85; Jim Monsonis, "The Brandeis University Reform Conference—A Report," *SDS Bulletin* [1] (March–April 1963), 12–13; Miller, *"Democracy Is in the Streets,"* 189.

42. *The Port Huron Statement,* SDS pamphlet (1962), reprinted in Miller, *"Democracy Is in the Streets,"* 373–74.

43. Nanc[y] Hollander to SDS Worklist, "Re: Campus Programming," December 5, 1963, and Al Haber to SDS National Council, "Report of the Economic Research and Action Project, October 1 to December 15," [1963], 2, SDS-2A, box 3, folder 9.

44. "National Council Minutes," December 1963, 3, SDS-2A, box 3, folder 9.

45. Joe Chabot, paraphrased in "National Council Minutes," December 1963, 5, SDS-2A, box 3, folder 9.

46. Lee Webb, "National Secretary's Report, 12/63," 1, SDS-2A, box 3, folder 9; Hayden, *Reunion*, 106, 110–11; Sale, *SDS*, 97.

47. Sharon Jeffrey, quoted in Miller, *"Democracy Is in the Streets,"* 184.

48. Miller, *"Democracy Is in the Streets,"* 51, 98, 145–47; Nick Egleson, paraphrased in "National Council Minutes," December 1963, 4, SDS-2A, box 3, folder 9.

49. Al Haber, paraphrased in "National Council Minutes," December 1963, 7, SDS-2A, box 3, folder 9; Al Haber, quoted in Sale, *SDS*, 107.

50. "National Council Minutes," December 1963, 4, SDS-2A, box 3, folder 9; Moody interview; Sale, *SDS*, 25–26; Flacks, *Making History*, 205.

51. Tom Hayden, paraphrased in "National Council Minutes," December 1963, 7, and "National Council Meeting Notes," December 1963 (handwritten), 1, SDS-2A, box 3, folder 9; Carson, *In Struggle*, 176.

52. Sharon Jeffrey, quoted in Miller, *"Democracy Is in the Streets,"* 54.

53. Sale, *SDS*, 129; Isserman, *If I Had a Hammer*, 214–15; Weinstein, *Ambiguous Legacy*, 130–31.

54. Al Haber, paraphrased in "National Council Meeting Notes," December 1963 (handwritten), 2, SDS-2A, box 3, folder 9.

55. Al Haber to SDS National Council, "Report of the Economic Research and Action Project, October 1 to December 15," [1963], 2, SDS-2A, box 3, folder 9.

56. Miller, *"Democracy Is in the Streets,"* 23, 30; Sale, *SDS*, 110.

57. Tom Hayden, paraphrased in Sale, *SDS*, 107.

58. Al Haber, paraphrased in "National Council Meeting Notes," December 1963 (handwritten), 2, SDS-2A, box 3, folder 9.

59. Hayden, *Reunion*, 125; Sharon Jeffrey, quoted in Miller, *"Democracy Is in the Streets,"* 191.

60. Oliver Fein, interview 1 with author, December 1, 1993.

61. Tom Hayden, editor's note, *SDS Bulletin* [1] (March–April 1963), 16; Al Haber, paraphrased in "National Council Meeting Notes," December 1963 (handwritten), 2, SDS-2A, box 3, folder 9.

62. "National Council Minutes," December 1963, 7, SDS-2A, box 3, folder 9.

63. Egleson interview.

64. Strauss interview.

65. Hayden, *Reunion*, 106.

66. Sharon Jeffrey, quoted in Miller, *"Democracy Is in the Streets,"* 187.

67. Rennie Davis, "Introduction," [1964], 3, SDS-2B, box 18, folder 2.

68. Hayden, *Reunion*, 106; Calvert, *Democracy from the Heart*, 228.

69. Carson, *In Struggle*, 175; Sarah Murphy, interview with author, November 24, 1999.

70. "National Council Minutes," December 1963, SDS-2A, box 3, folder 9.

71. Evans, *Personal Politics*, 112–13; Gitlin, *The Sixties*, 367.

72. Judith Bernstein, interview with author, November 14, 1999; Helen Garvy to Rennie Davis, January 5, [1965], SDS-2B, box 15, folder 11.

73. Evaluation, quoted in Evans, *Personal Politics*, 114, 116–20; Klatch, *A Generation Divided*, 177.

74. Carol Glassman, interview 1 with author, August 7, 1993; Murphy interview.

75. Richard Flacks, quoted in Evans, *Personal Politics*, 114.

76. Sale, *SDS*, 111; Breines, *Community and Organization*, 132; Fein interview 1.

77. Steve Max, "Correspondence," *SDS Bulletin* 2 (July 1964), 34.

78. Tom Hayden, paraphrased in "National Council Meeting Notes," April 1964 (handwritten), 31, SDS-2A, box 3, folder 10; Sale, *SDS*, 110–11.

79. Aronowitz, "When the New Left Was New," 23.

80. Moody and Murphy interviews; Jim Williams, interview with author, December 6, 1999.

81. "Convention Speaks on Community Organizing," *SDS Bulletin* 2 (July 1964), 18; Richard Flacks, "Letters on SDS," *SDS Bulletin* 3 (February 1965), 4; Michael Ansara, interview with author, November 23, 1999.

82. Stan Nadel, interview with author, November 3, 1999.

83. "Hayden Priority Proposal" [December 1963] and "National Council Minutes," December 1963, 9, SDS-2A, box 3, folder 9.

84. Jim Williams, "Reflections of a Southern Hillbilly SDSer," *SDS Bulletin* 2 (May 1964), 18.

85. Williams interview.

86. Isserman, *If I Had a Hammer*, 217.

87. Morrison and Morrison, *From Camelot to Kent State*, 225–33.

88. Steve Max, quoted in Evans, *Personal Politics*, 138.

89. Sharon Jeffrey, quoted in Miller, *"Democracy Is in the Streets,"* 192.

90. Sara Evans and Maurice Isserman dispute this point. Evans, *Personal Politics*, 154; Isserman, "The Not-So-Dark and Bloody Ground," 1002–3.

91. Marya Levenson, quoted in Evans, *Personal Politics*, 143.

92. Evans, *Personal Politics*, 138.

93. Berman, *A Tale of Two Utopias*, 57.

94. Williams interview; Sale, *SDS*, 95–96.

95. Fisher and Romanofsky, eds., *Community Organization for Urban Social Change*, xvii.

96. Rennie Davis to Steve Max, May 19, 1964, SDS-2B, box 15, folder 10; Boyte, *The Backyard Revolution*.

97. Fisher, *Let the People Decide*, 109.

98. Rayna Rapp, "Family and Class in Contemporary America," in Kling and Posner, eds., *Dilemmas of Activism*, 91–112.

99. Payne, *I've Got the Light of Freedom*, 101, 68.

100. Bernstein interview.

101. Ken McEldowney, interview with author, August 11, 1993; Gosse, *Where the Boys Are*, 255.

102. Carl Wittman, *Students and Economic Action*, SDS pamphlet (1963), reprinted in Teodori, ed., *The New Left*, 129.

103. Casey Hayden, personal communication with author, November 21, 1999; Vivian Rothstein, interview 1 with author, February 16, 1993.

104. Rennie Davis to Ed Rovner, July 21, 1964, SDS-2B, box 16, folder 3; Strauss interview.

105. Sale, *SDS*, 108–9.

106. Richard Flacks, quoted in Sale, *SDS*, 126.

NOTES TO CHAPTER 2

1. Carl Wittman and Tom Hayden, *An Interracial Movement of the Poor?* SDS pamphlet (n.d.), Lee D. Webb Papers, 1955–1968 [hereafter Webb Papers], box 1, folder 22; Paul Booth, interview with author, November 19, 1999; Jill Hamberg, interview with author, November 21, 1999.

2. Al Haber, paraphrased in "National Council Meeting Notes," December 1963 (handwritten), 2, SDS-2A, box 3, folder 9; Tom Kahn, "The Problem of the New Left," LID reprint from *Commentary* (July 1966), [3], Webb Papers, box 1, folder 6a.

3. Richard Rothstein, "Evolution of the ERAP Organizers," in Long, ed., *The New Left*, 276.

4. Carl Wittman and Tom Hayden, *An Interracial Movement of the Poor?* SDS pamphlet (n.d.), 1, Webb Papers, box 1, folder 22.

5. Carl Wittman and Tom Hayden, *An Interracial Movement of the Poor?* SDS pamphlet (n.d.), 1, 22, Webb Papers, box 1, folder 22; Todd Gitlin, interview with author, November 18, 1999.

6. Carl Wittman and Tom Hayden, *An Interracial Movement of the Poor?* SDS pamphlet (n.d.), 21, 25–26, Webb Papers, box 1, folder 22.

7. Carl Wittman and Tom Hayden, *An Interracial Movement of the Poor?* SDS pamphlet (n.d.), 25, Webb Papers, box 1, folder 22.

8. Paul Booth, "Prospectus for a Conference on Poverty in the United States," [1963], 1, Booth Papers, box 1, folder 1; Miller, *"Democracy Is in the Streets,"* 71, 218–19.

9. Hugh Heclo, "The Political Foundations of Antipoverty Policy," in Danziger and Weinberg, eds., *Fighting Poverty*, 320.

10. Harrington, *The Other America*, 4, 9.

11. Patterson, *America's Struggle against Poverty*, 151.

12. Paul Booth, "Prospectus for a Conference on Poverty in the United

States," [1963], 3, Booth Papers, box 1, folder 1; "Poverty in the United States," prospectus for a conference, n.d., SDS-2B, box 16, folder 8.

13. Ray Brown, *Our Crisis Economy: The End of the Boom*, SDS pamphlet (1963), 4–5, SDS-2B, box 16, folder 8; Sale, *SDS*, 99.

14. A. J. Hayes, quoted in Gilbert, *Another Chance*, 175; Weir, *Politics and Jobs*, 64–67.

15. Matusow, *The Unraveling of America*, 10–11; Davies, *From Opportunity to Entitlement*.

16. Paul Booth to Marshall Windmiller, February 22, 1964, Booth Papers, box 1, folder 3.

17. Rennie Davis to Paul Booth, January 19, 1964, Booth Papers, box 1, folder 3.

18. Conference on Community Organizing for Economic Issues, "Agenda," Ann Arbor, Michigan, April 1964, 3, SDS-2B, box 15, folder 5.

19. Katznelson and Pietrykowski, "Rebuilding the American State"; Lichtenstein, *The Most Dangerous Man in Detroit*, 389, 392.

20. S. M. Miller to Al Haber, December 26, 1963, SDS-2B, box 16, folder 1.

21. Carl Wittman and Tom Hayden, *An Interracial Movement of the Poor?* SDS pamphlet (n.d.), 25, Webb Papers, box 1, folder 22.

22. This project was soon "overshadowed by efforts to apply the vision to SDS's internal functioning." Flacks, "What Happened to the New Left?" 104.

23. Robert J. Ross, "Primary Groups in Social Movements: A Memoir and Interpretation," in Myers, ed., *Toward a History of the New Left*, 162; McCartin, *Labor's Great War*, 222, 225.

24. Rennie Davis to Robb Burlage, May 2, 1964, SDS-2B, box 17, folder 3. On the New Deal liberal vision, see Brinkley, "The Antimonopoly Ideal and the Liberal State."

25. Harrington, *The Other America*, 175; Lewis, *The Children of Sanchez*, preface.

26. Harvey and Reed, "Paradigms of Poverty," 278–79.

27. Al Haber, interview with author, September 11, 2000; Al Haber to POLIT folks, November 19, 1963, SDS-2B, box 18, folder 1.

28. Carl Wittman and Tom Hayden, *An Interracial Movement of the Poor?* SDS pamphlet (n.d.), 21, Webb Papers, box 1, folder 22.

29. SDS Economic Research and Action Project, "An Introductory Statement," [fall 1963], 2, SDS-2B, box 15, folder 5.

30. Weir, *Politics and Jobs*, 70–71; Davies, *From Opportunity to Entitlement*, 239; Gillette, *Launching the War on Poverty*, 89; Noble, *Welfare as We Knew It*, 88.

31. Todd Gitlin to Richard Rothstein, *ERAP Newsletter* (November 16–23, 1964), [19].

32. Paul Booth to Mr. and Mrs. Wittman, July 17, 1963, Booth Papers, box 1, folder 1.

33. Bob Ross, interview with author, November 1, 1999; Miller, *"Democracy Is in the Streets,"* 35.

34. *The Port Huron Statement*, SDS pamphlet (1962), reprinted in Miller, *"Democracy Is in the Streets,"* 333.

35. Mc Lanahan, Sørensen, and Watson, "Sex Differences in Poverty," 103.

36. Al Haber to Paul Booth, "Poverty Conference Program Draft," November 19, 1963, SDS-2B, box 18, folder 1; "Prospectus for Conference on Poverty in America," 1964, 2–3, SDS-2B, box 15, folder 5; Al Haber, "Readings on Poverty," *ERAP Newsletter* (November 30–December 7, 1964), 13; Evans, *Personal Politics*, 140.

37. Katz, *The Undeserving Poor*, 71; Gordon, *Pitied but Not Entitled*.

38. "Philadelphia Report," *ERAP Project Report* (June 20–July 1, 1964), 5, SDS-2B, box 15, folder 5; "University of Illinois Chicago Circle SDS White Paper," SDS Records, series 3 [hereafter SDS-3], box 38, folder 9.

39. Ehrenreich, *The Hearts of Men*; Goldin, *Understanding the Gender Gap*, 10; Linden-Ward and Green, *American Women in the 1960s*, xii.

40. Office of Economic Opportunity head Sargent Shriver, quoted in Diana Pearce, "Welfare Is Not *for* Women: Why the War on Poverty Cannot Conquer the Feminization of Poverty," in Gordon, ed., *Women, the State, and Welfare*, 272; Quadagno and Fobes, "The Welfare State and the Cultural Reproduction of Gender."

41. Carson, *In Struggle*, 176; Bill Mahoney to Robb Burlage, November 21, 1963, Robb Burlage Papers, 1956–1973 [hereafter Burlage Papers], box 3, folder 20; Alex Capron, "D.C. Residents," *SDS Bulletin* 2 (February 1964), 4–5.

42. "The Triple Revolution," quoted in Miller, *"Democracy Is in the Streets,"* 192; Sale, *SDS*, 100.

43. Unger, *The Best of Intentions*, 91. David Burner calls the Left's unwillingness to define such an alternative "one of the worst failures of the period." Burner, *Making Peace with the 60s*, 11.

44. See correspondence in SDS-2B, boxes 16–17, 28–29; Sale, *SDS*, 115. For a comparison of 1964 and 1997 dollars, see Derks, ed., *The Value of a Dollar*, 2.

45. Michael Harrington, quoted in Miller, *"Democracy Is in the Streets,"* 54.

46. Ken McEldowney to "Bob, et al.," March 12, 1964, SDS-2B, box 16, folder 2; Jack Conway to "Dear Friend," November 9, 1964, SDS-2B, box 17, folder 1; W. H. Ferry, A. J. Muste, and I. F. Stone to editors, *Studies on the Left* 4 (summer 1964), 98.

47. Calvert, *Democracy from the Heart*, 106.

48. Harry C. Boyte, "The Pragmatic Ends of Popular Politics," in Calhoun, ed., *Habermas and the Public Sphere*, 349.

49. Carl Wittman and Tom Hayden, *An Interracial Movement of the Poor?* SDS pamphlet (n.d.), 24, Webb Papers, box 1, folder 22.

50. C. Wright Mills, "Letter to the New Left," in Long, ed., *The New Left*, 22.

51. Ross interview; Kim Moody and Peter Davidowicz, "Comments on Original American Scene Document," n.d., SDS-2A, box 3, folder 9; Carl Wittman and Tom Hayden, *An Interracial Movement of the Poor?* SDS pamphlet (n.d.), 18, Webb Papers, box 1, folder 22.

52. Altbach, *Student Politics in America*, 221.

53. Sale, *SDS*, 89.

54. Vivian Rothstein, interview 2 with author, February 19, 1993; Steve Goldsmith, interview with author, February 18, 1993; Jim Williams, "Reflections of a Southern Hillbilly SDSer," *SDS Bulletin* 2 (May 1964), 19.

55. Potter, *A Name for Ourselves*, 147–48; Steve Max to Rennie Davis, [spring 1964], SDS-2B, box 15, folder 10.

56. Carl Wittman and Tom Hayden, *An Interracial Movement of the Poor?* SDS pamphlet, (n.d.), 21, 8–17, Webb Papers, box 1, folder 22; Carl Wittman, *Students and Economic Action*, SDS pamphlet (1963), reprinted in Teodori, ed., *The New Left*, 128; Carson, *In Struggle*, 90–91.

57. Todd Gitlin, "The Radical Potential of the Poor," in Teodori, ed., *The New Left*, 136–49; Hayden, quoted in Sale, *SDS*, 101.

58. Young, *An Infantile Disorder?* 54; Rossinow, *The Politics of Authenticity*, 2–4.

59. Richard Rothstein to Peter Freedman, November 22, 1964, SDS-2B, box 19, folder 1.

60. Carl Wittman and Tom Hayden, *An Interracial Movement of the Poor?* SDS pamphlet (n.d.), 17, Webb Papers, box 1, folder 22; Richard Flacks, "Organizing the Unemployed: The Chicago Project," April 7, 1964, 2, SDS-2B, box 21, folder 8.

61. Echols, "We Gotta Get Out of This Place," 16–17.

62. Breines, *Young, White, and Miserable*, 145–46.

63. Payne, *I've Got the Light of Freedom*, 266.

64. Jim Williams, "Notes on the Port Huron Statement," *SDS Bulletin* [1] (March–April 1963), 12.

65. Gitlin, "From Universality to Difference," 30.

66. Carl Wittman and Tom Hayden, *An Interracial Movement of the Poor?* SDS pamphlet (n.d.), 22, Webb Papers, box 1, folder 22; Potter, *A Name for Ourselves*, 144.

67. "Prospectus for Conference on Poverty in America," 1964, 2, SDS-2B, box 15, folder 5. In ERAP publications, the term "class" tended to denote an income or social status derived from wealth rather than from the relations and forces of production.

68. Carl Wittman and Tom Hayden, *An Interracial Movement of the Poor?*

SDS pamphlet (n.d.), 8, Webb Papers, box 1, folder 22; Cavallo, *A Fiction of the Past*, 236; Booth interview.

69. Fisher, *Let the People Decide*, 98; Breines, *Community and Organization*, 143; Bob Moses, quoted in Hodgson, *America in Our Time*, 207.

70. Richard Rothstein, "A Short History of ERAP," *SDS Bulletin* 4 [November 1965], special 3; Kazin, *The Populist Persuasion*, 198.

71. ERAP brochure (summer 1964), SDS-2B, box 15, folder 5.

72. Strauss interview; David Palmer, interview with author, September 9, 2000; Withorn, "To Serve the People," 345.

73. Cohen, *When the Old Left Was Young*, 267.

74. Richard Rothstein, "A Short History of ERAP," *SDS Bulletin* 4 [November 1965], special 1; Sale, *SDS*, 122–23.

75. Withorn, "To Serve the People," 307; Evans, *Personal Politics*, 112; SDS membership list for Pine Hill Convention, June 1964, and ERAP Institute attendance list, 1965, SDS-2A, box 4, folder 1.

76. Carl Wittman, *Students and Economic Action*, SDS pamphlet (1963), reprinted in Teodori, ed., *The New Left*, 129; Carl Wittman and Tom Hayden, *An Interracial Movement of the Poor?* SDS pamphlet (n.d.), 23, Webb Papers, box 1, folder 22.

77. Cohen, *When the Old Left Was Young*, 201; Booth interview; Tom Hayden, quoted in Sale, *SDS*, 101.

78. Anonymous ERAP organizer, February 1965, quoted in Richard Rothstein, "A Short History of ERAP," *SDS Bulletin* 4 [November 1965], special 5.

79. Epstein, *Political Protest and Cultural Revolution*, 36.

80. Todd Gitlin, "President's Report," *SDS Bulletin* 2 (April 1964), 3; Ehrenreich, *The Hearts of Men*.

81. Findley, "Tom Hayden," 36–50; Breines, *Community and Organization*, 129.

82. Breines, *Young, White, and Miserable*, 31; Evans, *Personal Politics*, 108.

83. Breines, *Young, White, and Miserable*, 74; Evans, *Personal Politics*, 20–23; Linden-Ward and Green, *American Women in the 1960s*, xii, 91–93; Goldin, *Understanding the Gender Gap*, 13.

84. Sharon Jeffrey, quoted in Miller, *"Democracy Is in the Streets,"* 184; Rothstein interview 1.

85. Glassman interview 1.

86. Rothstein interview 1.

87. McAdam, *Freedom Summer*, 57–58.

88. "ERAP: An Introduction," n.d., 2, SDS-2B, box 18, folder 2; Al Haber to POLIT folks, November 19, 1963, SDS-2B, box 18, folder 1.

89. SDS brochure [1966], SDS-3, box 46, folder 1; Carl Wittman and Tom Hayden, *An Interracial Movement of the Poor?* SDS pamphlet (n.d.), 15, Webb Papers, box 1, folder 22; Mattson, *Creating a Democratic Public*, 4.

90. Epstein, *Political Protest and Cultural Revolution*, 36.

91. "National Council Minutes," December 1963, 6, SDS-2A, box 3, folder 9; Carl Wittman and Tom Hayden, *An Interracial Movement of the Poor?* SDS pamphlet (n.d.), 17, Webb Papers, box 1, folder 22.

92. Rosenzweig, "Organizing the Unemployed," 40–41, 49; Leab, "'United We Eat,'" 305, 309.

93. George Brosi to Daniel Brower, July 6, 1964, SDS-2B, box 18, folder 4; "An Historical Perspective," *ERAP Project Report* (July 1–10, 1964), [16]; Rennie Davis, "ERAP Projects: Toward an Interracial Movement of the Poor," *SDS Bulletin* 2 (June 1964), 19; Nadel interview.

94. *What Is JOIN?* pamphlet [1964], SDS-2B, box 19, folder 7.

95. "Staff Needs for Chicago," April 12, 1964, SDS-2A, box 3, folder 10. Rennie Davis repeated the need for "a girl to handle office work" in a letter to Joe Chabot, April 19, 1964, SDS-2B, box 19, folder 1.

96. Bookman and Morgen, eds., *Women and the Politics of Empowerment*, 3–29.

97. Carl Wittman and Tom Hayden, *An Interracial Movement of the Poor?* SDS pamphlet (n.d.), 15–16, 20, Webb Papers, box 1, folder 22.

98. Fran Ansley, interview with author, December 9, 1999; Williams interview.

99. Al Haber, "The National Council. A Reply to the President's Report," *SDS Bulletin* 2 (March 1964), 23–24; Jeremy Brecher to Rennie Davis, March 2, 1964, SDS-2B, box 15, folder 6.

100. Steve Max, quoted in Sale, *SDS*, 104; Steve Max, interview with author, November 23, 1999.

101. Letter to Rennie Davis, February 27, [1964], SDS-2A, box 5, folder 3; Jim Williams, "Reflections of a Southern Hillbilly SDSer," *SDS Bulletin* 2 (May 1964), 19.

102. Peter Freedman to Richard Rothstein, November 25, 1964, SDS-2B, box 19, folder 1; Newfield, *A Prophetic Minority*, 138.

103. Kim Moody, "Thoughts on Organizing 'Poor Whites'" [1964], 1, SDS-2B, box 22, folder 13.

104. Rennie Davis, quoted in Sale, *SDS*, 110; Richard Flacks, "Organizing the Unemployed: The Chicago Project," April 7, 1964, SDS-2B, box 21, folder 8.

105. Potter, *A Name for Ourselves*, 149; Cavallo, *A Fiction of the Past*, 198.

106. McEldowney interview.

107. "Convention Speaks on Community Organizing," *SDS Bulletin* 2 (July 1964), 17.

108. Larry Gordon, "Chester: Model for the North," *SDS Bulletin* 2 (January 1964), 1, 17–19; "Prospectus for Summer Organizing Project in Chester, Pennsylvania," spring 1964, 3–4, SDS-2B, box 15, folder 5.

109. Carl Wittman, *Students and Economic Action*, SDS pamphlet (1963), reprinted in Teodori, ed., *The New Left*, 130; Ken McEldowney, "ERAP Report,"

SDS Bulletin 2 (April 1964), 10; C. Clark Kissinger, "1964 Convention Summary," *SDS Bulletin* 2 (July 1964), 32.

110. James O'Connor, "Towards a Theory of Community Unions," *Studies on the Left* 4 (spring 1964), 146. See also his "Towards a Theory of Community Unions II," *Studies on the Left* 4 (summer 1964), 99–102.

111. Flug, "Organized Labor and the Civil Rights Movement," 328–29.

112. Peter Davidowicz to SDS National Office, December 22, 1963, SDS-2A, box 3, folder 9.

113. Booth and Ross interviews.

114. Paul Millman, interview with author, November 17, 1999.

115. Carol Glassman, ERAP application, [1964], SDS-2B, box 26, folder 6; Nadel, Ross, Max, and Moody interviews.

116. "Hazard, KY.: Committee for Miners," *Studies on the Left* 5 (summer 1965), 92–93; Steve Max, personal communication, November 22, 2000.

117. Carl Wittman to Paul Booth, February 18, 1964, SDS-2B, box 19, folder 1; Sharon Jeffrey, quoted in Miller, *"Democracy Is in the Streets,"* 190.

NOTES TO CHAPTER 3

1. Sharon Jeffrey to Steve [Max?], May 4, 1964, SDS-2B, box 24, folder 5.

2. Sharon Jeffrey, Charlotte Phillips, and Oliver Fein to project applicants, May 9, 1964, SDS-2B, box 24, folder 5.

3. Project started in 1963: Chicago; projects started in 1964: Baltimore, Boston, Chester, Cleveland, Louisville, Newark, Philadelphia, and Trenton; those started, affiliated, or inspired in 1965: Cairo (Illinois), Hoboken, New Haven, and Oakland (California). New Left community organizing projects in Buffalo, New Brunswick, Cedar Heights (Maryland), Bellefonte (Pennsylvania), Champaign (Illinois), Des Moines, Knoxville, and Minneapolis corresponded, but never formally affiliated, with ERAP.

4. Gelfand, *A Nation of Cities*, 351; Mollenkopf, *The Contested City*, 93.

5. Joanne Grant, "Students Organizing the Poor in North's Cities," *National Guardian* (n.d.), news clipping, SDS-2B, box 23, folder 10.

6. "Newark Report to ERAP Executive Committee," August 8, 1964, 3, SDS-2B, box 15, folder 5; Milton Mankoff and Richard Flacks, "The Changing Social Base of the American Student Movement," in Altbach and Laufer, eds., *The New Pilgrims*, 46.

7. Strauss, Williams, and McEldowney interviews.

8. Unnamed Boston organizer, quoted in Donald M. Stewart, "Welfare and the Politics of Protest," May 1969, 18, Massachusetts Welfare Rights Organization Records, 1968–1972 [hereafter MWRO Records], box 4, folder 14.

9. Kathy Boudin, personal communication with author, January 31, 2000.

10. Community worker, quoted in Harwood, "Work and Community among Urban Newcomers," 118.

11. Corinna Fales, interview with author, November 13, 1999; Max interview.

12. Carson, *In Struggle*, 81; "Recipes for a Semi-Starvation Diet," n.d., SDS-2B, box 29, folder 2; Millman and Fales interviews.

13. Miller, *The Hippies and American Values*, 10, 88, 94.

14. Carol Glassman, ERAP application, [1964], SDS-2B, box 26, folder 6.

15. Evans, *Personal Politics*, 168.

16. "Report from the Cleveland Community Project," June 20–28, 1964, 1, SDS-2B, box 15, folder 5; Miller, *"Democracy Is in the Streets,"* 198; Gerwin, "The End of Coalition," 86.

17. Carl Wittman to Jill Hamberg, May 19, 1964, SDS-2B, box 23, folder 9.

18. Strauss interview.

19. Lee Webb, quoted in Sale, *SDS*, 108.

20. Hayden, *Reunion*, 123; Tom Hayden, quoted in Sale, *SDS*, 101.

21. Rabinowitz, *They Must Be Represented*, 35, 51; Stott, *Documentary Expression*, 8, 20–21, 30, 52.

22. Denning, *The Cultural Front*, 281.

23. Gitlin interview; Gitlin and Hollander, *Uptown*; D. Gorton, interview with author, September 11, 2000.

24. Sharon Jeffrey, paraphrased in "National Council Minutes," April 1964, 62, SDS-2A, box 3, folder 10; "Report from the Cleveland Community Project," June 20–28, 1964, 6, SDS-2B, box 15, folder 5.

25. Lee Webb, "Chicago," *SDS Bulletin* 2 (June 1964), 21–22; Nadel and Toni Helstein interviews.

26. Richard Rothstein, quoted in "Chicago: JOIN Project," *Studies on the Left* 5 (summer 1965), 108–9.

27. "Living in Poverty," *Wall Street Journal* (October 3, 1967), news clipping, Webb Papers, box 6, folder 22; Jones, *The Dispossessed*; Durr, "When Southern Politics Came North," 309.

28. Larry Bennett, "Postwar Redevelopment in Chicago: The Declining Politics of Party and the Rise of Neighborhood Politics," in Squires, ed., *Unequal Partnerships*, 163–64.

29. Gelfand, *A Nation of Cities*, 352–53; Teaford, *Cities of the Heartland*, 232–33, 235.

30. Chicago Fact Book Consortium, ed., *Local Community Factbook: Chicago Metropolitan Area*, 1980; Richard Rothstein to Peter Freedman, November 22, 1964, SDS-2B, box 19, folder 1.

31. Anne Thureson to Advisory Committee, January 14, 1965, SDS-2B, box 19, folder 5; "JOIN Community Union: Program for 1966," February 27,

1966, 40, SDS-2B, box 21, folder 9; "Living in Poverty," *Wall Street Journal* (October 3, 1967), news clipping, Webb Papers, box 6, folder 22.

32. Southern Woman Who Is a Member of JOIN, "Unemployment," *JOIN Newsletter* (August 8–14, 1966), SDS-2B, box 20, folder 3.

33. "JOIN Community Union: Program for 1966," February 27, 1966, 5, SDS-2B, box 21, folder 9.

34. Richard Rothstein, quoted in "Chicago: JOIN Project," *Studies on the Left* 5 (summer 1965), 111–12.

35. Jack Meltzer Associates, *Uptown: A Planning Report* 1 [1962], 1; City of Chicago, Department of Urban Renewal, "Uptown Conservation Area Staff Report" (1966), 3.

36. Peter Freedman, for the JOIN staff, to Dear Friend, [1965], SDS-2B, box 19, folder 1; Junior Ball, "A Playground for the Children," *JOIN Newsletter* (May 26, 1965), SDS-2B, box 20, folder 3.

37. Isabel Green, "Playground for Children?" *JOIN Newsletter* (May 14, 1965), SDS-2B, box 20, folder 3.

38. A Man Who Lives on Kenmore, "Day Labor Agencies Get Rich While Their Workers Stay Poor," *ERAP Newsletter* (April 8, 1965), [1]; Erastis Prichard, "Ready Man Steals Our Wages," *JOIN Newsletter* (July 15, 1965), SDS-2B, box 20, folder 3.

39. Dorothy Perez, "JOIN Building Inspectors," *JOIN Newsletter* (May 14, 1965), SDS-2B, box 20, folder 3.

40. "The Police and the Spanish-Speaking," *JOIN Newsletter* (March 19, 1965), SDS-2B, box 20, folder 3.

41. Judith Bernstein, quoted in "Chicago: JOIN Project," *Studies on the Left* 5 (summer 1965), 119.

42. "Living in Poverty," *Wall Street Journal* (October 3, 1967), news clipping, Webb Papers, box 6, folder 22; Schloss, "The Uptown Community Area," 8.

43. Chicago Organizing Project, JOIN, "Article for *Moderator*," February 4, 1965, SDS-2B, box 19, folder 4; Richard Rothstein, quoted in "Chicago: JOIN Project," *Studies on the Left* 5 (summer 1965), 111.

44. Casey Hayden, quoted in "Chicago: JOIN Project," *Studies on the Left* 5 (summer 1965), 116–17.

45. Guy, "The Media, the Police, and Southern White Migrant Identity."

46. Arnold R. Hirsch, "Chicago: The Cook County Democratic Organization and the Dilemma of Race, 1931–1987," in Bernard, ed., *Snowbelt Cities*, 79.

47. Peggy Terry, quoted in Terkel, *Race*, 52–53.

48. "National Council Minutes," December 1963, 6, SDS-2A, box 3, folder 9; Sale, *SDS*, 99.

49. "Newark," *SDS Bulletin* 2 (June 1964), 25; Aronowitz, "When the New Left Was New," 22–23.

50. Gerwin, "The End of Coalition," 135; "Team of 13 Students Busy in

Clinton Hill Jobs Drive," *Newark Evening News* (July 7, 1964), news clipping, SDS-2B, box 23, folder 10.

51. "Prospectus for a Newark Organizing-Research Project," [spring 1964], 1, SDS-2B, box 23, folder 9; Fisher, *Let the People Decide*, 93–94; Cunningham, *Newark*, 312.

52. Untitled Prospectus for Newark Project, [1964], 2, SDS-2B, box 23, folder 16; Wright, *Ready to Riot*, 14; "Prospectus for a Newark Organizing-Research Project," [spring 1964], 1, SDS-2B, box 23, folder 9.

53. Hayden, *Reunion*, 127.

54. Betty Moore, "Conference Reactions," *ERAP Newsletter* (March 4, 1965), [1].

55. Wright, *Ready to Riot*, 47, 49.

56. Carl Wittman, Harriet Stulman, and Jenny Roper, "Report on the Newark Project," *ERAP Project Report* (July 1–10, 1964), [3–4].

57. Harold Kaplan, "Urban Renewal in Newark," in Wilson, ed., *Urban Renewal*, 233; Tom Hayden, "Organizing the Poor," n.d., 2, SDS-2B, box 16, folder 6; Herbert J. Gans, "The Failure of Urban Renewal: A Critique and Some Proposals," in Bellush and Hausknecht, eds., *Urban Renewal*, 467–84.

58. Raymond A. Mohl, "Shifting Patterns of American Urban Policy since 1900," in Hirsch and Mohl, eds., *Urban Policy in Twentieth Century America*, 16; Douglas, "Reform in Newark," 104; Wright, *Ready to Riot*, 47–49.

59. Wright, *Ready to Riot*, 47; "If You Live in This Area, You're in Trouble," leaflet, *ERAP Newsletter* (January 7, 1965), [12]; resident, quoted in *We Got to Live Here*.

60. Linda Greenberg, *Monograph on Newark City Services*, section 2: "Recreation," July 6, 1964, SDS-2B, box 23, folder 16; Carl Wittman, Harriet Stulman, and Jenny Roper, "Report on the Newark Project," *ERAP Project Report* (July 1–10, 1964), [4]; Fales interview.

61. *Let's Look at the Record!* Clinton Hill Neighborhood Council pamphlet (1963), SDS-2B, box 23, folder 14; Robert C. Wood, "The Urban Crisis since the 1960s," in Winters, ed., *Riot to Recovery*, 25.

62. Resident, quoted in *We Got to Live Here*; Thabit, "Reducing Unemployment in Newark," 1.

63. "They Like Newark; Most Clinton Hill Folk for Staying," *Newark Evening News* (August 23, 1963), news clipping, SDS-2B, box 23, folder 14; Wright, *Ready to Riot*, 47.

64. Stanley B. Winters, "Urban Renewal and Civil Rights," [1964], 11, Webb Papers, box 1, folder 23.

65. "Newark," August 31, 1964, 1, Booth Papers, box 2, folder 9.

66. Stanley B. Winters, "Urban Renewal and Civil Rights," [1964], 11–12, Webb Papers, box 1, folder 23.

67. "Newark," handwritten notes, [spring 1964], SDS-2B, box 23, folder 12.

68. Newark Community Union, "Summer Report," [1964], 2, SDS-2B, box 23, folder 16; Hayden, *Reunion*, 144.

69. Oliver Fein to Lee Webb, January 18, 1964, SDS-2B, box 24, folder 5.

70. Oliver Fein and Charlotte Phillips to Rennie Davis et al., February 16, 1964, SDS-2B, box 24, folder 5; "Cleveland: Continuation of Projects," [summer 1964], 4, SDS-2B, box 15, folder 5.

71. Steve Berkowitz to Oliver Fein, February 7, 1965, SDS-2B, box 24, folder 5.

72. City of Cleveland, Overall Economic Development Program, *Progress Report* (March 28, 1969), 1; Teaford, *Cities of the Heartland*, 235.

73. Kirby, "The Southern Exodus," 597.

74. Thomas F. Campbell, "Cleveland: The Struggle for Stability," in Bernard, ed., *Snowbelt Cities*, 111, 114, 119.

75. Regional Church Planning Office, "Planning for Protestantism on Cleveland's Near West Side," report no. 4 (April 1961), 5, Paul and Betty Younger Papers, 1951–1976 [hereafter Younger Papers], container 1, folder 1.

76. Sharon Jeffrey, "Prospectus for the Cleveland Community Project," [1964], 1, SDS-2B, box 25, folder 4; Cleveland Fundraising Prospectus, [1965], 4, SDS-2B, box 17, folder 2.

77. "Report from the Cleveland Community Project," *ERAP Project Report* (June 20–July 1, 1964), SDS-2B, box 15, folder 5.

78. Marty Ruddenstein, "The Landlords Aren't Cold," *Cleveland Community News* (December 3, 1965), McEldowney Papers; "The Near West Side," *Cleveland Community Project Newsletter* (October 1964), SDS-2B, box 24, folder 12.

79. A Tenant, "Tenants Organize in Hillbilly Heaven," *ERAP Newsletter* (May 17, 1965), 2.

80. "Report from the Cleveland Community Project," *ERAP Project Report* (July 1–10, 1964), [10–11].

81. Mimi Feingold, quoted in Evans, *Personal Politics*, 130; "Report from the Cleveland Community Project," June 20–28, 1964, 5, SDS-2B, box 15, folder 5.

82. The program name changed in 1962. Abramovitz, *Regulating the Lives of Women*, 331.

83. Paul Alden Younger, "The Vicious Circle," *Concerns for Christian Citizens* 3 (April 1963), 2, Younger Papers, container 1, folder 1; Joan Bradbury, Sharon Jeffrey, and Oliver Fein, "The Cleveland Welfare System," [August 1964], 1, SDS-2B, box 25, folder 1; Gelfand, *A Nation of Cities*, 353; Lieberman, *Shifting the Color Line*, 167.

84. David L. Alexander et al., "Neglected Children: An Investigation of Life Under the Aid to Dependent Children Program," 1963, 19, Younger Papers, container 1, folder 12.

85. "The Near West Side," *Cleveland Community Project Newsletter* (October 1964), SDS-2B, box 24, folder 12.

86. Dorothy Hammer, speech at rally, *ERAP Newsletter* (January 27, 1965), [4]; Gwendolyn Gaston, "What Do We Do?" *ERAP Newsletter* (July 31, 1965), 10.

87. Charlotte Phillips and Oliver Fein, "Cleveland," *SDS Bulletin* 2 (June 1964), 23; Sharon Jeffrey, "Prospectus for the Cleveland Community Project," [1964], 1, SDS-2B, box 25, folder 4.

88. Sharon Jeffrey, "Report of Days Activities and Talks," April 28, 1964, SDS-2B, box 24, folder 5.

89. Paul Potter to Violet M. Gunther, January 21, 196[5], SDS-2B, box 28, folder 7; Sharon Jeffrey, Charlotte Phillips, and Oliver Fein to project applicants, May 9, 1964, SDS-2B, box 24, folder 5.

90. Rose, "The Politics of Social Reform in Cleveland," 172–73; Sharon Jeffrey, "Report on Discussion," April 28, 1964, SDS-2B, box 25, folder 3; Craig, *Just a Woman*, 16, 31.

91. Oliver Fein to Lee Webb, January 18, 1964, SDS-2B, box 24, folder 5.

92. CORE Cleveland Chapter, "Background Information," n.d., Ruth Turner to Dear Friend, December 14, 1963, CORE Cleveland Chapter, "Agenda," n.d., and "An Open Letter to the Power Structure," n.d., Bonnie Gordon Papers, 1958–1969, box 1, folder 3; Rose, "The Politics of Social Reform in Cleveland," 87; Flug, "Organized Labor and the Civil Rights Movement," 325.

93. Rennie Davis to Chester Hartman, March 16, 1964, SDS-2B, box 16, folder 2; "Report from Boston," *ERAP Project Report* (July 1–10, 1964), [14–15].

94. Ansara interview.

95. Pat Hammond to Rennie Davis, November 18, 1964, SDS-2B, box 23, folder 4; "Approximate Budget and Financial Needs for SDS," [1965], Burlage Papers, box 3, folder 22.

96. "Boston," *SDS Bulletin* 2 (June 1964), 20; Boston Action Centers Prospectus, [fall 1964], SDS-2B, box 23, folder 8; Medoff and Sklar, *Streets of Hope*, 1, 7.

97. Formisano, *Boston against Busing*, 25; Brady, "City of Boston," 2.

98. Medoff and Sklar, *Streets of Hope*, 12–13; Mark I. Gelfand, "Boston: Back to the Politics of the Future," in Bernard, ed., *Snowbelt Cities*, 50.

99. Boston Action Centers Prospectus, [fall 1964], 4, SDS-2B, box 23, folder 8.

100. Boston Redevelopment Authority, Planning Department, "Housing in Boston" (July 1967), 3–9; Burke, "The Amazing BRA Story," 7–9; Medoff and Sklar, *Streets of Hope*, 17–18. Indeed, by 1964, 63 percent of families relocated under urban renewal were nonwhite. Lowe, *Cities in a Race with Time*, 207.

101. Boston Action Centers Prospectus, [fall 1964], 2, SDS-2B, box 23, folder 8.

102. Yvonne Ruelas, "A Poem for Roxbury," *ERAP Newsletter* (July 31, 1965), 6.

103. Massachusetts General Court, Joint Committee on Social Welfare, "Report" (November 1968); Massachusetts Consumers' Council, "Special Report on 'The Increasing Costs of the Necessities of Life, Notably Foods'" (February 1967).

104. *Had Us a Time,* film about the Cleveland Community Conference, February 1965, transcript, part 2, SDS-2B, box 24, folder 11.

105. "Dudley St. Report," *ERAP Newsletter* (February 5, 1965), 5; Marya Levenson to Rennie et al., May 24, 1965, SDS-2B, box 23, folder 5; Boston Redevelopment Authority and Harvard University, "A Report on the Schools of Boston" (May 1962), section 2, 68–72; Formisano, *Boston against Busing*, 37.

106. "Dudley St. Report," *ERAP Newsletter* (February 5, 1965), 6; Boston Action Centers Prospectus, [fall 1964], 4, SDS-2B, box 23, folder 8.

107. Donald M. Stewart, "Welfare and the Politics of Protest," May 1969, 45, MWRO Papers, box 4, folder 14; Lowe, *Cities in a Race with Time*, 267–68.

108. Thernstrom, *Poverty, Planning, and Politics*, 27.

109. Pat Hammond to Dear Friends, February 17, 1965, SDS-2B, box 23, folder 5; Boston Action Centers Prospectus, [fall 1964], 4–5, SDS-2B, box 23, folder 8.

110. Noel Day to Rennie Davis, March 17, 1964, SDS-2B, box 16, folder 2; Pat Hammond to Rennie Davis, November 18, 1964, SDS-2B, box 23, folder 5; Boston Action Centers Prospectus, [fall 1964], 1, SDS-2B, box 23, folder 8; Formisano, *Boston against Busing*, 11, 37.

111. Donald M. Stewart, "Welfare and the Politics of Protest," May 1969, 12–14, 45, MWRO Records, box 4, folder 14.

112. Teaford, *Cities of the Heartland*, 230.

113. Carol Glassman, interview with Bernard Goldstein, June 18, 1965, 9, Newark Community Union Project Oral History Transcripts, 1965 [hereafter NCUP Oral History Transcripts]; "Cleveland Report," quoted in Miller, *"Democracy Is in the Streets,"* 213.

114. Miller, "Saul Alinsky," 13.

115. Sidney Plotkin, "Enclave Consciousness and Neighborhood Activism," in Kling and Posner, eds., *Dilemmas of Activism*, 218–39.

116. Kaplan, "Female Consciousness and Collective Action"; Rayna Rapp, "Family and Class in Contemporary America," in Kling and Posner, eds., *Dilemmas of Activism*, 98–99.

NOTES TO CHAPTER 4

1. Daniel Schechter to Lee Webb, [fall 1963], SDS-2A, box 3, folder 9.

2. Stein, "Between Organization and Movement," 98.

3. Slayton, *Back of the Yards*, 196–98; Stein, "Between Organization and Movement," 100–101.

4. Robert Fisher and Joseph M. Kling, "Leading the People: Two Approaches to the Role of Ideology in Community Organizing," in Kling and Posner, eds., *Dilemmas of Activism*, 83–84.

5. Horwitt, *Let Them Call Me Rebel*, 525.

6. Rothstein interview 2; Helen Garvy, interview with author, November 7, 1999; Ross and Bancroft interviews.

7. Strauss interview.

8. Stein, "Between Organization and Movement," 108.

9. "Introduction to Survey," [winter 1964–65], SDS-2B, box 20, folder 7.

10. Hayden, *Reunion*, 143.

11. Pre-interview conversation with Vivian Rothstein, January 1993.

12. "Trenton Project-Housing Survey," [summer 1964], SDS-2B, box 24, folder 3.

13. "Training Institute of the Economic Research and Action Project," June 6–11, 1964, 2, SDS-2B, box 15, folder 5; project letter, quoted in John Bancroft, "The Newsletter," *ERAP Newsletter* (August 27, 1965), 6.

14. Rennie Davis to Project Directors, [June 1964], SDS-2B, box 15, folder 5; Fisher, *Let the People Decide*, 108.

15. Nanc[y] Gitlin [Hollander], ["A Day in the Life of an ERAP Organizer"], 3, Staughton Lynd Papers, 1940–1977 [hereafter Lynd Papers], box 7, folder 4; Chicago Project Survey Data, [1965], SDS-2B, box 20, folder 8.

16. Carol Glassman, interview with Bernard Goldstein, May 14, 1965, 9, NCUP Oral History Transcripts.

17. Hayden, *Reunion*, 143–44.

18. "Report from Trenton," *ERAP Project Report* (June 20–July 1, 1964), [14].

19. Moody interview.

20. Carl Wittman and Tom Hayden, "Newark," *SDS Bulletin* 3 (October 1964), 16; Jill Hamberg, interview with Bernard Goldstein, February 11, 1965, 27, NCUP Oral History Transcripts; Fales interview.

21. Jefferson and Warren, quoted in Douglas M. Davis, "Tom Hayden—The White Stokely," *New York/World Journal Tribune* (January 1, 1967), 4, news clipping, "Newark Community Union Project" Information File.

22. Oliver Fein, interview 2 with author, December 15, 1993; Chicago Organizing Project, JOIN, "Article for *Moderator*," February 4, 1965, 1, SDS-2B, box 19, folder 4.

23. Hill, ed., *Whiteness*.

24. Goldsmith interview; Zeiger Wildflower, quoted in Evans, *Personal Politics*, 139; Leni Zeiger Wildflower, interviews 1 and 2 with author, August 28 and September 20, 1993.

25. Rennie Davis, quoted in "Chicago: JOIN Project," *Studies on the Left* 5 (summer 1965), 113; Rennie Davis, interview with author, November 23, 1999.

26. Ansley interview.

27. Richard Rothstein, "A Short History of ERAP," *SDS Bulletin* 4 [November 1965], special 2; Breines, *Community and Organization*, 142–43.

28. Jean Tepperman, interview with author, December 6, 1999.

29. Eric Mann, interview with author, December 15, 1999.

30. Carol Glassman, interview with Bernard Goldstein, May 14, 1965, 2, NCUP Oral History Transcripts; woman organizer, quoted in Zeiger Wildflower interview 2.

31. McEldowney interview; Bernice Johnson Reagon, quoted in Greenberg, ed., *A Circle of Trust*, 122.

32. Ansley, Millman, and Strauss interviews.

33. Tepperman interview; Dickie Magidoff, interview with author, November 27, 1999.

34. "Report from the Cleveland Community Project," *ERAP Project Report* (July 1–10, 1964), [9]; Rothstein interview 2.

35. Cathy Wilkerson, *Rats, Washtubs, and Block Organizations,* SDS pamphlet [1964], 4–5, Webb Papers, box 1, folder 6a; Evans, *Personal Politics*, 141; Hyman, "Immigrant Women and Consumer Protest," 98; Neil Betten and Michael J. Austin, "The Cincinnati Unit Experiment, 1917–1920," in Betten and Austin, eds., *The Roots of Community Organizing*, 39.

36. Milton Mankoff and Richard Flacks, "The Changing Social Base of the American Student Movement," in Altbach and Laufer, eds., *The New Pilgrims*, 46; Jim Williams, "Louisville," *SDS Bulletin* 2 (July 1964), 13.

37. "Newark," August 2, 1964, 2, SDS-2B, box 15, folder 5; Housing Violation Form, n.d., SDS-2B, box 20, folder 1; "Report from the Cleveland Community Project," *ERAP Project Report* (June 20–July 1, 1964), [26], SDS-2B, box 15, folder 15.

38. Seth Koven, "The Dangers of Castle-Building—Surveying the Social Survey," and Martin Bulmer, Kevin Bales, and Kathryn Kish Sklar, "Introduction," in Bulmer, Bales, and Sklar, eds., *The Social Survey in Historical Perspective*, 368–70, 42.

39. "Chicago Report," *ERAP Newsletter* (November 23–30, 1964), 1–3; Rennie Davis, "Projects: ERAP," *SDS Bulletin* 2 (February 1964), 7.

40. "Report from the Cleveland Community Project," *ERAP Project Report* (July 1–10, 1964), [9]; Seth Koven, "The Dangers of Castle-Building—Surveying the Social Survey," in Bulmer, Bales, and Sklar, eds., *The Social Survey in Historical Perspective*, 368–69.

41. Craig, *Just a Woman*, 17, 31; Rennie Davis, "Ann Arbor Report," *ERAP Newsletter* (January 20, 1965), 2.

42. "Cleveland Summer Organizing Project," April 12, 1964, SDS-2A, box 3, folder 10.

43. Stein, "Between Organization and Movement," 105.

44. Sharon Jeffrey, quoted in Miller, *"Democracy Is in the Streets,"* 199.

45. Hayden, *Reunion*, 131; Sharon Jeffrey, quoted in Evans, *Personal Politics*, 132; Evan Metcalf to Larry Gordon and Nick Egleson, *ERAP Newsletter* (July 23, 1965), [20].

46. Marilyn Katz, interview with author, December 8, 1999.

47. "Songs from Newark," *ERAP Newsletter* (February 11, 1965), [22].

48. Craig, *Just a Woman*, 11–12, 16–17.

49. Egleson and Garvy interviews.

50. Sharon Jeffrey, quoted in Miller, *"Democracy Is in the Streets,"* 203; Hazel Williams, "CUFAW," *ERAP Newsletter* (July 31, 1965), [10].

51. Dovie Thurman, quoted in Terkel, *Race*, 57.

52. Cathy Wilkerson, *Rats, Washtubs, and Block Organizations*, SDS pamphlet [1964], 4, Webb Papers, box 1, folder 6a; Rothstein interview 2.

53. Davis, *Spearheads for Reform*; Darlene Clark Hine, "The Housewives' League of Detroit: Black Women and Economic Nationalism," in Hewitt and Lebsock, eds., *Visible Women*, 223–41; Lawson and Barton, "Sex Roles in Social Movements."

54. "ERAP Staff Evaluation Questionnaire," September 1964, SDS-2B, box 25, folder 11; Cathy Wilkerson, *Rats, Washtubs, and Block Organizations*, SDS pamphlet [1964], 5, Webb Papers, box 1, folder 6a.

55. Kaplan, "Female Consciousness and Collective Action"; Bookman and Morgen, eds., *Women and the Politics of Empowerment*; McCourt, *Working Class Women and Grass Roots Politics*; Naples, *Grassroots Warriors*, 181.

56. Casey Hayden, quoted in Evans, *Personal Politics*, 145; Charlotte Fein, "Report on First Meeting of Fulton Road Cluster," November 6, 1964, 1, SDS-2B, box 25, folder 2.

57. Carol Glassman, "Women and the Welfare System," in Morgan, ed., *Sisterhood Is Powerful*, 112; Garvy interview.

58. Delgado, *Organizing the Movement*, 191; Orleck, "'We Are That Mythical Thing Called the Public'"; Giddings, *When and Where I Enter*; Milkman, ed., *Women, Work, and Protest*.

59. Moody interview; Carol Glassman, interview with Bernard Goldstein, July 2, 1965, 8, NCUP Oral History Transcripts.

60. Cathy Wilkerson, *Rats, Washtubs and Block Organizations*, SDS pamphlet [1964], 4–5, Webb Papers, box 1, folder 6a.

61. Kim Moody, "ERAP, Ideology, and Social Change," [1964–65], 2, SDS-2B, box 22, folder 13; "Chester," July 1964, 3, SDS-2B, box 15, folder 5.

62. Glenn Thureson, "Chicago Report," *ERAP Newsletter* (October 26–

November 2, 1964), [9]; Rennie Davis, quoted in "Chicago: JOIN Project," *Studies on the Left 5* (summer 1965), 113.

63. Echols, "We Gotta Get Out of This Place," 18.

64. Jill Hamberg, interview with Bernard Goldstein, April 29, 1965, 11, NCUP Oral History Transcripts; Gertrude Nickerson, quoted in Sara Davidson, "Part Mata Hari, Part Robin Hood," [1966], news clipping, Reuther Collection, Citizens' Crusade Against Poverty [hereafter CCAP], box 3, folder "Poverty/Rights Action Center 1966"; Mann interview.

65. Sharon Jeffrey to Rennie Davis, May 12, 1964, SDS-2B, box 24, folder 5; Casey Hayden and Judith Bernstein, quoted in "Chicago: JOIN Project," *Studies on the Left 5* (summer 1965), 118; Helen Garvy, "Report," January 20, 1966, Helen Garvy personal collection; Crocker, *Social Work and Social Order*, 214.

66. Ross interview.

67. Rennie Davis, "ERAP Summer . . . Unresolved Issues," *SDS Bulletin 3* (September 1964), 2; Fein interview 1; Cleveland project staff to applicant, April 23, 1965, SDS-2B, box 24, folder 6.

68. Stein, "Between Organization and Movement," 105–8.

69. Simmons, *Organizing in Hard Times*, 116.

70. Bouchier, *Radical Citizenship*, 71; Calvert, *Democracy from the Heart*, 118; Nadel interview.

71. Payne, *I've Got the Light of Freedom*, 101.

72. Casey Hayden, "Notes on Organizing Poor Southern Whites," *ERAP Newsletter* (August 27, 1965), 11; Payne, *I've Got the Light of Freedom*, 129.

73. Breines, *Community and Organization*, 57.

74. Horwitt, *Let Them Call Me Rebel*, 525; Neil Betten and Michael J. Austin, "The Conflict Approach to Community Organizing: Saul Alinsky and the CIO," in Betten and Austin, eds., *The Roots of Community Organizing*, 158.

75. Mansbridge, *Beyond Adversary Democracy*.

76. Delgado, *Beyond the Politics of Place*.

77. "Report on the Newark Project," *ERAP Project Report* (July 1–10, 1964), [5]; Pat Hammond, "Dudley St. Report," *ERAP Newsletter* (February 25, 1965), [3–4]; "Report from the Cleveland Community Project," *ERAP Project Report* (July 1–10, 1964), [12].

78. Richard Rothstein, paraphrased in Breines, *Community and Organization*, 61.

79. Carl Wittman and Tom Hayden, "Newark," *SDS Bulletin 3* (October 1964), 17; "Chicago Report," *ERAP Newsletter* (February 5, 1965), [9]; Carson, *In Struggle*, 151.

80. Newark project, quoted in Evans, *Personal Politics*, 136; Bancroft interview.

81. "Interview with Evan Metcalf," tape 44, April 19, 1969, James P.

O'Brien Collection; Casey Hayden, "Notes on Organizing Poor Southern Whites," *ERAP Newsletter* (August 27, 1965), 9.

82. Payne, *I've Got the Light of Freedom*, 71.

83. Ross interview; Neil Betten and Michael J. Austin, "The Conflict Approach to Community Organizing: Saul Alinsky and the CIO," in Betten and Austin, eds., *The Roots of Community Organizing*, 154; community participant, quoted in *Had Us a Time*, transcript, part 2, 13, SDS-2B, box 24, folder 11.

84. Fisher, *Let the People Decide*, 107; Moody interview; Rothstein interview 1; Kathy Boudin and Carol McEldowney, "Welfare Grievance Committee Training Program—An Evaluation," [April 1967], McEldowney Papers.

85. Payne, *I've Got the Light of Freedom*, 129.

86. Max interview.

87. Richard Rothstein, quoted in Breines, *Community and Organization*, 142.

88. Richard Rothstein, "A Short History of ERAP," *SDS Bulletin* 4 [November 1965], special 3; Mann interview.

89. Carson, *In Struggle*, 177.

90. Moody interview.

91. Richard Rothstein, "Chicago Report: JOIN's History and Structure," *ERAP Newsletter* (October 5, 1965), 16; Marya Levenson to Members of MAW, *ERAP Newsletter* (January 17, 1966), 3–4; Casey Hayden, "Notes on Organizing Poor Southern Whites," *ERAP Newsletter* (August 27, 1965), 9.

92. Sharon Jeffrey, quoted in Miller, *"Democracy Is in the Streets,"* 203.

93. Naples, *Community Activism and Feminist Politics*, 341.

94. "Cleveland Report," July 23, 1964, 5, SDS-2B, box 15, folder 5; Pope, *Biting the Hand*, 43.

95. Jill Hamberg, pre-interview conversation with author, July 1993; Delgado, *Organizing the Movement*, 192–93.

96. Payne, *I've Got the Light of Freedom*, 268; Robnett, *How Long? How Long?* 120.

97. Dovie Thurman, quoted in Terkel, *Race*, 58.

98. Craig, *Just a Woman*, 19; Mendel-Reyes, *Reclaiming Democracy*, 121.

99. Phillips, *Engendering Democracy*, 43.

100. Mrs. Ellis, paraphrased in Charlotte Fein, "Report on Second Meeting of Fulton Road Cluster," November 16, 1964, 1, SDS-2B, box 25, folder 2; Booth interview.

101. Carol Glassman, interview with Bernard Goldstein, June 18, 1965, 7, NCUP Oral History Transcripts.

102. "Cleveland," August 9, 1964, 1, SDS-2B, box 15, folder 5; Miller, *"Democracy Is in the Streets,"* 204.

103. "Cleveland," *ERAP Report* (August 8–16, 1964), [10], SDS-2B, box 15, folder 5; Susie Moore, "CUFAW Fights for 100% Welfare," *ERAP News-*

letter (May 17, 1965), 3; "Proposal for an Elected Executive Committee," [1967], Vivian Rothstein personal collection.

104. Jill Hamberg, interview with Bernard Goldstein, April 1, 1965, 15, NCUP Oral History Transcripts; Richard Rothstein, quoted in Breines, *Community and Organization*, 61.

105. Richard Rothstein, "Evolution of the ERAP Organizers," in Long, ed., *The New Left*, 272–88.

106. Richard Rothstein, "Chicago Report: JOIN's History and Structure," *ERAP Newsletter* (October 5, 1965), 16–20; "Proposal for an Elected Executive Committee," [1967], Vivian Rothstein personal collection.

107. Horwitt, *Let Them Call Me Rebel*, 525; Gornick, *The Romance of American Communism*, 194–95.

108. John Mendelhoff to Rennie Davis, January 31, 1965, SDS-2B, box 23, folder 5; Carol Glassman, interview 2 with author, August 28, 1993.

109. Miller, *"Democracy Is in the Streets,"* 225.

NOTES TO CHAPTER 5

1. Eyerman and Jamison, *Social Movements*, 149.

2. "Cleveland," *ERAP Report* (August 8–16, 1964), [11], SDS-2B, box 15, folder 5; Glassman interview 1; "Philadelphia Report," *ERAP Newsletter* (October 26–November 2, 1964), [5].

3. Moody interview; Kim Moody, "Baltimore," *SDS Bulletin* 3 (October 1964); "Chicago Report," *ERAP Newsletter* (October 19–29, 1964), [1–3].

4. "Philadelphia Report," *ERAP Newsletter* (October 26–November 2, 1964), [5]; George Graham to Richard Rothstein, "Correspondence," *ERAP Newsletter* (February 11, 1965), [18]; Mike Zweig, quoted in Gerwin, "The End of Coalition," 97.

5. John Herling, "Unions Plan Difficult Job: Organizing the Unemployed," *[Philadelphia] Evening Bulletin* (May 18, 1964), news clipping, Booth Papers, box 3, folder 8.

6. Lee Webb, quoted in Sale, *SDS*, 134; Paul Potter, *A Name for Ourselves*, 145; Weir, *Politics and Jobs*, 92; Matusow, *The Unraveling of America*, 178.

7. Connie Brown, interview with author, November 19, 1993; "Meeting of the Economic Committee of the National Council," January 16, 1964, Ann Arbor, SDS-2B, box 15, folder 4.

8. Richard Flacks, "The Unemployed," correspondence between Flacks and Rennie Davis, *SDS Bulletin* 3 (November–December 1964), 6–7; Jim Williams and Steve Max, "The New Congress: An Appraisal," *SDS Bulletin* 3 (February 1965), 2, 15.

9. Katznelson, *City Trenches*, 6; Gerwin, "The End of Coalition," 111–12; Hayden, *Reunion*, 131.

10. Weir, *Politics and Jobs*, 9, 46, 93; Davies, *From Opportunity to Entitlement*, 9.

11. Katznelson and Pietrykowski, "Rebuilding the American State," 306; Weir, *Politics and Jobs*, 98; Davies, *From Opportunity to Entitlement*, 242.

12. Todd Gitlin to Rennie Davis, July 9, 1964, SDS-2B, box 19, folder 1.

13. Potter, *A Name for Ourselves*, 146; Moody interview.

14. Richard Flacks, "Organizing the Unemployed: The Chicago Project," April 7, 1964, 1, SDS-2B, box 21, folder 8.

15. This use of "lumpenproletariat" later was criticized by others who saw it as a misreading of Marx, who reserved the term for deviant and criminal elements. Piven and Cloward, *Poor People's Movements*, xxiv; Mann and Tepperman interviews.

16. Nadel interview.

17. Richard Rothstein, paraphrased in "Ann Arbor Report," *ERAP Newsletter* (November 16–23, 1964), 2.

18. Steve Max, "Words, Butter, No Parsnips: Remarks on the Nature of Community Political Organization," *SDS Bulletin* 2 (May 1964), 19–21.

19. Kim Moody, "ERAP, Ideology, and Social Change," [1964–65], 2, SDS-2B, box 22, folder 13.

20. Baker, "The Domestication of Politics"; Gosse, "'To Organize in Every Neighborhood,'" 114.

21. "Report from the Cleveland Community Project," *ERAP Project Report* (July 1–10, 1964), [10].

22. "Report from the Cleveland Community Project," *ERAP Project Report* (July 1–10, 1964), [12]; "Cleveland Report," July 23, 1964, 3, SDS-2B, box 15, folder 5.

23. Carl Wittman, paraphrased in "Ann Arbor Report," *ERAP Newsletter* (November 16–23, 1964), 3.

24. Sidney Plotkin, "Enclave Consciousness and Neighborhood Activism," in Kling and Posner, eds., *Dilemmas of Activism*, 227.

25. Hayden, *Reunion*, 134.

26. Iva Pearce, "Playground," *ERAP Newsletter* (July 17, 1965), 8; Mercer-Jackson Tenants Council to Dear Sir, [1964], SDS-2B, box 24, folder 2; "Remove the Hulks!" SDS-2B, box 20, folder 1; "Where Do the Kids in Glenville Play?" *The Drummer* (October 11, 1965), news clipping, SDS-2B, box 25, folder 3; Junior Ball, "A Playground for the Children," *JOIN Newsletter* (May 26, 1965), SDS-2B, box 20, folder 3; "The Traffic Light Mystery," *Newark Community Union News* (October 12, 1965), SDS-2B, box 23, folder 1.

27. Castells, *The City and the Grassroots*.

28. [Paul Potter], "Thoughts on Power Structures and Diamond Cutting," n.d., 11, SDS-2B, box 17, folder 8; Fein interview 2.

29. Joseph A. Spencer, "Tenant Organization and Housing Reform in New

York City: The Citywide Tenants' Council, 1936–1943," in Fisher and Romanofsky, eds., *Community Organization*, 138–39.

30. Larry Gordon, "Newark," July 24, 1964, 2, SDS-2B, box 15, folder 5; Carl Wittman, Harriet Stulman, and Jenny Roper, "Report on the Newark Project," *ERAP Project Report* (July 1–10, 1964), [4].

31. "Newark," *ERAP Report* (August 8–16, 1964), [7]; Stanley Aronowitz, "New York City: After the Rent Strikes," *Studies on the Left* 5 (winter 1965), 85–86. Because rent strikes were not legally sanctioned in New Jersey, as they were in New York, NCUP had less success with this strategy than did the Harlem rent strikers.

32. Nelson, "Client Evaluations of Social Programs," 37–39; Mann, *Micro-Politics*, 27.

33. Casey Hayden, "Notes on Organizing Poor Southern Whites," *ERAP Newsletter* (August 27, 1965), 8.

34. Evan Metcalf, "Personal Notes on Alienation Organizing," *ERAP Newsletter* (July 23, 1965), [23].

35. Carl Wittman, Harriet Stulman, and Jenny Roper, "Report on the Newark Project," *ERAP Project Report* (July 1–10, 1964), [4]; Casey Hayden, quoted in "Chicago: JOIN Project," *Studies on the Left* 5 (summer 1965), 117.

36. Glassman interview 2.

37. Casey Hayden, "Notes on Organizing Poor Southern Whites," *ERAP Newsletter* (August 27, 1965), 9; Payne, *I've Got the Light of Freedom*, 68.

38. Lawrence Witmer and Gibson Winter, "Strategies of Power in Community Organizations," March 21, 1968, West Side Federation (Chicago, Ill.) Records, 1966–1968, 44.

39. Robert Fisher and Joseph M. Kling, "Leading the People: Two Approaches to the Role of Ideology in Community Organizing," in Kling and Posner, eds., *Dilemmas of Activism*, 36; Gosse, "'To Organize in Every Neighborhood,'" 127–29.

40. Dickie Magidoff to "CCPniks," November 29, 1964, SDS-2B, box 24, folder 5.

41. "Chicago, Illinois," *ERAP Newsletter* (February 1964), 7; JOIN leaflets, SDS-2B, box 19, folder 7.

42. Arnold R. Hirsch, "Chicago: The Cook County Democratic Organization and the Dilemma of Race, 1931–1987," in Bernard, ed., *Snowbelt Cities*, 63–90; Glenn Thureson, "Chicago Report," *ERAP Newsletter* (October 26–November 2, 1964), [9]; Bob Ross, "The Poverty of Influence and Low Income Supporters of the Chicago Machine," March 1965, 8, Webb Papers, box 1, folder 5.

43. Withorn, *Serving the People*, 3–5, 21–22; Ehrenreich, *The Altruistic Imagination*, 160.

44. Carl Wittman to Paul Booth, February 18, 1964, SDS-2B, box 19, folder 1; Withorn, *Serving the People*, 57.

45. "An Evaluation of the Trenton Project," [1964], SDS-2B, box 24, folder 2; "Welfare Organizing—Some Questions," [1966], and Kathy Boudin and Carol McEldowney, "Welfare Grievance Committee Training Program—An Evaluation," [April 1967], McEldowney Papers.

46. "Training Institute of the Economic Research and Action Project," June 6–11, 1964, SDS-2B, box 15, folder 5; Pat Hammond, "Dudley St. Report," *ERAP Newsletter* (February 25, 1965), [3].

47. Withorn, *Serving the People*, 21–22; McCarthy, ed., *Lady Bountiful Revisited*.

48. Richard Rothstein, quoted in Withorn, *Serving the People*, 57; "To Change a City!" School of Community Organization, [1966], Booth Papers, box 2, folder 5; Walkowitz, *Social Workers and the Politics of Middle-Class Identity*; "Agenda for JOIN Retreat," October [1966?], SDS-2B, box 20, folder 6.

49. Lillian Craig to Judy, [spring 1965], SDS-2B, box 24, folder 7.

50. Ross interview.

51. William Wingell, "Student Project to Aid the Jobless," *Presbyterian Life* (October 1, 1961), 9, news clipping, SDS-2B, box 19, folder 6; Glenn Thureson, "Chicago Report," *ERAP Newsletter* (October 26–November 2, 1964), [9]; Millman interview.

52. Richard Rothstein, quoted in "Chicago JOIN Project," *Studies on the Left* (summer 1965), 122–23; "Baltimore Report," *ERAP Newsletter* (March 11, 1965), [15].

53. Withorn, "To Serve the People," 347; Cathy Wilkerson, *Rats, Washtubs, and Block Organizations*, SDS pamphlet [1964], 3, Webb Papers, box 1, folder 6a; Salem, *To Better Our World*, 253.

54. Bobby Joe Wright, quoted in Gitlin and Hollander, *Uptown*, 425; Casey Hayden, "Notes on Organizing Poor Southern Whites," *ERAP Newsletter* (August 27, 1965), 8.

55. Stanley Aronowitz, quoted in Withorn, *Serving the People*, 58; Carson, *In Struggle*, 80.

56. Margaret McCarty, quoted in "Welfare Mothers Drive Launched," *Baltimore Afro-American* (July 2, 1966), news clipping, Reuther Collection, CCAP, box 3, folder "Poverty/Rights Action Center 1966"; "Welfare Organizing—Some Questions," [1966], McEldowney Papers.

57. "Cleveland Report," July 23, 1964, 1, SDS-2B, box 15, folder 5; "JOIN Community Union: Program for 1966," February 27, 1966, 9, SDS-2B, box 21, folder 9.

58. Elaine Maramick to Pat Hammond, *ERAP Newsletter* (November 16–23, 1964), [20]; Gertrude Nickerson, quoted in Sara Davidson, "Part Mata Hari, Part Robin Hood," [1966], news clipping, Reuther Collection, CCAP, box 3, folder "Poverty/Rights Action Center 1966"; Pope, *Biting the Hand*, 43–44, 72.

59. Fundraising Proposal to the Citizens' Crusade Against Poverty, draft, n.d., SDS-2B, box 28, folder 7.

60. "Cleveland Report," July 23, 1964, 2, SDS-2B, box 15, folder 5; Cleveland Welfare Rights Movement, "Proposal for Staff Support," June 1967, Younger Papers, carton 1, folder 9.

61. "The Buying Club," and "Are You Tired of High Food Prices?" leaflets, Vivian Rothstein personal collection; Jim "Skipper" Sisk, fund-raising appeal, n.d., SDS-2B, box 19, folder 7.

62. Frank, *Purchasing Power*; Rennie Davis, "ERAP Projects: Toward an Interracial Movement of the Poor," *SDS Bulletin* 2 (June 1964), 19.

63. Delores Maxwell, "The Cleveland Children's Community," *Free Press* 1 (July 18, 1966).

64. Calvin West, Jr., "Why I Like Freedom School," n.d., John Bancroft personal collection; "The Community School," n.d., SDS-3, box 36, folder 10.

65. Bill Ayers, interview 2 with author, November 30, 1999; Silver and Silver, *An Educational War on Poverty*, 324–25.

66. "Newark Report," July 24, 1964, 1, SDS-2B, box 15, folder 5; "Talking Clinton Hill," *ERAP Newsletter* (February 11, 1965), [23].

67. "JOIN Wins Welfare Case," *JOIN Newsletter* (June 25, 1965), SDS-2B, box 20, folder 3; "The Apparatchik," *New Republic* (July 24, 1965), news clipping, SDS-2B, box 18, folder 2.

68. Nelson, "Client Evaluations of Social Programs," 37–39; Naples, *Grassroots Warriors*, 186–87; Pope, *Biting the Hand*, 43–44, 72.

69. Elvie Jordan, "The Welfare Grievance Committee," typescript of speech, n.d., McEldowney Papers.

70. Nelson, "Help-Seeking from Public Authorities," 175–92; Gordon, "What Does Welfare Regulate?" 609–30.

71. Rennie Davis, "ERAP Summer . . . Unresolved Issues," *SDS Bulletin* 3 (September 1964), 2; "JOIN Community Union: Program for 1966," February 27, 1966, 42, SDS-2B, box 21, folder 9.

72. Mann, *Micro-Politics*, 27; Robert Fisher and Joseph M. Kling, "Leading the People: Two Approaches to the Role of Ideology in Community Organizing," in Kling and Posner, eds., *Dilemmas of Activism*, 36.

73. Cruikshank, "The Will to Empower," 38; Potter, *A Name for Ourselves*, 141.

74. Donald M. Stewart, "Welfare and the Politics of Protest," May 1969, 32, MWRO Records, box 4, folder 14; Withorn, *Serving the People*, 51.

75. Connie Brown, "Cleveland: Conference of the Poor," *Studies on the Left* 5 (spring 1965), 72; Delgado, *Organizing the Movement*, 197.

76. Cruikshank, "The Will to Empower," 41, 52.

77. "Statement of a Public Assistance Mother," *ERAP Newsletter* (March 4, 1965), [7].

78. "Report from the Cleveland Community Project," *ERAP Project Report* (June 20–July 1, 1964), [27], SDS-2B, box 15, folder 5; Tom Hayden, "Welfare Liberalism and Social Change," 496.

79. Todd Gitlin, "On Organizing the Poor in America," *New Left Notes* 1 (December 23, 1966), 4; Bob Smiddie, "Cleveland West Plans a Play," *ERAP Newsletter* (August 27, 1965), 3.

80. Kim Moody, "Thoughts on Organizing 'Poor Whites,'" [1964], 2, SDS-2B, box 22, folder 13; "Report from the Cleveland Community Project," *ERAP Project Report* (June 20–July 1, 1964), [28], SDS-2B, box 15, folder 5; Bernstein interview.

81. Carl Wittman and Tom Hayden, *An Interracial Movement of the Poor?* SDS pamphlet (n.d.), 7–8, Webb Papers, box 1, folder 22.

82. Fran Ansley, quoted in Richard Hoffman, "Uptown Out to Recapture Its Sparkle," *Chicago American* (March 19, 1967), Chicago Newspaper Clipping Files; Ansley interview.

83. Cleveland ERAP, "Poverty and Community Movements," conference prospectus, December 1964, 3, SDS-2B, box 17, folder 2.

84. Payne, *I've Got the Light of Freedom*, 70–71.

85. Cleveland ERAP, "Poverty and Community Movements," conference prospectus, December 1964, SDS-2B, box 17, folder 2.

86. Mann interview.

87. Naples, *Community Activism and Feminist Politics*, 332.

88. Virginia Bowers, quoted in Terkel, *Coming of Age*, 228; Dovie Thurman, quoted in Terkel, *Race*, 59–60.

89. Lillian Craig, "The Power of a Few," *ERAP Newsletter* (January 27, 1965), [3].

90. Dovie Thurman, quoted in Terkel, *Race*, 58.

91. Ross interview; Ralph Thurman, quoted in Jack A. Smith, "Chicago's Poor Whites Fighting the System," *National Guardian* (September 24, 1966), news clipping, Todd Gitlin and Nanc[y] Hollander Papers, 1961–1970 [hereafter Gitlin and Hollander Papers], box 1, folder 9.

92. Barbara Jackson, "My Viewpoints of the Cleveland Conference," *Newark Community News*, no. 18 [1965], SDS-2B, box 23, folder 13; Jill Hamberg, interview with Bernard Goldstein, February 25, 1965, 5, NCUP Oral History Transcripts; Lillian Craig, "Community People's Conference," *ERAP Newsletter* (February 25, 1965), [2].

93. Stein, "Between Organization and Movement," 110; Naples, *Community Activism and Feminist Politics*, 337.

94. Harwood, "Work and Community among Urban Newcomers," 149; Bernstein, *Guns or Butter*, 97.

95. Jean Brown, "What Is JOIN???" *JOIN Community Union*, no. 25 (September 31, 1965), SDS-2B, box 20, folder 3; Craig, *Just a Woman*, 39.

96. Dorothy Perez, "The Need for JOIN," n.d., SDS-2B, box 20, folder 2.

97. Phyllis Jackson, "Open Letter," *ERAP Newsletter* (February 19, 1965), [4].

98. JOIN Organizers, "Take a Step into America," in Baritz, comp., *The American Left*, 411.

99. "Parallel Organizing: An Alternative to the 'Interracial Movement of the Poor,'" n.d., SDS-3, box 46, folder 8.

100. Lillian Craig, "The Power of a Few," *ERAP Newsletter* (January 27, 1965), [3]; Margaret McCarty, quoted in "Welfare Mothers Drive Launched," *Baltimore Afro-American* (July 2, 1966), news clipping, Reuther Collection, CCAP, box 3, folder "Poverty/Rights Action Center 1966."

101. Omi and Winant, *Racial Formation*, 93–95.

102. Anndrena Belcher, quoted in Terkel, *The Great Divide*, 316; Durr, "When Southern Politics Came North," 312; Guy, "The Media, the Police, and Southern White Migrant Identity," 336.

103. "Parallel Organizing: An Alternative to the 'Interracial Movement of the Poor,'" n.d., SDS-3, box 46, folder 8.

104. John Case, "Welfare Work," *Dirt and Flowers*, no. 2 (July 30, 1966), 11, SDS-3, box 36, folder 10; Todd Gitlin, "The Radical Potential of the Poor," in Teodori, ed., *The New Left*, 141.

105. Robert Fisher and Joseph M. Kling, "Leading the People: Two Approaches to the Role of Ideology in Community Organizing," in Kling and Posner, eds., *Dilemmas of Activism*, 80; Tom Hayden, "Organizing the Poor," n.d., SDS-2B, box 16, folder 6; Gerlad Kellum and Wally Thompson, "JOIN Holds Big Dance," *JOIN Newsletter* (May 14, 1965), SDS-2B, box 20, folder 3.

106. Walt Popper to Rennie Davis, June 21, 1964, SDS-2B, box 23, folder 18.

107. Tom Hayden, quoted in Newfield, *A Prophetic Minority*, 142; Hayden, *Reunion*, 126.

108. Marie Kennedy and Chris Tilly with Mauricio Gaston, "Transformative Populism and the Development of a Community of Color," in Kling and Posner, eds., *Dilemmas of Activism*, 306.

109. Strauss interview; Jack A. Smith, "Chicago's Poor Whites Fighting the System," *National Guardian* (September 24, 1966), news clipping, Gitlin and Hollander Papers, box 1, folder 9.

110. Peter Countryman, "Race and the Movement," *ERAP Newsletter* (August 21, 1965), 9; Delgado, *Organizing the Movement*, 195.

111. Rodgers, *Contested Truths*, 212.

112. Kazin, *The Populist Persuasion*, 1; George Fontaine, "Special Conference Issue," *Newark Community News*, no. 18 [1965], SDS-2B, box 23, folder 13; Jean Joachin, *Community Union News* [January 15, 1966], McEldowney Papers.

113. Kazin, *The Populist Persuasion*, 2; Mrs. Alcantar, "What Is Our Democracy??" *JOIN Newsletter* (September 23–October 7, 1966), SDS-2B, box 20, folder 3.

114. Hartog, "The Constitution of Aspiration."

115. Sandra Echols, "Why We Demonstrated," *Welfare Grievance Committee News* (August 26, 1966), McEldowney Papers.

116. Dorothy Hammer, "My Personal View," *ERAP Newsletter* (March 4, 1965), [8]; Naples, *Community Activism and Feminist Politics*, 342.

117. Joan Bradbury, "ERAP: Cleveland," *SDS Bulletin* 3 (September 1964), 7.

118. Naples, *Community Activism and Feminist Politics*, 4; Ames with Ellsworth, *Women Reformed, Women Empowered*, 99–102; Jetter, Orleck, and Taylor, eds., *The Politics of Motherhood*, 4.

NOTES TO CHAPTER 6

1. "Report: Newark Project," *ERAP Project Report* (June 20–July 1, 1964), [4], SDS-2B, box 15, folder 5.

2. "Community People's Conference," *ERAP Newsletter* (February 11, 1965), [1].

3. Miller, *"Democracy Is in the Streets,"* 148–49; Mattson, *Creating a Democratic Public*, 4–5.

4. Prudence S. Posner, "Introduction," in Kling and Posner, eds., *Dilemmas of Activism*, 15.

5. Mattson, *Creating a Democratic Public*, 83.

6. Paul Booth, quoted in Newfield, *A Prophetic Minority*, 138.

7. Dickie Magidoff, "On Campus Programming," *SDS Bulletin* 3 (February 1965), 5.

8. Teaford, *The Rough Road to Renaissance*, 5–6.

9. Steve Max, "Words, Butter, No Parsnips: Remarks on the Nature of Community Political Organization," *SDS Bulletin* 2 (May 1964), 21.

10. Richard Flacks, "Letters on SDS," *SDS Bulletin* 3 (February 1965), 4.

11. Carl Oglesby, quoted in Morgan, *The 60s Experience*, 277.

12. Barbara Lois Jackson, "My Viewpoints of the Cleveland Conference," *ERAP Newsletter* (March 4, 1965), 2.

13. Betty Moore, quoted in "Newark Report," *ERAP Newsletter* (April 26, 1965), 6.

14. Sinsheimer, "The Freedom Vote of 1963."

15. Norm Fruchter, interview with author, December 7, 1999.

16. George Fontaine, "Special Conference Issue," *Newark Community News*, no. 18 [1965], SDS-2B, box 23, folder 13.

17. Mann interview.

18. Ross interview; Lichtenstein, *The Most Dangerous Man in Detroit*, 394–95; Calvert, *Democracy from the Heart*, 12.

19. "Cleveland Report," September 20–27, 1964, SDS-2B, box 15, folder

5; Joan Bradbury to National Office People, August 31, 1964, SDS-2B, box 24, folder 8.

20. "Chicago Report," *ERAP Newsletter* (October 19–26, 1964), 1; Lawson, "From Boycotts to Ballots," 188.

21. Carl Lorig, "Lack of Education Ties People to Poverty," *JOIN Community Union Newsletter*, no. 24 (September 31, 1965), SDS-2B, box 20, folder 3.

22. Dorothy Hammer, "Representative," *Cleveland Community News* 1 (July 19, 1965), Social Protest Collection, carton 16, folder 19.

23. Lawson, "From Boycotts to Ballots," 186.

24. Evan Metcalf, "Discussion of Politics," *ERAP Newsletter* (July 31, 1965), 9.

25. Glassman interview 2; Mann interview.

26. Organizers, quoted in Parenti, "Power and Pluralism," 514; Hayden, *Reunion*, 139–41.

27. Parenti, "Power and Pluralism," 515–16.

28. Fruchter and Mann interviews.

29. Judith Bernstein to "Dear Ken," *ERAP Newsletter* (April 26, 1965), [23].

30. Bonilla, "Migrants, Citizenship, and Social Pacts," 85; Hayden, *Reunion*, 140.

31. For this misperception, see Ellis, *The Dark Side of the Left*, 126.

32. Parenti, "Power and Pluralism," 515.

33. Hayden, *Reunion*, 147.

34. Richard Rothstein, "A Short History of ERAP," *SDS Bulletin* 4 [November 1965], special 4.

35. Economic Opportunity Act, quoted in Matusow, *The Unraveling of America*, 245.

36. Richard Rothstein, "Yale Political Notes," n.d., SDS-2B, 2, box 21, folder 8.

37. Mike Miller, "Notes on Dealing with the War on Poverty," *ERAP Newsletter* (October 12–19, 1964), [14].

38. Todd Gitlin, "President's Report," *SDS Bulletin* 2 (April 1964), 2; Mary Grace, "Special Conference Issue," *Newark Community News*, no. 18 [1965], SDS-2B, box 23, folder 13.

39. Walter Reuther, quoted in Lichtenstein, *The Most Dangerous Man in Detroit*, 390; Sargent Shriver, quoted in *ERAP Newsletter* (December 11, 1964), 10; Ehrenreich, *The Altruistic Imagination*, 170.

40. Greenstone and Peterson, *Race and Authority in Urban Politics*, 19–20.

41. "Philadelphia Report," *ERAP Newsletter* (November 30–December 7, 1964), 3.

42. Bob Moore, "Baltimore Project Acts," *SDS Bulletin* 3 (February 1965), 7; "Baltimore Report," *ERAP Newsletter* (February 25, 1965), [B]; Moody interview.

43. "Chicago Report," *ERAP Newsletter* (March 11, 1965), [7–8]; Doro-

thy Perez, Ron Nicholas, and Richard Rothstein for JOIN to Sargent Shriver, June 8, 1965, SDS-2B, box 19, folder 4.

44. Carole King, "Poem for a Rat March on the Poverty Board," *ERAP Newsletter* (August 21, 1965), 1.

45. Alice Aarons and Carole King, "Reports on Cleveland's Rat March," *ERAP Newsletter* (August 27, 1965), 4–5.

46. "Chicago Report," *ERAP Newsletter* (April 1, 1965), [4].

47. Phyllis Jackson, "Open Letter," *ERAP Newsletter* (February 19, 1965), [4].

48. "Convention Statement: SDS and the 1964 Elections," *SDS Bulletin* 2 (July 1964), 20; Norm Fruchter and Robert Kramer, "An Approach to Community Organizing Projects," *Studies on the Left* 6 (March–April 1966), 51.

49. Dorothy Perez, "Welfare Suggestion," *ERAP Newsletter* (April 8, 1965), [5]; Stokely Carmichael, quoted in Breines, *Community and Organization*, 139.

50. Rose, "The Politics of Social Reform in Cleveland," 185; "This Is War?" *Cleveland Community Project* 2 (February 1965), SDS-2B, box 24, folder 12.

51. Sargent Shriver to Everett Dirksen, July 19, 1965, SDS-2B, box 19, folder 4; Rev. Lynward Stevenson, quoted in Rice, "In the Trenches of the War on Poverty," 155.

52. Ralph W. Findley to Theodore Berry, November 15, 1965, Records of the Office of Economic Opportunity, Record Group 381 [hereafter OEO, RG 381], folder "Cleveland, Ohio."

53. Rose, "The Politics of Social Reform in Cleveland," 185–86; Zarefsky, *President Johnson's War on Poverty*, 131–33.

54. Deton J. Brooks to Sargent Shriver, July 19, 1967, OEO, RG 381, folder "CAP Chicago Illinois, July 1967–December 1967"; "JOIN's Plans for the Urban Progress Center Accepted—Sort Of," *JOIN Newsletter* (February 7, 1966), SDS-2B, box 20, folder 3.

55. Bob Moore and Kim Moody, "Baltimore Report," January 28, 1965, SDS-2B, box 16, folder 6.

56. Hayden, *Reunion*, 145; Unger, *The Best of Intentions*, 158.

57. Jill Hamberg, interview with Bernard Goldstein, March 25, 1965, 4, NCUP Oral History Transcripts; Hayden, *Reunion*, 146; Gerwin, "The End of Coalition," 157–65.

58. Glassman interview 2; Fruchter interview.

59. "Chicago Report," November 17, 1964, SDS-2B, box 21, folder 8; Bob Moore and Kim Moody, "Baltimore Report," January 28, 1965, 7, SDS-2B, box 16, folder 6.

60. Mike Miller, "Notes on Dealing with the War on Poverty," *ERAP Newsletter* (October 12–19, 1964), [13].

61. Dovie Coleman, quoted in "Press Release," December 6, 1965, SDS-2B,

box 21, folder 4; Bob Moore, "Baltimore Project Acts," *SDS Bulletin* 3 (February 1965), 7.

62. JOIN Employment Committee, "War on Poverty Proposal," [1966], SDS-2B, box 21, folder 3.

63. Jill Hamberg, interview with Bernard Goldstein, February 11, 1965, 10, NCUP Oral History Transcripts.

64. JOIN petition, [1965], SDS-2B, box 21, folder 6; Guy, "The Media, the Police, and Southern White Migrant Identity," 342.

65. Roger Manela, "Playground Report," *ERAP Newsletter* (July 31, 1965), 5–6; Linn Drive–Lakeview Community Unions Recreation Center Proposal, [1965], SDS-2B, box 25, folder 3; "Uptown Residents Will Build Playground," press release, September 9, 1965, SDS-2B, box 20, folder 8; Todd Gitlin, "The Radical Potential of the Poor," in Teodori, ed., *The New Left*, 147.

66. Carol Glassman, "A Night of the People," *New Left Notes* 1 (March 4, 1966), 1.

67. Fein interview 2; Unger, *The Best of Intentions*, 158; Rice, "In the Trenches of the War on Poverty," 195.

68. Rothstein interview 2; "Please Don't Wait, It May Be Too Late," leaflet (n.d.), Vivian Rothstein personal collection.

69. Fee, "Public Health in Baltimore"; Carson, *Settlement Folk*, 70; Rice, "In the Trenches of the War on Poverty," 150.

70. Harold Kaplan, "Urban Renewal in Newark," in Wilson, ed., *Urban Renewal*, 241; "What Do We, the People of the Near West Side, Know about Urban Renewal?" leaflet [1966–67], McEldowney Papers.

71. Vernon Grizzard, "Letters," *SDS Bulletin* 3 (November–December 1964), 31; Uptown resident, quoted in Rev. Daniel Marcum, "Urban Renewal Will Mean People Removal," *JOIN Newsletter* (October 18–November 1, 1966), SDS-2B, box 20, folder 3.

72. "What Do We, the People of the Near West Side, Know about Urban Renewal?" leaflet [1966–67], McEldowney Papers; Bennett, "Uptown," 24.

73. Bob Wable, "Voice from the Slum," *JOIN Newsletter* (January 20–February 15, 1967), SDS-2B, box 20, folder 3.

74. Sidney Plotkin, "Enclave Consciousness and Neighborhood Activism," in Kling and Posner, eds., *Dilemmas of Activism*, 227; "What Do We, the People of the Near West Side, Know about Urban Renewal?" leaflet [1966–67], McEldowney Papers.

75. New Independent Committee for Better Urban Renewal, "We Demand," *ERAP Newsletter* (November 6, 1964), [14]; JOIN Community Union to Reverend H. Kris Rennow, September 15, 1966, Lynd Papers, box 6, folder 1; Wright, *Building the Dream*, 236.

76. "Urban Renewal Action Committee," leaflet [1966], McEldowney Papers.

77. Morgan, "Democracy in Eclipse?" 28 n. 23.

78. Gillette, *Launching the War on Poverty*, 203; Rice, "In the Trenches of the War on Poverty," 221; Kramer, *Participation of the Poor*, 261.

79. Mollenkopf, *The Contested City*, 90.

80. Gerwin, "The End of Coalition," 167; Fales interview; Glassman interview 2.

81. Derek Winans, quoted in Douglas M. Davis, "Tom Hayden—The White Stokely," *New York/World Journal Tribune* (January 1, 1967), 6, news clipping, "Newark Community Union Project" Information File.

82. Marya Levenson, quoted in Evans, *Personal Politics*, 143.

83. "Newark Project Report," *ERAP Newsletter* (July 23, 1965), [5]; Carol Glassman, interview with Bernard Goldstein, July 2, 1965, 3–6, NCUP Oral History Transcripts.

84. Roldo S. Bartimole and Murray Gruber, "Cleveland: Recipe for Violence," *Nation* (June 26, 1967), 816; Dorothy Osborn, Masil Day, Iva Pearce, Lillian Craig, and Harriet Sizemore, "Why Should Children Fear Policemen?" *ERAP Newsletter* (July 17, 1965), 7.

85. "Demonstration," *Uptown News* (August 16, 1966), news clipping, Gitlin and Hollander Papers, box 1, folder 9; Mrs. Heyman, quoted in Gerwin, "The End of Coalition," 99; Virginia Richardson, "The Way the Law Treats You If You're Poor," *JOIN Newsletter* (July 15, 1965), SDS-2B, box 20, folder 3.

86. J. C. Nichols, paraphrased in Carol Glassman, interview with Bernard Goldstein, May 14, 1965, 20, NCUP Oral History Transcripts; "The Police and the Spanish-Speaking," *JOIN Newsletter* (March 19, 1965), SDS-2B, box 20, folder 3.

87. "Let Your Voice Be Heard," leaflet (n.d.), SDS-2B, box 19, folder 7; Mrs. Alcantar, "200 People Marched!" *JOIN Community Union Newsletter* 2 (August 15–21, 1966), SDS-2B, box 20, folder 3.

88. Norm Fruchter and Robert Kramer, "An Approach to Community Organizing Projects," *Studies on the Left* 6 (March–April 1966), 52; Fogelson, *Big-City Police*, 283–97; Carol Glassman, interview with Bernard Goldstein, July 2, 1965, 11, NCUP Oral History Transcripts.

89. Todd Gitlin, "The Radical Potential of the Poor," in Teodori, ed., *The New Left*, 147–48.

90. "We Demand," *Free Press* 1 (July 28, 1966), Lynd Papers, box 6, folder 7; Fogelson, *Big-City Police*, 283–97.

91. "Outline for Program with Welfare Mothers," [1964], SDS-2B, box 25, folder 2.

92. Nanc[y] Hollander, "Cleveland," *SDS Bulletin* 2 (July 1964), 12; "Cleveland," July 27, 1964, 5, SDS-2B, box 15, folder 5.

93. Rennie Davis, "Ann Arbor Report," *ERAP Newsletter* (January 20, 1965), 2; Frances Fox Piven, "Ideology and the State: Women, Power, and the

Welfare State," and Linda Gordon, "The New Feminist Scholarship on the Welfare State," in Gordon, ed., *Women, the State, and Welfare.*

94. JOIN, "Welfare Bill of Rights," n.d., SDS-2B, box 20, folder 1; "Welfare Bill of Rights," [Hoboken], n.d., Helen Garvy personal collection; "Welfare Bill of Rights," *CUFAW Newsletter* (December 1965), McEldowney Papers.

95. Margaret McCarty, quoted in "Welfare Mothers Drive Launched," *Baltimore Afro-American* (July 2, 1966), news clipping, Reuther Collection, CCAP, box 3, folder "Poverty/Rights Action Center 1966."

96. Mary Murphy, "On the Welfare System," *ERAP Newsletter* (November 8, 1965), 4.

97. Carole King, "Action Now!" *Free Press* (July 5, 1966), McEldowney Papers.

98. Davis, *Brutal Need*; Harriet Stulman to Edward V. Sparer, January 28, 1965, SDS-2B, box 19, folder 4.

99. Susie Moore, "CUFAW Fights for 100% Welfare," *ERAP Newsletter* (May 17, 1965), 3; "CUFAW's Last Trip to Columbus," *ERAP Newsletter* (July 31, 1965), 10.

100. JOIN, "Press Release," December 22, 1965, SDS-2B, box 21, folder 5; Statement of Dovie Thurman before the Legislative Advisory Committee on Public Aid, January 9, 1966, SDS-2B, box 21, folder 5.

101. John Case, "Welfare Work," *Dirt and Flowers*, no. 2 (July 30, 1966), 9, SDS-3, box 36, folder 10.

102. Sharon Jeffrey, "Report on Discussion," April 28, 1964, SDS-2B, box 25, folder 3; Carole King, "Action Now!" *Free Press* (July 5, 1966), McEldowney Papers.

103. "Cleveland Report," *ERAP Newsletter* (November 16–23, 1964), [7]; "Cleveland Report," *ERAP Newsletter* (April 1, 1965), [6].

104. Barbara and Dick Skillen, "More Food for People under Welfare," *ERAP Newsletter* (February 5, 1965), [5].

105. Carol Glassman, "Women and the Welfare System," in Morgan, ed., *Sisterhood Is Powerful*, 105; Kornbluh, "To Fulfill Their 'Rightly Needs,'" 78.

106. Mary V. Hockenberry, "Welfare Mothers Organize in Chicago," *ERAP Newsletter* (October 5, 1965), 11.

107. Frank Blalock, "JOIN Begins to Act on Food Stamp Plan," *ERAP Newsletter* (April 8, 1965), [3]; Dorothy Perez, "Food Stamps," *JOIN Newsletter* (May 26, 1965), SDS-2B, box 20, folder 3.

108. CUFAW to President Johnson, August 12, 1964, SDS-2B, box 25, folder 2; Mary V. Hockenberry, "Welfare Mothers Organize in Chicago," *ERAP Newsletter* (October 5, 1965), 11.

109. *CUFAW Newsletter* (December 1965), McEldowney Papers.

110. Sandra Echols and Bertha Rice, quoted in Louise A. Lind, "Protesting Moms 'Buy,' Don't Pay," *Cleveland Plain Dealer* (August 20, 1966), and "Spe-

cial Demonstration Issue," *Welfare Grievance Committee News* (August 26, 1966), McEldowney Papers.

111. Stein, ed., *The Crisis of Welfare in Cleveland*, v.

112. "Welfare Bill of Rights," *CUFAW Newsletter* (December 1965), McEldowney Papers; "'Welfare Mothers' Rally," *Boston Herald* (July 1, 1966), news clipping, Reuther Collection, CCAP, box 3, folder "Poverty/Rights Action Center 1966."

113. "Cleveland Report," July 23, 1964, 6, SDS-2B, box 15, folder 5.

114. Doris Bland and Gertrude M. Nickerson, "Boston: Letter to the Commissioner," *ERAP Newsletter* (January 17, 1966), 2.

115. John Case, "Welfare Work," *Dirt and Flowers*, no. 2 (July 30, 1966), 9, SDS-3, box 36, folder 10; "Walk for Decent Welfare," leaflet (summer 1966), McEldowney Papers; Ayers interview 2; Mann interview; Edin, *There's a Lot of Month Left*.

116. "Community Union Meeting Notes," *Community Union News* [January 15, 1966], McEldowney Papers.

117. Craig, *Just a Woman*, 57.

118. Tillmon, "Welfare Is a Woman's Issue," 316.

119. "Statement of a Public Assistance Mother," *ERAP Newsletter* (March 4, 1965), [7]; Lowe, *Cities in a Race with Time*, 287.

120. Carole King, paraphrased in "The Question of 'Employability,'" *Welfare Grievance Committee News* (July 5, 1966), McEldowney Papers; Kornbluh, "The Goals of the National Welfare Rights Movement," 68, 72.

121. Casey Hayden, quoted in "Chicago: JOIN Project," *Studies on the Left* 5 (summer 1965), 117.

122. Casey Hayden, "Thoughts of Young Radicals: Raising the Question of Who Decides," *New Republic* (January 22, 1966), 9.

123. "Welfare Bill of Rights," *CUFAW Newsletter* (December 1965), McEldowney Papers; "M.A.W.'s Demands," n.d., Younger Papers, carton 3, folder 3; Princess Redfeather, "Servants of the People," *JOIN Community Union Newsletter* 2 (June 13, 1966), SDS-2B, box 20, folder 3; Pope, *Biting the Hand*, 56.

124. "Welfare Bill of Rights," *CUFAW Newsletter* (December 1965), and Welfare Grievance Committee, "Press Release," October 24, 1966, McEldowney Papers.

125. Linda Gordon, "Putting Children First: Women, Maternalism, and Welfare in the Early Twentieth Century," in Kerber, Kessler-Harris, and Sklar, eds., *U.S. History as Women's History*, 83.

126. Phronie Simpson, "When the Welfare Inspectors Came," *ERAP Newsletter* (June 30, 1965), 3.

127. Lillian Craig, "Morals—What Are Morals?" *ERAP Newsletter* (July 23, 1965), [24]; "'Welfare Mothers' Rally," *Boston Herald* (July 1, 1966),

news clipping, Reuther Collection, CCAP, box 3, folder "Poverty/Rights Action Center 1966."

128. Phronie Simpson, "The Welfare Department," *ERAP Newsletter* (June 30, 1965), 2.

129. Craig, *Just a Woman*, 18; Garvy interview; Glassman interview 2.

130. John Case, "Welfare Work," *Dirt and Flowers*, no. 2 (July 30, 1966), 9, SDS-3, box 36, folder 10.

131. Dorothy Perez, "Statement before the Advisory Council on Public Welfare," March 1965, SDS-2B, box 19, folder 14; JOIN, "Welfare Bill of Rights," n.d., SDS-2B, box 20, folder 1.

132. Judith Bernstein, quoted in "Chicago: JOIN Project," *Studies on the Left* 5 (summer 1965), 124–25.

133. Official, quoted in Jo Ann Levine, "Welfare Protest Planned," *Christian Science Monitor* (June 29, 1966), news clipping, Reuther Collection, CCAP, box 3, folder "Poverty/Rights Action Center 1966"; Donald M. Stewart, "Welfare and the Politics of Protest," May 1969, 34–35, MWRO Records, box 4, folder 14.

134. Kornbluh, "The Goals of the National Welfare Rights Movement," 66.

135. Brown interview.

136. Goodwin, *Gender and the Politics of Welfare Reform*, 7.

137. Hayden personal communication.

138. Sherna Berger Gluck in collaboration with Maylei Blackwell, Sharon Cotrell, and Karen S. Harper, "Whose Feminism, Whose History? Reflections on Excavating the History of (the) U.S. Women's Movement(s)," in Naples, ed., *Community Activism and Feminist Politics*, 31–56. For discussions of "maternalism," see "Symposium: Maternalism as a Paradigm," *Journal of Women's History* 5 (fall 1993), 95–131.

NOTES TO CHAPTER 7

1. Craig, *Just a Woman*, 33.

2. Miller, *"Democracy Is in the Streets,"* 216; Carol McEldowney, personal journals, McEldowney Papers; Boudin personal communication; Strauss and Magidoff interviews; Oliver Fein, interview 3 with author, January 12, 1994; Charlotte Phillips, interview with author, December 5, 1993; Craig, *Just a Woman*, 33.

3. Matusow, *The Unraveling of America*; Aronowitz, "When the New Left Was New," 23.

4. Marya Levenson, quoted in Sale, *SDS*, 145.

5. Sharon Jeffrey to Dickie Magidoff, November 1964, SDS-2B, box 24, folder 5.

6. Hayden, *Reunion*, 143.

7. Richard Rothstein, "Evolution of the ERAP Organizers," in Long, ed., *The New Left*, 285.

8. Carol Glassman, interview with Bernard Goldstein, July 2, 1965, 20, NCUP Oral History Transcripts.

9. "JOIN Signs Collective Bargaining Agreement," press release, May 26, 1966, SDS-2B, box 20, folder 6; Ralph, *Northern Protest*, 64, 262 n. 63.

10. Ayers interview 2.

11. Clark Kissinger, quoted in Steven Kelman, "SDS: Troubled Voice of the New Left," *New Leader* (September 27, 1965), 10, Reuther Collection, UAW President's Office, box 523, folder 18; "Sixteen Plagues," *New Left Notes* 1 (December 23, 1966), 7.

12. Tepperman interview; Paul Booth, "On Programmatic Radicalism," [summer 1967], Booth Papers, box 1, folder 8.

13. Gerwin, "The End of Coalition," 141; Glassman interview 2.

14. Davis interview; Hayden personal communication.

15. Judith Bernstein, quoted in "Chicago: JOIN Project," *Studies on the Left* 5 (summer 1965), 112.

16. Carol Glassman, interview with Bernard Goldstein, June 18, 1965, 7, NCUP Oral History Transcripts.

17. Hayden, *Reunion*, 147.

18. Todd Gitlin, "The Dynamics of the New Left," *motive* 31 (November 1970), 43; Sharon Jeffrey, quoted in Miller, *"Democracy Is in the Streets,"* 190, 199; Rothstein interview 2.

19. Strauss interview.

20. Cathy Wilkerson, *Rats, Washtubs and Block Organizations,* SDS pamphlet [1964], 3, Webb Papers, box 1, folder 6a; Hayden personal communication; Bernstein and Goldsmith interviews; Rothstein interview 1.

21. Sharon Jeffrey, "CUFAW Meeting Report," October 12, [1964], SDS-2B, box 25, folder 2.

22. Rennie Davis, quoted in "Chicago: JOIN Project," *Studies on the Left* 5 (summer 1965), 113–14; "Newark Report," August 31, 1964, Booth Papers, box 2, folder 9; Hayden, *Reunion*, 131.

23. "Report from the Cleveland Community Project," *ERAP Project Report* (June 20–July 1, 1964), [26], SDS-2B, box 15, folder 5.

24. Boudin personal communication.

25. Sara Preston, "Community Organization Survey Questions," [1966], [20], Lynd Papers, box 7, folder 4; Uptown Goodfellows Organizers, "Proposal," n.d., 2, Gitlin and Hollander Papers, box 1, folder 9; Gitlin and Hollander, *Uptown*, 380–81.

26. Peggy Terry and Youngblood, "JOIN/NCU to End Rumors," *New Left Notes* 3 (February 26, 1968), 5, 8.

27. Elaine Plaisance, quoted in Fraser, ed., *1968*, 65; Donald M. Stewart,

"Welfare and the Politics of Protest," May 1969, 31, 46, MWRO Papers, box 4, folder 14.

28. Donald W. Jackson, "Letter," *ERAP Newsletter* (October 5, 1965), 13.

29. Hayden, *Reunion*, 161; Fales and Strauss interviews.

30. Moody interview; JOIN, "Coordinator's Report," May 8, 1967, Lynd Papers, box 6, folder 2.

31. Massey and Denton, *American Apartheid*, 1, 14; Jones, *The Dispossessed*, 241–49.

32. "December Conference Impressions," *New Left Notes* (January 28, 1966), 4; Evans, *Personal Politics*, 149–50.

33. Goldsmith and Nadel interviews; Evans, *Personal Politics*, 151, 149; Rennie Davis to Lee Webb and Vernon Grizzard, January 15, [1965], SDS-2B, box 17, folder 6.

34. Evans, *Personal Politics*, 149.

35. Toni Helstein interview.

36. Tepperman interview.

37. Rennie Davis, quoted in "Chicago: JOIN Project," *Studies on the Left* 5 (summer 1965), 113; Vivian Rothstein, quoted in Evans, *Personal Politics*, 146.

38. Hayden personal communication.

39. Breines, *Community and Organization*, 63; Miller, *"Democracy Is in the Streets,"* 215; Carol Glassman, interview with Bernard Goldstein, July 2, 1965, 15, NCUP Oral History Transcripts.

40. Jill Hamberg, interview with Bernard Goldstein, February 18, 1965, 26, NCUP Oral History Transcripts; "Crisis in JOIN Continues," [1964], SDS-2B, box 19, folder 1.

41. Sharon Jeffrey, quoted in Miller, *"Democracy Is in the Streets,"* 207; "Chicago Project," September 25, 1964, 3, SDS-2B, box 15, folder 5.

42. Rennie Davis to Carl Wittman, January 19, [1965], SDS-2B, box 19, folder 2; Sale, *SDS*, 140; Calvert, *Democracy from the Heart*, 118.

43. Nick Egleson to Oliver and Charlotte Fein, July 13, 1964, SDS-2B, box 24, folder 5; Hayden, *Reunion*, 130.

44. Evans, *Personal Politics*, 152–53.

45. Unnamed woman organizer, quoted in Evans, *Personal Politics*, 153; Rothstein interview 1.

46. Duberman, *Stonewall*, 220; Carl Wittman, "A Gay Manifesto," *Liberation* (February 1970), 24; Hayden, *Reunion*, 130.

47. Boudin personal communication; Goldsmith interview.

48. Jill Hamberg, interview with Bernard Goldstein, April 1, 1965, 15, NCUP Oral History Transcripts; Bancroft interview.

49. Richard Rothstein, "Evolution of the ERAP Organizers," in Long, ed., *The New Left*, 286.

50. McEldowney and Magidoff interviews; Jack Kittredge, interview with author, November 15, 1999.

51. Breines, *Community and Organization*, 131–32.

52. Potter, *A Name for Ourselves*, 151; Rothstein interview 2.

53. Gitlin, *The Sixties*, 186; Steve Bookshester, Letter, *ERAP Newsletter* (April 8, 1965), [8].

54. Parenti, "Power and Pluralism," 517.

55. "Fake JOIN Leaflet," n.d., SDS-2B, box 20, folder 2; "Fake NCUP Newsletter," n.d., SDS-2B, box 23, folder 11.

56. Richard Rothstein, quoted in "Chicago: JOIN Project," *Studies on the Left* 5 (summer 1965), 121–22; "Relations with Other Groups," *New Left Notes* 2 (July 10, 1967), 2.

57. "Philadelphia Report," *ERAP Newsletter* (November 30–December 3, 1964), 2; Jill Hamberg, interview with Bernard Goldstein, February 11, 1965, 6, NCUP Oral History Transcripts.

58. Jacob Sampson, quoted in Stewart McDonald, "Building Owner Claims Embezzlement," (September 7, 1966), news clipping, Gitlin and Hollander Papers, box 1, folder 9.

59. "Cleveland Report," *ERAP Newsletter* (July 17, 1965), 6; Williams interview.

60. Strauss and Goldsmith interviews.

61. Evans, *Personal Politics*, 139; Donner, *Protectors of Privilege*, 73.

62. Pre-interview conversation with Vivian Rothstein, January 1993.

63. Parenti, "Power and Pluralism," 519; Fales interview.

64. Hayden, *Reunion*, 149.

65. Sitkoff, *The Struggle for Black Equality*, 209.

66. Ralph, *Northern Protest*.

67. Isserman and Kazin, *America Divided*, 177.

68. Noble, *Welfare as We Knew It*, 96; Weir, *Politics and Jobs*, 83.

69. Wittner, *Cold War America*, 273–74.

70. Martin Luther King, Jr., quoted in Wittner, *Cold War America*, 273–74; Rice, "In the Trenches of the War on Poverty," 208; Matusow, *The Unraveling of America*, 160.

71. Dickie Magidoff to Rennie Davis, August 17, 1964, SDS-2B, box 24, folder 5.

72. Gitlin, *The Sixties*, 180; Miller, *"Democracy Is in the Streets,"* 226–27.

73. Katz interview.

74. Bailis, *Bread or Justice*, 147, 169.

75. Carl Oglesby, quoted in Fraser, ed., *1968*, 109.

76. Paul Potter on Tom Hayden, quoted in Gitlin, *The Sixties*, 166; Richard Rothstein, "Evolution of the ERAP Organizers," in Long, ed., *The New Left*, 274.

77. Klatch, *A Generation Divided*, 109.

78. Payne, *I've Got the Light of Freedom*, 360, 374–75.

79. Breines, *Community and Organization*, 55.

80. Mann interview; Paul Mattick, Jr., "The Old Left and the New Left," *New Left Notes* 4 (January 15, 1969), 7.

81. Anderson, *The Movement and the Sixties*.

82. Egleson interview.

83. Carson, *In Struggle*, 291.

84. Dovie Thurman, quoted in Terkel, *Race*, 60–61.

85. Farber, *The Age of Great Dreams*, 265–66.

86. "National Community Union," *Radicals in the Professions* 1 (February 1968), 13; Peggy Terry, quoted in Terkel, *Race*, 54.

87. NOC Staff, "Peggy Terry Campaign," *New Left Notes* 3 (October 7, 1968), 7.

88. Poverty/Rights Action Center, "Summary Report of Welfare Action Meeting," May 27, 1966, Social Action Vertical File, folder "NWRO (Poverty/Rights Action Center)."

89. "Walk for Decent Welfare," leaflet (summer 1966), and "March to Columbus," *Free Press* (July 5, 1966), McEldowney Papers; Piven and Cloward, *Poor People's Movements*, 290–91.

90. Delegate list from National Welfare Rights Meeting, Chicago, August 6–7, 1966, Social Action Vertical File, folder "NWRO (Poverty/Rights Action Center)."

91. "Officers of NWRO," February 1, 1968, and "National Coordinating Committee of the NWRO," February 14 and August 20, 1968, George Wiley Papers, 1949–1975 [hereafter Wiley Papers], box 8, folder 7.

92. Davis, *Moving the Mountain*, 350–53.

93. Jean Tepperman, quoted in Echols, *Daring to Be Bad*, 86.

94. Calvert, *Democracy from the Heart*, 117.

95. Carl Wittman, "A Gay Manifesto," *Liberation* (February 1970), 24.

96. Levy, *The New Left and Labor*, 48–49, 46–47.

97. Goldsmith, Moody, and Williams interviews.

98. Flug, "Organized Labor and the Civil Rights Movement," 343–44.

99. Larry Spence, quoted in Breines, *Community and Organization*, 31; Rossinow, *The Politics of Authenticity*, 194.

100. Sale, *SDS*, 339; Heather Booth, "Chicago Conference: What Role for Professionals," *Radicals in the Professions* 1 (February 1968), 2–5.

101. Phillips interview.

102. Millman interview.

103. Miller, *"Democracy Is in the Streets,"* 266–70, 281–82, 295–96, 308.

104. Evans, *Personal Politics*, 182; Rothstein interview 2.

105. Jacobs, *The Way the Wind Blew*; Sale, *SDS*, 648–49.

106. Mann interview.

107. Palmer interview.

108. Tepperman and Magidoff interviews; Rossinow, *The Politics of Authenticity*, 251.

109. Phillips interview.

110. Glassman interview 1.

111. Rothstein interviews.

112. Evans, *Personal Politics*, 154; Echols, "We Gotta Get Out of This Place," 22.

113. Katz, Bernstein, and Ansley interviews; Evans, *Personal Politics*, 148; Zeiger Wildflower interview 2.

114. "*NLN* Talks to Phil Hutchings," *New Left Notes* 3 (October 7, 1968), 12; Phil Hutchings, quoted in Carson, *In Struggle*, 291; Dovie Thurman, quoted in Terkel, *Race*, 60.

115. Doug Blakely, a.k.a. Youngblood, "Seriousness in the Movement: Students and the Revolution," *New Left Notes* 2 (November 27, 1967), 3.

116. D. J. R. Bruckner, "Ticket Mate of Cleaver Still Fighting: Peggy Terry Sees Struggle Involving Classes, Not Races," *Los Angeles Times* (February 20, 1969), news clipping, Steve Goldsmith personal collection.

117. Strobel, "Organizational Learning in the Chicago Women's Liberation Union," 148.

118. Jean Tepperman, "Two Jobs: Women Who Work in Factories," in Morgan, ed., *Sisterhood Is Powerful*, 115; Tepperman interview.

119. Katz interview.

120. Davis, "Welfare Rights and Women's Rights," 159.

121. Carol Glassman, "Women and the Welfare System," in Morgan, ed., *Sisterhood Is Powerful*, 115.

122. Doris Bland, in *NOW!* (February 2, 1968).

123. Davis, "Welfare Rights and Women's Rights," 145; Gordon, "What Does Welfare Regulate?"

124. MAW activist, quoted in Marya Levenson, "Welfare Organizing: Its Goals and Methods," [1968–69], [3], MWRO Records, box 4, folder 12; Bailis, *Bread or Justice*, 11, 57.

125. Freeman, "The Tyranny of Structurelessness"; Strobel, "Organizational Learning in the Chicago Women's Liberation Union."

126. Unnamed organizer, quoted in Sale, *SDS*, 219; Heineman, *Campus Wars*, 159.

127. Egleson, Davis, and Ayers interviews; Sale, *SDS*, 524.

128. Mann and Goldsmith interviews; Sale, *SDS*, 579–80.

129. Mike James, "Chicago Organizing School," *New Left Notes* 2 (April 24, 1967), 3.

130. Max interview.

131. Glassman interview 1; Hayden, *Reunion*, 161.

132. David Gerwin, unpublished prospectus in author's possession, 4.

133. Rothstein interview 2; Richard Rothstein, "Organizing in the Heart of America," *Radicals in the Professions* 1 (December 1967), 1, 17–18; Nadel interview.

134. Gitlin and Hollander, *Uptown*, 434; Clarus Backes, "Migrants," *Chicago Tribune Magazine* (September 29, 1968), news clipping, Chicago Newspaper Clipping Files.

135. Katz interview.

136. Hayden, *Reunion*, 168.

137. Craig, *Just a Woman*, 19–20; Marge Grevatt, quoted in Craig, *Just a Woman*, 21.

138. Robert G. McGruder, "Stokes Forms Welfare Crisis Commission," *Cleveland Plain Dealer* (January 3, 1968), "Welfare Crisis Commission" Clipping File; "This Is Your Life—Carole King," 1969, Wiley Papers, box 26, folder 6.

139. Hayden, *Reunion*, 170.

140. Fisher, *Let the People Decide*, 109; Ross interview.

141. Delgado, *Organizing the Movement*, 13.

142. Horwitt, *Let Them Call Me Rebel*, 544; Rothstein interview 2; Epstein, *Political Protest and Cultural Revolution*, 36; Bouchier, *Radical Citizenship*, 104.

143. Meyer and Whittier, "Social Movement Spillover."

NOTES TO THE CONCLUSION

1. Weinstein, *Ambiguous Legacy*, 132; Breines, *Community and Organization*, 145.

2. Piven and Cloward, *Poor People's Movements*, xiii.

3. Neil Betten and Michael J. Austin, "The Cincinnati Unit Experiment, 1917–1920," in Betten and Austin, eds., *The Roots of Community Organizing*, 35.

4. Alinsky, *Reveille for Radicals*, 201.

5. Paul Booth, "On Programmatic Radicalism," [summer 1967], Booth Papers, box 1, folder 8.

6. Payne, *I've Got the Light of Freedom*, 306.

7. Zeiger Wildflower interview 2.

8. Williams interview.

9. Flacks, *Making History*.

10. Mann interview.

11. Simmons, *Organizing in Hard Times*, 125; Payne, *I've Got the Light of Freedom*, 359.

12. Tom Hayden, quoted in Greenberg, ed., *A Circle of Trust*, 33.

13. Robnett, *How Long? How Long?* 137; Fein interview 3.

14. Vivian Rothstein, quoted in Evans, *Personal Politics*, 147; Fales interview.

15. Payne, *I've Got the Light of Freedom*, 331.

16. Craig, *Just a Woman*, 53; Dovie Coleman, "Self-Explanation on an Over-All Thing—That's Pressure," n.d., Wiley Papers, box 25, folder 1.

17. Craig, *Just a Woman*, 55.

18. Dovie Thurman, quoted in Terkel, *Race*, 63.

19. Tony Kronman, letter, reprinted in *Discussion Bulletin* (spring 1965), Supplement for the December 1964 National Council Meeting; Palmer interview.

20. Klatch, *A Generation Divided*, 334; Moody and Tepperman interviews.

21. Craig, *Just a Woman*, 45. Used throughout the Civil Rights Movement, this song was "often sung at moments of internal organizational crisis" to inspire unity. Bernice Johnson Reagon, liner notes for *Voices of the Civil Rights Movement*.

Selected Bibliography

PRIMARY SOURCES

Manuscript Collections

Archives of Labor and Urban Affairs, Wayne State University, Detroit
    Walter P. Reuther Collection
        Citizens' Crusade Against Poverty
        UAW President's Office

Bancroft Library, University of California, Berkeley
    Social Protest Collection, 1960–1982

Cleveland Public Library
    "Welfare Crisis Commission" Clipping File

Hoover Institution on War, Revolution, and Peace, Stanford University, Stanford, California
    New Left Collection, 1964–1988

Municipal Reference Library, Chicago
    Chicago Newspaper Clipping Files

National Archives, Washington, D.C.
    Records of the Office of Economic Opportunity, Record Group 381, Inspection and Civil Rights Reports

Newark Public Library
    "Newark Community Union Project" Information File

Schlesinger Library on the History of Women in America, Radcliffe College, Cambridge, Massachusetts
    "Welfare Mothers" Vertical File

State Historical Society of Wisconsin, Madison
    Stanley Aronowitz Papers, 1962–1965
    Paul Booth Papers, 1956–1970
    Robb Burlage Papers, 1956–1973
    Michael Davis Papers, 1965–1970
    Todd Gitlin and Nancy Hollander Papers, 1961–1970
    Bonnie Gordon Papers, 1958–1969

Charles Levenstein Papers, 1963–1967
Staughton Lynd Papers, 1940–1977
Massachusetts Welfare Rights Organization Records, 1968–1972
Carol McEldowney Papers, 1964–1968
Social Action Vertical File
Students for a Democratic Society Records, 1958–1970
Lee D. Webb Papers, 1955–1968
West Side Federation (Chicago, Illinois) Records, 1966–1968
George Wiley Papers, 1949–1975

Tamiment Institute Library, New York University, New York
Students for a Democratic Society Records, 1934–1936; 1946–1966

Western Reserve Historical Society, Cleveland
Paul and Betty Younger Papers, 1951–1976

Periodicals

ERAP Newsletter
ERAP Project Report
Liberation
Nation
New Left Notes
New Republic
Radicals in the Professions
SDS Bulletin
Studies on the Left

Government Publications, Reports, and Pamphlets

Boston Public Library
Boston Redevelopment Authority. Planning Department. "Housing in Boston." July 1967.
Boston Redevelopment Authority, and Harvard University. "A Report on the Schools of Boston." May 1962.
Brady, Patricia. "The City of Boston: History, Planning, and Development." Mayor's Office in conjunction with the Boston Redevelopment Authority. 1978.
Burke, Alice. "The Amazing BRA Story." *Boston Traveler* (April 3, 1963). Boston City Council Reprint.
Massachusetts General Court. Joint Committee on Social Welfare. "Report." November 1968.
Massachusetts Consumers' Council. "Special Report on 'The Increasing Costs of the Necessities of Life, Notably Foods.'" February 1967.

Chicago Public Library, Special Collections Department, Government Publications.

Jack Meltzer Associates. *Uptown: A Planning Report.* Vol. 1. [1962].

Municipal Reference Library, Chicago.

Bennett, Larry. "Uptown: Port of Entry, Hotbed of Movements, Contested Territory." June 1991.

City of Chicago. Department of Urban Renewal. "Uptown Conservation Area Staff Report." 1966.

Schloss, Bert P. "The Uptown Community Area and the Southern White In-Migrant." May 1957.

Warren, Elizabeth. *Chicago's Uptown.* Chicago: Loyola University Center for Urban Policy, 1979.

Newark Public Library.

City of Newark. "Economic Base Study." November 1964.

Mayor's Commission on Group Relations. *Newark: A City in Transition.* Vol. 1, *The Characteristics of the Population.* January 1959.

Thabit, Walter. "Reducing Unemployment in Newark, New Jersey." August 15, 1964.

Western Reserve Historical Society, Cleveland.

City of Cleveland. Overall Economic Development Program. *Progress Report.* March 28, 1969.

Stein, Herman D., ed. *The Crisis of Welfare in Cleveland: Report of the Mayor's Commission.* Cleveland: Case Western Reserve University, 1969.

Oral, Photograph, and Film Sources

Interviews by Author

Michael Ansara, November 23, 1999

Fran Ansley, December 9, 1999

Bill Ayers, November 23 and 30, 1999

John Bancroft, November 7, 1999

Judith Bernstein, November 14, 1999

Paul Booth, November 19, 1999

Kathy Boudin, January 31, 2000

George Brosi, November 24 and December 6, 1999

Connie Brown, November 19, 1993

Rennie Davis, November 23, 1999

Nick Egleson, November 13, 1993

Corinna Fales, November 13, 1999

Oliver Fein, December 1 and 15, 1993, January 12, 1994

Norm Fruchter, December 7, 1999

Helen Garvy, November 7, 1999
Todd Gitlin, November 18, 1999
Carol Glassman, August 7 and 28, 1993
Steve Goldsmith, February 18, 1993
D. Gorton, September 11, 2000
Al Haber, September 11, 2000
Jill Hamberg, November 21, 1999
Casey Hayden, November 21, 1999
Nina Helstein, September 17, 2000
Toni Helstein, September 17, 2000
Nanci Hollander, September 26, 1993
Michael James, December 1, 1999
Marilyn Katz, December 8, 1999
Jack Kittredge, November 15, 1999
Dickie Magidoff, November 27, 1999
Eric Mann, December 15, 1999
Steve Max, November 23, 1999
Ken McEldowney, August 11, 1993
Paul Millman, November 17, 1999
Kim Moody, November 18, 1999
Sarah Murphy, November 24, 1999
Stan Nadel, November 3, 1999
David Palmer, September 9, 2000
Robert Pardun, November 27, 1999
Charlotte Phillips, December 5, 1993
Bob Ross, November 1, 1999
Vivian Rothstein, February 16 and 19, 1993
Danny Schechter, November 14, 1999
Dave Strauss, November 29, 1999
Jean Tepperman, December 6, 1999
Jim Williams, December 6, 1999
Leni Zeiger Wildflower, August 28 and September 20, 1993

State Historical Society of Wisconsin, Iconography and Film Archives, Madison
    We Got To Live Here, film directed by Norm Fruchter
    James P. O'Brien Collection

Tamiment Institute Library, New York University, New York
    Interviews by Bernard Goldstein with Carol Glassman and Jill Hamberg,
        Newark Community Union Project Oral History Transcripts, 1965

*Voices of the Civil Rights Movement: Black American Freedom Songs, 1960–
    1966.* Smithsonian Folkways Recordings, 1997.

SECONDARY SOURCES

Books

Abramovitz, Mimi. *Regulating the Lives of Women: Social Welfare Policy from Colonial Times to the Present*. Boston: South End, 1988.

Adelson, Alan. *SDS*. New York: Scribner, 1972.

Alinsky, Saul D. *Reveille for Radicals*. Chicago: University of Chicago Press, 1946.

Altbach, Philip G. *Student Politics in America: A Historical Analysis*. New York: McGraw-Hill, 1974.

Albach, Philip G., and Robert S. Laufer, eds. *The New Pilgrims: Youth Protest in Transition*. New York: David McKay, 1972.

Ames, Linda J., with Jeanne Ellsworth. *Women Reformed, Women Empowered: Poor Mothers and the Endangered Promise of Head Start*. Philadelphia: Temple University Press, 1997.

Anderson, Terry H. *The Movement and the Sixties*. New York: Oxford University Press, 1995.

Bacciocco, Edward J., Jr. *The New Left in America: Reform to Revolution, 1956–1970*. Stanford, Calif.: Hoover Institution Press, 1974.

Bailey, Robert J. *Radicals in Urban Politics: The Alinsky Approach*. Chicago: University of Chicago Press, 1974.

Bailis, Lawrence Neil. *Bread or Justice: Grassroots Organizing in the Welfare Rights Movement*. Lexington, Mass.: D. C. Heath, 1974.

Baritz, Loren, comp. *The American Left: Radical Political Thought in the Twentieth Century*. New York: Basic Books, 1971.

Bellush, Jewel, and Murray Hausknecht, eds. *Urban Renewal: People, Politics, and Planning*. Garden City, N.Y.: Anchor, 1967.

Berman, Paul. *A Tale of Two Utopias: The Political Journey of the Generation of 1968*. New York: Norton, 1996.

Bernard, Richard M., ed. *Snowbelt Cities: Metropolitan Politics in the Northeast and Midwest since World War II*. Bloomington: Indiana University Press, 1990.

Bernstein, Irving. *Guns or Butter: The Presidency of Lyndon Johnson*. New York: Oxford University Press, 1996.

Betten, Neil, and Michael J. Austin, eds. *The Roots of Community Organizing, 1917–1939*. Philadelphia: Temple University Press, 1990.

Bookman, Ann, and Sandra Morgen, eds. *Women and the Politics of Empowerment*. Philadelphia: Temple University Press, 1988.

Bouchier, David. *Radical Citizenship: The New American Radicalism*. New York: Schocken, 1987.

Boyte, Harry C. *The Backyard Revolution: Understanding the New Citizen Movement*. Philadelphia: Temple University Press, 1980.

Breines, Wini. *Community and Organization in the New Left, 1962–1968: The Great Refusal*. Rev. ed. New Brunswick: Rutgers University Press, 1989.

———. *Young, White, and Miserable: Growing Up Female in the Fifties*. Boston: Beacon, 1992.

Brown, Elaine. *A Taste of Power: A Black Woman's Story*. New York: Pantheon, 1992.

Bulmer, Martin, Kevin Bales, and Kathryn Kish Sklar, eds. *The Social Survey in Historical Perspective, 1880–1940*. Cambridge: Cambridge University Press, 1991.

Burner, David. *Making Peace with the 60s*. Princeton: Princeton University Press, 1996.

Burns, Stewart. *Social Movements of the 1960s: Searching for Democracy*. Boston: Twayne, 1990.

Calhoun, Craig, ed. *Habermas and the Public Sphere*. Cambridge: MIT Press, 1992.

———. *Social Theory and the Politics of Identity*. Cambridge: Blackwell, 1994.

Calvert, Gregory Nevala. *Democracy from the Heart: Spiritual Values, Decentralization, and Democratic Idealism in the Movement of the 1960s*. Eugene, Ore.: Communitas, 1991.

Carson, Clayborne. *In Struggle: SNCC and the Black Awakening in the 1960s*. Cambridge: Harvard University Press, 1981.

Carson, Mina. *Settlement Folk: Social Thought and the American Settlement Movement, 1885–1930*. Chicago: University of Chicago Press, 1990.

Castells, Manuel. *The City and the Grassroots: A Cross-Cultural Theory of Urban Social Movements*. London: Edward Arnold, 1983.

Cavallo, Dominick. *A Fiction of the Past: The Sixties in American History*. New York: St. Martin's, 1990.

Chafe, William H. *The Unfinished Journey: America since World War II*. New York: Oxford University Press, 1986.

Chicago Fact Book Consortium, ed. *Local Community Fact Book: Chicago Metropolitan Area, 1980*. Chicago: University of Illinois at Chicago, 1985.

Cluster, Dick, ed. *They Should Have Served That Cup of Coffee: Seven Radicals Remember the '60s*. Boston: South End, 1979.

Cohen, Mitchell, and Dennis Hale, eds. *The New Student Left: Anthology*. Boston: Beacon, 1966.

Cohen, Robert. *When the Old Left Was Young: Student Radicals and America's First Mass Student Movement, 1929–1941*. New York: Oxford University Press, 1993.

Craig, Lillian, with Marge Grevatt. *Just a Woman: Memoirs of Lillian Craig*. Cleveland: Orange Blossom Press, 1981.

Crocker, Ruth Hutchinson. *Social Work and Social Order: The Settlement*

Movement in Two Industrial Cities, 1889–1930. Urbana: University of Illinois Press, 1992.

Cunningham, John T. *Newark.* Newark: New Jersey State Historical Society, 1988.

Danziger, Sheldon H., and Daniel H. Weinberg, eds. *Fighting Poverty: What Works and What Doesn't.* Cambridge: Harvard University Press, 1986.

Davies, Gareth. *From Opportunity to Entitlement: The Transformation and Decline of Great Society Liberalism.* Lawrence: University Press of Kansas, 1996.

Davis, Allen F. *Spearheads for Reform: The Social Settlements and the Progressive Movement, 1890–1914.* New York: Oxford University Press, 1967.

Davis, Flora. *Moving the Mountain: The Women's Movement in America since 1960.* New York: Simon and Schuster, 1991.

Davis, Martha F. *Brutal Need: Lawyers and the Welfare Rights Movement, 1960–1973.* New Haven: Yale University Press, 1993.

DeBenedetti, Charles, with Charles Chatfield. *An American Ordeal: The Antiwar Movement of the Vietnam Era.* Syracuse: Syracuse University Press, 1990.

Delgado, Gary. *Organizing the Movement: The Roots and Growth of ACORN.* Philadelphia: Temple University Press, 1986.

———. *Beyond the Politics of Place: New Directions in Community Organizing.* 2d and rev. ed. Berkeley: Chardon, 1997.

Denning, Michael. *The Cultural Front: The Laboring of American Culture in the Twentieth Century.* London: Verso, 1996.

Derks, Scott, ed. *The Value of a Dollar: Prices and Income in the United States, 1860–1999.* Lakeville, Conn.: Grey House, 1999.

Donner, Frank. *Protectors of Privilege: Red Squads and Police Repression in Urban America.* Berkeley: University of California Press, 1990.

Duberman, Martin. *Stonewall.* New York: Dutton, 1993.

Echols, Alice. *Daring to Be Bad: Radical Feminism in America, 1967–1975.* Minneapolis: University of Minnesota Press, 1989.

Edin, Kathryn. *There's a Lot of Month Left at the End of the Money: How Welfare Recipients Make Ends Meet in Chicago.* New York: Garland, 1993.

Ehrenreich, Barbara. *The Hearts of Men: American Dreams and the Flight from Commitment.* Garden City, N.Y.: Anchor, 1983.

Ehrenreich, John H. *The Altruistic Imagination: A History of Social Work and Social Policy in the United States.* Ithaca: Cornell University Press, 1985.

Ellis, Richard J. *The Dark Side of the Left: Illiberal Egalitarianism in America.* Lawrence: University Press of Kansas, 1998.

Epstein, Barbara. *Political Protest and Cultural Revolution: Nonviolent Direct Action in the 1970s and 1980s.* Berkeley: University of California Press, 1991.

Evans, Sara. *Personal Politics: The Roots of Women's Liberation in the Civil*

Rights Movement and the New Left. New York: Knopf, 1979; New York: Vintage Books, 1980.

Eyerman, Ron, and Andrew Jamison. *Social Movements: A Cognitive Approach*. University Park: Pennsylvania State University Press, 1991.

Farber, David. *The Age of Great Dreams: America in the 1960s*. New York: Hill and Wang, 1994.

Fisher, Robert. *Let the People Decide: Neighborhood Organizing in America*. Boston: Twayne, 1984.

Fisher, Robert, and Joseph Kling, eds. *Mobilizing the Community: Local Politics in the Era of the Global City. Urban Affairs Annual Review* 41. Newbury Park, Calif.: Sage, 1993.

Fisher, Robert, and Peter Romanofsky, eds. *Community Organization for Urban Social Change: A Historical Perspective*. Westport, Conn.: Greenwood, 1981.

Flacks, Richard. *Youth and Social Change*. Chicago: Markham, 1971.

———. *Making History: The Radical Tradition in American Life*. New York: Columbia University Press, 1988.

Fogelson, Robert M. *Big-City Police*. Cambridge: Harvard University Press, 1977.

Formisano, Ronald D. *Boston against Busing: Race, Class, and Ethnicity in the 1960s and 1970s*. Chapel Hill: University of North Carolina Press, 1991.

Fox, Kenneth. *Metropolitan America: Urban Life and Urban Policy in the United States, 1940–1980*. Jackson: University of Mississippi Press, 1986.

Frank, Dana. *Purchasing Power: Consumer Organizing, Gender, and the Seattle Labor Movement, 1919–1929*. Cambridge: Cambridge University Press, 1994.

Fraser, Ronald, ed. *1968: A Student Generation in Revolt*. New York: Pantheon, 1988.

Fraser, Steven, and Gary Gerstle, eds. *The Rise and Fall of the New Deal Order, 1930–1980*. Princeton: Princeton University Press, 1989.

Funiciello, Theresa. *Tyranny of Kindness: Dismantling the Welfare System to End Poverty in America*. New York: Atlantic Monthly Press, 1993.

Gelfand, Mark I. *A Nation of Cities: The Federal Government and Urban America, 1933–1965*. New York: Oxford University Press, 1975.

Giddings, Paula. *When and Where I Enter: The Impact of Black Women on Race and Sex in America*. New York: Bantam, 1984.

Gilbert, James. *Another Chance: Postwar America, 1945–1985*. 2d ed. Chicago: Dorsey, 1986.

Gillette, Michael L. *Launching the War on Poverty: An Oral History*. New York: Twayne, 1996.

Gitlin, Todd. *The Sixties: Years of Hope, Days of Rage*. Toronto: Bantam, 1987.

Gitlin, Todd, and Nanc[y] Hollander. *Uptown: Poor Whites in Chicago.* New York: Harper and Row, 1970.

Goldin, Claudia. *Understanding the Gender Gap: An Economic History of American Women.* New York: Oxford University Press, 1990.

Goodwin, Joanne L. *Gender and the Politics of Welfare Reform: Mothers' Pensions in Chicago, 1911–1929.* Chicago: The University of Chicago Press, 1997.

Gordon, Linda. *Pitied but Not Entitled: Single Mothers and the History of Welfare.* New York: Free Press, 1994.

————, ed. *Women, the State, and Welfare.* Madison: University of Wisconsin Press, 1990.

Gornick, Vivian. *The Romance of American Communism.* New York: Basic Books, 1977.

Gosse, Van. *Where the Boys Are: Cuba, Cold War America, and the Making of the New Left.* London: Verso, 1993.

Greenberg, Cheryl Lynn, ed. *A Circle of Trust: Remembering SNCC.* New Brunswick: Rutgers University Press, 1998.

Greenstone, J. David, and Paul E. Peterson. *Race and Authority in Urban Politics: Community Participation and the War on Poverty.* New York: Russell Sage, 1973.

Hamberg, Jill, with Paul Booth, Mimi Feingold, and Carl Wittman. *Where It's At: A Research Guide for Community Organizing.* Boston: New England Free Press, 1967.

Hamilton, Dona Cooper, and Charles V. Hamilton. *The Dual Agenda: Race and Social Welfare Policies of Civil Rights Organizations.* New York: Columbia University Press, 1997.

Handler, Joel F., and Yeheskel Hasenfeld. *The Moral Construction of Poverty: Welfare Reform in America.* Newbury Park, Calif.: Sage, 1991.

Harrington, Michael. *The Other America: Poverty in the United States.* New York: Macmillan, 1962.

Hayden, Tom. *Reunion: A Memoir.* New York: Random House, 1988.

Heineman, Kenneth J. *Campus Wars: The Peace Movement at American State Universities in the Vietnam Era.* New York: New York University Press, 1993.

Hertz, Susan Handley. *The Welfare Mothers Movement: A Decade of Change for Poor Women?* Washington, D.C.: University Press of America, 1981.

Hewitt, Nancy A., and Suzanne Lebsock, eds. *Visible Women: New Essays on American Activism.* Urbana: University of Illinois Press, 1994.

Hill, Mike, ed. *Whiteness: A Critical Reader.* New York: New York University Press, 1997.

Hirsch, Arnold R., and Raymond A. Mohl, eds. *Urban Policy in Twentieth Century America.* New Brunswick: Rutgers University Press, 1993.

Hodgson, Godfrey. *America in Our Time*. Garden City, N.Y.: Doubleday, 1976.

Horwitt, Sanford D. *Let Them Call Me Rebel: Saul Alinsky: His Life and Legacy*. New York: Knopf, 1989.

Isserman, Maurice. *If I Had a Hammer . . . The Death of the Old Left and the Birth of the New Left*. New York: Basic Books, 1987.

Isserman, Maurice, and Michael Kazin. *America Divided: The Civil War of the 1960s*. New York: Oxford University Press, 2000.

Jackson, Larry R., and William A. Johnson. *Protest by the Poor: The Welfare Rights Movement in New York City*. Lexington, Mass.: D. C. Heath, 1974.

Jacobs, Ron. *The Way the Wind Blew: A History of the Weather Underground*. London: Verso, 1997.

Jetter, Alexis, Annelise Orleck, and Diana Taylor, eds. *The Politics of Motherhood: Activist Voices from Left and Right*. Hanover, N.H.: University Press of New England, 1997.

Jones, Jacqueline. *The Dispossessed: America's Underclasses from the Civil War to the Present*. New York: Basic Books, 1992.

Katz, Michael B. *The Undeserving Poor: From the War on Poverty to the War on Welfare*. New York: Pantheon, 1990.

———, ed. *The "Underclass" Debate: Views from History*. Princeton: Princeton University Press, 1993.

Katznelson, Ira. *City Trenches: Urban Politics and the Patterning of Class in the United States*. New York: Pantheon, 1981.

Kazin, Michael. *The Populist Persuasion: An American History*. Rev. ed. Ithaca: Cornell University Press, 1998.

Kerber, Linda K., Alice Kessler-Harris, and Kathryn Kish Sklar, eds. *U.S. History as Women's History: New Feminist Essays*. Chapel Hill: University of North Carolina Press, 1995.

Klatch, Rebecca E. *A Generation Divided: The New Left, the New Right, and the 1960s*. Berkeley: University of California Press, 1999.

Kling, Joseph M., and Prudence S. Posner, eds. *Dilemmas of Activism: Class, Community, and the Politics of Local Mobilization*. Philadelphia: Temple University Press, 1990.

Kramer, Ralph M. *Participation of the Poor: Comparative Community Case Studies in the War on Poverty*. Englewood Cliffs, N.J.: Prentice-Hall, 1969.

Larner, Jeremy, and Irving Howe, eds. *Poverty: Views from the Left*. New York: William Morrow, 1968.

Levy, Peter B. *The New Left and Labor in the 1960s*. Urbana: University of Illinois Press, 1994.

Lewis, Oscar. *The Children of Sanchez*. New York: Random House, 1961.

———. *La Vida: A Puerto Rican Family in the Culture of Poverty—San Juan and New York*. New York: Random House, 1966.

Lichtenstein, Nelson. *The Most Dangerous Man in Detroit: Walter Reuther and the Fate of American Labor.* New York: Basic Books, 1995.

Lieberman, Robert C. *Shifting the Color Line: Race and the American Welfare State.* Cambridge: Harvard University Press, 1998.

Linden-Ward, Blanche, and Carol Hurd Green. *American Women in the 1960s: Changing the Future.* New York: Twayne, 1993.

Long, Priscilla, ed. *The New Left: A Collection of Essays.* Boston: Porter Sargent, 1969.

Lowe, Jeanne. *Cities in a Race with Time: Progress and Poverty in America's Renewing Cities.* New York: Random House, 1967.

Mann, Patricia S. *Micro-Politics: Agency in a Postfeminist Era.* Minneapolis: University of Minnesota Press, 1994.

Mansbridge, Jane J. *Beyond Adversary Democracy.* Chicago: University of Chicago Press, 1980.

Massey, Douglas S., and Nancy A. Denton. *American Apartheid: Segregation and the Making of the Underclass.* Cambridge: Harvard University Press, 1993.

Mattson, Kevin. *Creating a Democratic Public: The Struggle for Urban Participatory Democracy during the Progressive Era.* University Park: Pennsylvania State University Press, 1998.

Matusow, Allen J. *The Unraveling of America: A History of Liberalism in the 1960s.* New York: Harper and Row, 1984.

McAdam, Doug. *Freedom Summer.* New York: Oxford University Press, 1988.

McCarthy, Kathleen D., ed. *Lady Bountiful Revisited: Women, Philanthropy, and Power.* New Brunswick: Rutgers University Press, 1990.

McCartin, Joseph A. *Labor's Great War: The Struggle for Industrial Democracy and the Origins of Modern American Labor Relations, 1912–1921.* Chapel Hill: University of North Carolina Press, 1997.

McCourt, Kathleen. *Working Class Women and Grass Roots Politics.* Bloomington: Indiana University Press, 1977.

Medoff, Peter, and Holly Sklar. *Streets of Hope: The Fall and Rise of an Urban Neighborhood.* Boston: South End, 1994.

Mendel-Reyes, Meta. *Reclaiming Democracy: The Sixties in Politics and Memory.* New York: Routledge, 1995.

Milkman, Ruth, ed. *Women, Work, and Protest: A Century of U.S. Women's Labor History.* London: Routledge and Kegan Paul, 1985.

Miller, James. *"Democracy Is in the Streets": From Port Huron to the Siege of Chicago.* New York: Simon and Schuster, 1987.

Miller, Timothy. *The Hippies and American Values.* Knoxville: University of Tennessee Press, 1991.

Mollenkopf, John H. *The Contested City.* Princeton: Princeton University Press, 1983.

Morgan, Edward P. *The 60s Experience: Hard Lessons about Modern America.* Philadelphia: Temple University Press, 1991.

Morgan, Robin, ed. *Sisterhood Is Powerful: An Anthology of Writings from the Women's Liberation Movement.* New York: Vintage, 1970.

Morris, Aldon D. *The Origins of the Civil Rights Movement: Black Communities Organizing for Change.* New York: Free Press, 1984.

Morrison, Joan, and Robert K. Morrison. *From Camelot to Kent State: The Sixties Experience in the Words of Those Who Lived It.* New York: Times Books, 1987.

Myers, R. David, ed. *Toward a History of the New Left: Essays from within the Movement.* Brooklyn, N.Y.: Carlson, 1989.

Naples, Nancy A. *Grassroots Warriors: Activist Mothering, Community Work, and the War on Poverty.* New York: Routledge, 1998.

———, ed. *Community Activism and Feminist Politics: Organizing across Race, Class, and Gender.* New York: Routledge, 1998.

Newfield, Jack. *A Prophetic Minority.* New York: New American Library, 1966.

Noble, Charles. *Welfare as We Knew It: A Political History of the American Welfare State.* New York: Oxford University Press, 1997.

Omi, Michael, and Howard Winant. *Racial Formation in the United States: From the 1960s to the 1980s.* New York: Routledge, Kegan Paul, 1986.

O'Neill, William L. *Coming Apart: An Informal History of America in the 1960s.* New York: Quadrangle, 1978.

Patterson, James T. *America's Struggle against Poverty, 1900–1985.* Rev. ed. Cambridge: Harvard University Press, 1986.

Payne, Charles M. *I've Got the Light of Freedom: The Organizing Tradition and the Mississippi Freedom Struggle.* Berkeley: University of California Press, 1995.

Phillips, Anne. *Engendering Democracy.* University Park: Pennsylvania State University Press, 1991.

Piven, Frances Fox, and Richard A. Cloward. *Poor People's Movements: Why They Succeed, How They Fail.* New York: Pantheon, 1977; New York: Vintage, 1979.

Plotnick, Robert D., and Felicity Skidmore. *Progress against Poverty: A Review of the 1964–1974 Decade.* New York: Academic Press, 1975.

Pope, Jacqueline. *Biting the Hand That Feeds Them: Organizing Women on Welfare at the Grass Roots Level.* New York: Praeger, 1989.

Potter, Paul. *A Name for Ourselves: Feelings about Authentic Identity, Love, Intuitive Politics, Us.* Boston: Little, Brown, 1971.

Quadagno, Jill. *The Color of Welfare: How Racism Undermined the War on Poverty.* New York: Oxford University Press, 1994.

Rabinowitz, Paula. *They Must Be Represented: The Politics of Documentary.* London: Verso, 1994.

Ralph, James R., Jr. *Northern Protest: Martin Luther King, Jr., Chicago, and the Civil Rights Movement*. Cambridge: Harvard University Press, 1993.

Robnett, Belinda. *How Long? How Long? African-American Women in the Struggle for Civil Rights*. New York: Oxford University Press, 1997.

Rodgers, Daniel T. *Contested Truths: Keywords in American Politics since Independence*. New York: Basic Books, 1987.

Rossinow, Doug. *The Politics of Authenticity: Liberalism, Christianity, and the New Left in America*. New York: Columbia University Press, 1998.

Sale, Kirkpatrick. *SDS*. New York: Random House, 1973.

Salem, Dorothy. *To Better Our World: Black Women in Organized Reform, 1890–1920*. Brooklyn, N.Y.: Carlson, 1990.

Schwartz, Joel. *The New York Approach: Robert Moses, Urban Liberals, and Redevelopment of the Inner City*. Columbus: Ohio State University Press, 1993.

Silver, Harold, and Pamela Silver. *An Educational War on Poverty: American and British Policy-Making, 1960–1980*. Cambridge: Cambridge University Press, 1991.

Simmons, Louise B. *Organizing in Hard Times: Labor and Neighborhoods in Hartford*. Philadelphia: Temple University Press, 1994.

Sitkoff, Harvard. *The Struggle for Black Equality, 1954–1980*. New York: Hill and Wang, 1981.

Slayton, Robert A. *Back of the Yards: The Making of a Local Democracy*. Chicago: University of Chicago Press, 1986.

Squires, Gregory D., ed. *Unequal Partnerships: The Political Economy of Urban Redevelopment in Postwar America*. New Brunswick: Rutgers University Press, 1989.

Stott, William. *Documentary Expression and Thirties America*. London: Oxford University Press, 1973.

Teaford, Jon C. *The Rough Road to Renaissance: Urban Revitalization in America, 1940–1985*. Baltimore: Johns Hopkins University Press, 1990.

———. *Cities of the Heartland: The Rise and Fall of the Industrial Midwest*. Bloomington: Indiana University Press, 1993.

Teodori, Massimo, ed. *The New Left: A Documentary History*. Indianapolis: Bobbs-Merrill, 1969.

Terkel, Studs. *Division Street: America*. New York: Pantheon, 1967.

———. *The Great Divide: Second Thoughts on the American Dream*. New York: Pantheon, 1988.

———. *Race: How Blacks and Whites Think and Feel about the American Obsession*. New York: New Press, 1992.

———. *Coming of Age: The Story of Our Century by Those Who've Lived It*. New York: New Press, 1995.

Thernstrom, Stephan. *Poverty, Planning, and Politics in the New Boston: The Origins of ABCD*. New York: Basic Books, 1969.

Tischler, Barbara L., ed. *Sights on the Sixties.* New Brunswick: Rutgers University Press, 1992.

Unger, Irwin. *The Best of Intentions: The Triumphs and Failures of the Great Society under Kennedy, Johnson, and Nixon.* New York: Doubleday, 1996.

Viorst, Milton. *Fire in the Streets: America in the 1960s.* New York: Simon and Schuster, 1979.

Walkowitz, Daniel J. *Social Workers and the Politics of Middle-Class Identity.* Chapel Hill: University of North Carolina Press, 1999.

Weinstein, James. *Ambiguous Legacy: The Left in American Politics.* New York: New Viewpoints, 1975.

Weir, Margaret. *Politics and Jobs: The Boundaries of Employment Policy in the United States.* Princeton: Princeton University Press, 1992.

West, Guida. *The National Welfare Rights Organization: The Social Protest of Poor Women.* New York: Praeger, 1981.

West, Guida, and Rhoda Lois Blumberg, eds. *Women and Social Protest.* New York: Oxford University Press, 1990.

Whitfield, Stephen J. *A Critical American: The Politics of Dwight Macdonald.* Hamden, Conn.: Archon, 1984.

Wilson, James Q., ed. *Urban Renewal: The Record and the Controversy.* Cambridge: MIT Press, 1966.

Winters, Stanley B., ed. *Riot to Recovery: Newark after Ten Years.* Washington, D.C.: University Press of America, 1979.

Withorn, Ann. *Serving the People: Social Services and Social Change.* New York: Columbia University Press, 1984.

Wittner, Lawrence S. *Cold War America: From Hiroshima to Watergate.* Expanded ed. New York: Rinehart and Winston, 1978.

Wright, Gwendolyn. *Building the Dream: A Social History of Housing in America.* New York: Pantheon, 1981.

Wright, Nathan, Jr. *Ready to Riot.* New York: Holt, Rinehart, and Winston, 1968.

Young, Nigel. *An Infantile Disorder? The Crisis and Decline of the New Left.* London: Routledge and Kegan Paul, 1977.

Zarefsky, David. *President Johnson's War on Poverty: Rhetoric and History.* University, Ala.: University of Alabama Press, 1986.

Articles and Essays

Aronowitz, Stanley. "When the New Left Was New." In *The '60s without Apology,* ed. Sohnya Sayres et al., 11–34. Minneapolis: University of Minnesota Press, 1984.

Baker, Paula. "The Domestication of Politics: Women and American Political Society, 1780–1920." *American Historical Review* 89 (June 1984): 620–47.

Barlow, Andrew. "The Student Movement of the 1960s and the Politics of Race." *Journal of Ethnic Studies* 19 (fall 1991): 1–22.

Berman, Paul. "Don't Follow Leaders." *New Republic* (August 10 and 17, 1987): 28–35.

Bonilla, Frank. "Migrants, Citizenship, and Social Pacts." *Radical America* 23 (1989): 81–89.

Breines, Winifred. "Whose New Left?" *Journal of American History* 75 (September 1988): 528–45.

Brinkley, Alan. "The Antimonopoly Ideal and the Liberal State: The Case of Thurman Arnold." *Journal of American History* 80 (September 1993): 557–79.

Cruikshank, Barbara. "The Will to Empower· Technologies of Citizenship and the War on Poverty." *Socialist Review* 23 (October–December 1994)· ?9–55.

Davis, Martha F. "Welfare Rights and Women's Rights in the 1960s." *Journal of Policy History* 8, no. 1 (1996): 144–65.

Durr, Kenneth. "When Southern Politics Came North: The Roots of White Working-Class Conservatism in Baltimore, 1940–1964." *Labor History* 37 (summer 1996): 309–31.

Echols, Alice. "We Gotta Get Out of This Place: Notes toward a Remapping of the Sixties." *Socialist Review* 22 (April–June 1992). 9–33.

Eynon, Bret. "Community in Motion: The Free Speech Movement, Civil Rights, and the Roots of the New Left." *Oral History Review* 17 (spring 1989): 39–69.

Fee, Elizabeth. "Public Health in Baltimore: Childhood Lead Paint Poisoning, 1930–1970." *Maryland Historical Magazine* 87 (fall 1992): 267–93.

Findley, Tim. "Tom Hayden: The Rolling Stone Interview, Part 1." *Rolling Stone* (October 26, 1972): 36–50.

Flacks, Richard. "The Liberated Generation: An Exploration of the Roots of Student Protest." *Journal of Social Issues* 23 (July 1967): 52–75.

———. "What Happened to the New Left?" *Socialist Review* 19 (January–March 1989): 91–110.

Fleming, Cynthia Griggs. "Black Women Activists and the SNCC: The Case of Ruby Doris Smith Robinson." *Journal of Women's History* 4 (winter 1993): 64–82.

Flug, Michael. "Organized Labor and the Civil Rights Movement of the 1960s: The Case of the Maryland Freedom Union." *Labor History* 31 (summer 1990): 322–46.

Freeman, Jo. "The Tyranny of Structurelessness." *Berkeley Journal of Sociology* 17 (1972–73): 151–64.

Garver, Paul, and George Abbott White. "What Was Old, What Was New? The New Left and American Exceptionalism." *Journal of American Studies* 22 (April 1988): 67–76.

Gitlin, Todd. "From Universality to Difference: Notes on the Fragmentation of the Idea of the Left." *Contention* 2 (winter 1993): 15–40.

———. "Beyond Identity Politics: A Modest Precedent." In *Audacious Democracy: Labor, Intellectuals, and the Social Reconstruction of America*, ed. Steven Fraser and Joshua B. Freeman, 152–63. Boston: Houghton Mifflin, 1997.

Gordon, Linda. "What Does Welfare Regulate?" *Social Research* 55 (winter 1988): 609–30.

Gosse, Van. "'To Organize in Every Neighborhood, in Every Home': The Gender Politics of American Communists between the Wars." *Radical History Review* 50 (spring 1991): 109–41.

Guy, Roger. "The Media, the Police, and Southern White Migrant Identity in Chicago, 1955–1970." *Journal of Urban History* 26 (March 2000): 329–49.

Hartog, Hendrik. "The Constitution of Aspiration and 'The Rights That Belong to Us All.'" In *The Constitution and American Life*, ed. David Thelen, 353–74. Ithaca: Cornell University Press, 1988.

Harvey, David L., and Michael Reed. "Paradigms of Poverty: A Critical Assessment of Contemporary Perspectives." *International Journal of Politics, Culture, and Society* 6 (winter 1992): 269–97.

Hayden, Tom. "Welfare Liberalism and Social Change." In *The Great Society Reader: The Failure of American Liberalism*, ed. Marvin E. Gettleman and David Mermelstein, 476–501. New York: Random House, 1967.

Hyman, Paula E. "Immigrant Women and Consumer Protest: The New York City Kosher Meat Boycott of 1902." *American Jewish History* 70 (September 1980): 91–105.

Isserman, Maurice. "The Not-So-Dark and Bloody Ground: New Works on the 1960s." *American Historical Review* 94 (October 1989): 990–1010.

Kaplan, Temma. "Female Consciousness and Collective Action: The Case of Barcelona, 1910–1918." *Signs* 7 (spring 1982): 545–66.

Katznelson, Ira, and Bruce Pietrykowski. "Rebuilding the American State: Evidence from the 1940s." *Studies in American Political Development* 5 (fall 1991): 301–39.

Kelley, Robin D. G. "Birmingham's Untouchables: The Black Poor in the Age of Civil Rights." In *Race Rebels: Culture, Politics, and the Black Working Class*. New York: Free Press, 1994.

———. "Identity Politics and Class Struggle." *New Politics* 6 (winter 1997): 84–96.

Kirby, Jack Temple. "The Southern Exodus, 1910–1960: A Primer for Historians." *Journal of Southern History* 49 (November 1983): 585–600.

Kornbluh, Felicia. "To Fulfill Their 'Rightly Needs': Consumerism and the National Welfare Rights Movement." *Radical History Review* 69 (fall 1997): 76–113.

———. "The Goals of the National Welfare Rights Movement: Why We Need Them Thirty Years Later." *Feminist Studies* 24 (spring 1998): 65–78.

Lawson, Ronald, and Stephen E. Barton. "Sex Roles in Social Movements: A Case Study of the Tenant Movement in New York City." *Signs* 6 (winter 1980): 230–47.

Lawson, Steven F. "From Boycotts to Ballots: The Reshaping of National Politics." In *New Directions in Civil Rights Studies*, ed. Armstead L. Robinson and Patricia Sullivan, 184–210. Charlottesville: University Press of Virginia, 1991.

Leab, Daniel J. "'United We Eat': The Creation and Organization of the Unemployed Councils of 1930." *Labor History* 8 (fall 1967): 302–15.

Martin, Patricia Yancey. "Rethinking Feminist Organizations." *Gender and Society* 4 (June 1990): 182–206.

Mc Lanahan, Sara S., Annemette Sørenson, and Dorothy Watson. "Sex Differences in Poverty, 1950–1980." *Signs* 15 (autumn 1989): 102–22.

Meyer, David S., and Nancy Whittier. "Social Movement Spillover." *Social Problems* 41 (May 1994): 277–98.

Miller, Alan S. "Saul Alinsky: America's Radical Reactionary." *Radical America* 21 (January–February 1987): 11–18.

Morgan, Edward P. "Democracy in Eclipse? Media Culture and the Postmodern 'Sixties.'" *New Political Science* 40 (summer 1997): 5–31.

Nelson, Barbara J. "Help-Seeking from Public Authorities: Who Arrives at the Agency Door?" *Policy Studies* 12 (August 1980): 175–92.

———. "Client Evaluations of Social Programs." In *The Public Encounter: Where State and Citizen Meet*, ed. Charles T. Goodsell, 23–42. Bloomington: Indiana University Press, 1981.

Orleck, Annelise. "'We Are That Mythical Thing Called the Public': Militant Housewives during the Great Depression." *Feminist Studies* 19 (spring 1993): 147–72.

Parenti, Michael. "Power and Pluralism: A View from the Bottom." *Journal of Politics* 32 (August 1970): 501–30.

Quadagno, Jill, and Catherine Fobes. "The Welfare State and the Cultural Reproduction of Gender: Making Good Girls and Boys in the Job Corps." *Social Problems* 42 (May 1995): 171–90.

Rosenzweig, Roy. "Organizing the Unemployed: The Early Years of the Great Depression, 1929–1933." *Radical America* 10 (July–August 1976): 37–60.

Sacks, Karen Brodkin. "Toward a Unified Theory of Class, Race, and Gender." *American Ethnologist* 16 (August 1989): 534–50.

Sinsheimer, Joseph A. "The Freedom Vote of 1963: New Strategies of Racial Protest in Mississippi." *Journal of Southern History* 55 (May 1989): 217–44.

Skocpol, Theda. "Legacies of New Deal Liberalism." *Dissent* 30 (winter 1983): 33–44.

Staples, Brent. "Blaming Nixon." *New York Times Book Review* (January 16, 2000): 10.

Stein, Arlene. "Between Organization and Movement: ACORN and the Alinsky Model of Community Organizing." *Berkeley Journal of Sociology* 31 (1986): 93–115.

Strobel, Margaret. "Organizational Learning in the Chicago Women's Liberation Union." In *Feminist Organizations: Harvest of the New Women's Movement*, ed. Myra Marx Ferree and Patricia Yancey Martin, 145–64. Philadelphia: Temple University Press, 1995.

"Symposium: Maternalism as a Paradigm." *Journal of Women's History* 5 (fall 1993): 95–131.

Tillmon, Johnnie. "Welfare Is a Woman's Issue." In *America's Working Women: A Documentary History—1600 to the Present*, rev. and updated, ed. Rosalyn Baxandall and Linda Gordon, with Susan Reverby, 314–18. New York: Norton, 1995. First published in *Liberation News Service*, no. 451 (February 26, 1972).

Tucker, Bruce. "Inner-City Activism in the 1960s: An Oral History Interview." *U.S. Catholic Historian* 2 (winter 1993): 101–12.

White, Lucie E. "*Goldberg v. Kelly* on the Paradox of Lawyering for the Poor." *Brooklyn Law Review* 56 (fall 1990): 861–87.

Pamphlets and Unpublished Works

Douglas, Philip Le B. "Reform in Newark: The Response to Crisis, 1953–1972." Senior thesis, Woodrow Wilson School of Public and International Affairs, Princeton University, 1972.

Gerwin, David Milton. "The End of Coalition: The Failure of Community Organizing in Newark in the 1960s." Ph.D. dissertation, Columbia University, 1998.

Harwood, Edwin S. "Work and Community among Urban Newcomers: A Study of the Social and Economic Adaptation of Southern Migrants in Chicago." Ph.D. dissertation, University of Chicago, 1966.

O'Brien, James Putnam. "The Development of a New Left in the United States, 1960–1965." Ph.D. dissertation, University of Wisconsin-Madison, 1971.

O'Neil, Dennis. *SDS 101: From the Inside*. Freedom Road Socialist Organization, 1987.

Rice, Leila Meier. "In the Trenches of the War on Poverty: The Local Implementation of the Community Action Program, 1964–1969." Ph.D. dissertation, Vanderbilt University, 1997.

Rose, Kenneth Wayne. "The Politics of Social Reform in Cleveland, 1945–1967: Civil Rights, Welfare Rights, and the Response of Civic Leaders." Ph.D. dissertation, Case Western Reserve University, 1988.

Withorn, Ann. "To Serve the People: An Inquiry into the Success of Service Delivery as a Social Movement Strategy." Ph.D. dissertation, Brandeis University, 1977.

Index

About the Author

Jennifer Frost is an assistant professor of history at the University of Northern Colorado.